KAFKA

KAFKA

PIETRO CITATI

Translated from the Italian by
Raymond Rosenthal

Alfred A. Knopf   New York   1990

THIS IS A BORZOI BOOK
PUBLISHED BY ALFRED A. KNOPF, INC.

Copyright © 1989 by Alfred A. Knopf, Inc.

All rights reserved under International and Pan-American
Copyright Conventions. Published in the United States
by Alfred A. Knopf, Inc., New York, and simultaneously in
Canada by Random House of Canada Limited, Toronto.
Distributed by Random House, Inc., New York.

Originally published in Italy by RCS Rizzoli Libri S.p.A., Milan,
in 1987. Copyright © 1987 RCS Rizzoli Libri S.p.A., Milano

Library of Congress Cataloging-in-Publication Data
Citati, Pietro.
[Kafka. English]
Kafka / Pietro Citati; translated from the Italian
by Raymond Rosenthal.
p. cm.
Translation of: Kafka.
Includes index.
ISBN 0-394-56840-0
1. Kafka, Franz, 1883–1924. 2. Authors, Austrian—
20th century— Biography. I. Title.
PT2621.A26Z662513 1989
833'.912—dc20
[B]   88-45766
CIP

Manufactured in the United States of America

FIRST AMERICAN EDITION

Contents

KAFKA

CHAPTER ONE

The Man at the Window

All the people who met Franz Kafka in his youth or maturity had the impression that he was surrounded by a "wall of glass." There he stayed, behind that very transparent glass, walking gracefully, gesticulating, speaking; he smiled like a meticulous and buoyant angel; and his smile was the last flower born of a gentleness that gave itself and immediately pulled back, spent itself and jealously closed in upon itself. He seemed to say: "I am like you, I am a man like you, I suffer and rejoice as you do." But the more he participated in the destiny and sufferings of others, the more he excluded himself from the game, and that subtle shadow of invitation and exclusion on the edge of his lips told us that he could never be present, that he lived far away, very far away, in a world that did not belong even to him.

What did they see, the others, behind the delicate glass wall? He was a tall man, thin and lithe, who carried his long body around as though it had been given to him as a gift. He had the impression that he would never grow up and would never know the weight, stability and horror of what others with incomprehensible joy called "maturity." He once confessed to Max Brod: "I shall never experience manhood, from being a child I shall immediately become an old man with white hair." Everybody was attracted by his large eyes which he held very wide open, at times staring, and which in photographs, struck by the sudden flash of magnesium, seemed those of a man possessed or of a visionary. His eyelashes were long; his pupils are described now as brown, now gray, now steel-blue, now simply dark; while a passport assures us that they were "dark gray-blue." When he looked at himself in the mirror, he found that his gaze was "incredibly energetic"; but others never stopped commenting on and interpreting his eyes, as though only they offered a door to his soul. Some considered them full of sadness; some felt observed and scrutinized; some saw them light up suddenly, glisten with golden granules, then turn pensive or even forbidding; some saw them imbued with now a mild, now a corrosive irony; some perceived in them surprise and a strange cunning; some, who loved him a great deal, pursuing his enigma in a thousand ways, thought that he, like Tolstoy, knew something of which other men knew nothing; some found his eyes impenetrable; and some, finally, believed that at times a stony calm, a mortal void, a funereal estrangement dominated his gaze.

Very rarely did he speak of his own initiative; perhaps it seemed to him insupportable arrogance to come out on life's stage without being summoned. His voice was soft, thin and melodious: only illness was to make it muffled and almost raucous. He never said anything insignificant; everything that is everyday was alien to him or was transfigured by the light of his inner world. If the subject inspired him, he spoke with facility, elegance, vivacity, at times with enthusiasm; he let himself go, as though it were possible to say everything to everyone; he formed his sentences with the pleasure of an artisan satisfied with his craft; and he accompanied his words with the play of his long, ethereal fingers. He often contracted his eyebrows, wrinkled his forehead, pushed out his lower lip, joined his hands, rested them open on his desk or pressed one against his heart, like an old melodramatic actor or a new mime of the silent films. When he laughed, he bent back his head, barely opened his mouth, and closed his eyes until they became the thinnest of slits. But whether the spirit of his soul was gay or sad he never lost that gift of the gods: supreme naturalness. He, of all people, who thought he was and indeed was contradictory and contorted—nothing but a relic, a stone, a broken piece of wood stuck in a torn-up field, a fragment left over from other fragments, nothing but cries and laceration—left the impression that all his gestures expressed "calm in motion." He attained quiet in his life even before he attained it in his writing. Nothing can awaken a deeper impression in men. They came to him, anxious or uncertain or simply curious, old friends, already recognized writers, unhappy and megalomaniac youths, and they drew from this an impression of well-being and almost of joy. In his presence everyday life changed. Everything seemed new: everything appeared seen for the first time; often it seemed new in a very sad way, but without ever excluding a last possibility of conciliation.

When he made an appointment with his friends, he always came late. He arrived at a run, an embarrassed smile on his face, and held his hand over his heart, as though to say: "I am innocent." The actor Itzhak Löwy waited for him in front of his house for a very long time. When he saw the light burning in Kafka's room, he speculated: "He's still writing"; then the light suddenly went out but remained on in the next room, and at that Löwy said to himself: "He's having dinner"; the light went on again in Kafka's room, where he, obviously, was brushing his teeth; when it went out, Löwy thought that he must be hastily descending the stairs; but look! now it went on again, perhaps Kafka had forgotten something. . . . Kafka explained that he himself loved to wait: a long wait, with unhurried glances at the watch and an indifferent pacing to and fro, pleased him as much as lying down on the couch with his legs stretched out and his hands in his pockets. Waiting gave a purpose to his life, which otherwise seemed so indeterminate to him: he had a fixed point before him, which marked his time and assured him that he existed. Perhaps he forgot to say that coming late was for him a way of eluding time: defeating it, wearing it down little by little and escaping its regular beat.

His friends saw him from a distance, dressed always in a clean, tidy way, never elegant: gray or dark blue suits, like a clerk. For a long period of time, enveloped in his dream of asceticism and stoic impassibility, he wore only one suit for the office, the street, his writing desk, summer and winter; and well into November, while everyone else wore heavy overcoats, he appeared in the street "like a madman in a summer suit and a small summer hat," almost as though wanting to impose a single uniform on the diversity of life. As soon as he saw his friends, he seemed happy. Even though he communicated with them only "with his finger-tips," he had a Chinese formality, which was born from the weariness of his heart and an almost unprecedented refinement of the spirit. He offered himself with ironic grace: a Carroll-like levity, the levity of a Hasidic saint or a romantic imp; a whimsical imagination, hovering and errant—the delicacies of Oriental poetry, delightful *marivaudages*, games with smoke, the heart and death.

When he was with friends, he liked to exhibit his talent as a mime. Now he would imitate someone twirling his walking stick, the gesture of his hands, the movement of his fingers. Now he imitated the complexities of a person's character, and his inner mimicry was so potent and perfect as to become unconscious. Often he read books he loved: with gaiety and rapture, eyes shining with emotion, a rapid voice, capable of re-creating rhythm by means of the secret vibration of song, causing the intonations to stand out with extreme precision, savoring certain expressions and repeating them or empha-sizing them with insistence, until Flaubert or Goethe or Kleist, he who was reading, his friends or sisters would all fuse in that room into a single person. This was his dream of power—the only one that he, the enemy of all power, ever wished to realize. As a boy he had dreamt that he was in a large hall crowded with people and was reading aloud *The Sentimental Education*, from beginning to end without stopping, without ever interrupting himself, for all the necessary nights and mornings and evenings, just as later he would dream of writing *Amerika* or *The Castle* all in one breath. The others would listen to him, never getting tired, completely fascinated.

When the evening was over, Kafka returned home with his birdlike lightness. He walked with a quick step, slightly bent, his head a bit inclined, wavering as though the gusts of wind were dragging him now to one side of the street, now to the other; he rested his crossed hands on his shoulders, and his long stride, along with the dark color of his face, often caused him to be mistaken for a half-breed Indian. Thus he passed, in the depths of the night, absorbed in his thoughts, before the palaces, churches, monuments and synagogues, turning into the picturesque and dark side alleys that traverse Prague. This was his way of taking leave of life and sapping strength from the certain unhappiness of the following day.

At eight in the morning he punctually arrived in his office at the Institute for Workmen's Accident Insurance for the Kingdom of Bohemia. At his desk covered by a disheveled pile of papers and dossiers, he dictated to the typist; every so often his mind halted, vacant of all ideas, and the typist dozed off, lit his pipe or looked out the window. He participated in meetings, drew up documents and reports, carried out surveys. He was considered an excellent employee: "indefatigable, diligent and ambitious . . . a very zealous worker, of uncommon talent and extraordinarily scrupulous in the performance of his duties." His superiors did not know that he was not in the least "ambitious." He worked there, in that din, among that crowd of clerks and porters and injured workers only because he knew that he must not devote all his time to literature. He feared that literature would suck him in, like a vortex, until he would lose his way in its boundless territories. He could not afford to be free. He needed constriction: he must devote his day to some extraneous activity, and only then would he be able to carve out from his quotidian prison those precious hours, those nocturnal hours, in which his pen pursued the unknown world that someone had ordered him to bring to life. Office work gave him the subtle pleasure, which he savored as few others did, of being irresponsible: no autonomous decision, no handwritten sheet and, at the bottom of the sheets, not the name but the initials F.K. But what great tension this double life demanded! He grappled with the immense and tortuous work of the office and with the phantoms of his nights; he had no ease, he had no time; he had few hours left to sleep; and more than once he thought that he would be torn to shreds by this conflict, or that madness was the only path to salvation.

He returned home, to his other prison—"so much more oppressive since it seemed a bourgeois home exactly the same as all others"—around a quarter past two in the afternoon. He said he lived there like a stranger, great though his love was for father, mother and sisters. He did not participate in the family rituals, the card games, the gatherings. Sometimes a shy good-night kiss from his mother brought him closer to her. "This is fine," he said. "I never dared," his mother answered, "I thought you didn't like it. But if you do, I too am very happy about it"; and she smiled at him with a forgotten tenderness somehow resurrected for the moment. He did share the communal food. While the others ate meat—that meat brought back to his memory vivid with hatred and disgust all the violence that men had sown over the earth, and the minuscule filaments between one tooth and the next seemed to him germs of putrefaction and fermentation like those of a dead rat between two stones—he poured onto the table nature's rich cornucopia. He had always loved the food of vegetarian restaurants: green cabbage with fried eggs, whole wheat bread, semolina with raspberry syrup, lettuce with cream, gooseberry wine; and the soft foods of the sanatoriums—apple jam, mashed potatoes, liquid legumes, fruit juices, sweet omelets—which glided swiftly, almost unnoticed, down the throat. He tried to outdo those diets; and yogurt, Simon's bread, walnuts and filberts, chestnuts, dates, figs, grapes, almonds, raisins, sugar, bananas, apples, pears, oranges, pineapples filled him with that gentle nourishment which had to sustain him during his nocturnal labors.

Then he retired to his room, which was a passageway, or rather, a rackety connecting path between the living room and his parents' bedroom. There was a bed, a closet, a small old desk with a few books and many notebooks. On the walls there perhaps still hung reproductions from the apartment on the Zeltnergasse: a print of *The Ploughman* by Hans Thoma and the plaster cast of a small ancient relief, a Macnad who danced while brandishing an animal's thigh. The desk was not always tidy; from the drawer poured out pamphlets, old newspapers, catalogues, picture postcards, torn or open letters, forming a kind of ramp; a brush lay there, bristles down, his change purse was open in case he wanted to pay for something, from the bunch of keys one protruded, ready to be used, and the tie was still partly knotted around the collar. With his sensitivity sharpened by neurosis he could not stand noises: it seemed to him he lived and wrote in the "noise headquarters of the entire apartment," "with a constant tremor on his brow." Doors slammed, and their noise drowned out the hasty steps of parents and sisters. The stove door in the kitchen banged. His father flung open the door to his room and passed close to him, dragging along his rustling robe; somebody was scraping the ashes from the stove in the next room; his sister Valli asked at random, as though across a Parisian alleyway, whether Father's hat had been brushed; more hissings, more shouts; the house's entrance door croaked like a hoarse throat; then it opened with the brief chirp of a female voice and closed again with a deep masculine thump; and then there was the more tender, more desperate noise of two canaries. . . .

With painful weariness he threw himself down on the couch and stared at the light. When the door to his room was struck simultaneously by the light from the foyer and that from the kitchen, a greenish glow poured over the glass pane. If it was struck only by the kitchen light, the closer pane turned a deep azure, the other an azure so whitish that the design on the frosted glass dissolved completely. The lights and shadows cast by the electric street lights were jumbled, superimposed and hard to understand. The illumination projected by the traveling tram onto the ceiling went by milky, veiled and in mechanical jerks, while at the first fresh and full reverberation of the street lamps, a luminous dot slithered along the equator of an earth globe, leaving it a brownish color like that of a russet apple. In the end, like Gregor Samsa and Joseph K., Kafka went to the window that looked out on the river and the hill. It was late: he no longer felt the weight of the light. Now he contemplated with meticulous attention everything he could make out in the dusk; now his empty and unfocused gaze, which rose from the heart's unknown turmoils and complications, obliterated things; now he entrusted to his motionless gaze his quiet melancholy, his flight from existence, his desire to live no longer; now he stared into the faces of the passersby and at the colors of the houses, and tried to establish a relationship between himself and the objects, and among the objects themselves, as though he might be able to find in the streets "any arm whatsoever to which he could attach himself." Perhaps in that gaze, only in that gaze, he found liberation and salvation; that "unknown nourishment" for which he had always longed.

———

When he was about twenty, he experienced with Oskar
Pollak, a young art critic killed during the First World War,
one of those pure and exclusive friendships which can be
born only from the delicate fires of youth. He existed only
for his friend; and the tension was so great that at every
instant he feared his friend might become a stranger and
desert him. This was a friendship rife with reticences,
caution and respect; he said that he ignored the other and that
the other ignored him; he distrusted the words they exchanged, and thought they could not communicate with one
another: "When we talk to each other, the words are hard, we
walk on them as on an uneven pavement. On the more subtle
points our feet swell and it is not our fault. We almost hinder
each other mutually, I run into you, and you . . . I dare not,
and you . . . We are dressed in dominos with masks over our
faces, we make (yes, I above all) clumsy gestures and then
suddenly we are sad and tired. Have you ever been as tired
with someone else as you are with me? . . . When we talk to
each other we are always hindered by things that we want to
say and cannot say that way, but we express ourselves so that
we mutually misunderstand each other or don't even listen to
each other or deride each other. . . ." And yet suddenly,
despite those uncertain, stammered, treacherous words with
"swollen feet," he reached out to his friend impulsively,
offering him all of himself. "I take a piece of my heart,
carefully wrap it in a few sheets of written paper and give it
to you." Then this shy, reticent man who did not possess
himself, separated from all things by an insurmountable
barrier, became his friend: lived through his friend: thought
with his mind, loved through his heart, saw with his
eyes—because he had not yet learned how to see for himself.
"You were for me, besides many other things," he confessed
to him later on, "also a sort of window from which I could
look out into the streets."

While he spoke to or walked with or wrote to Pollak,
Kafka split in two: he sat at his desk and another self

was present at Pollak's meeting with a girl; he lay, beatific, in bed and another self performed, like an ironic and indifferent actor, his part on the streets. His friend was only one of these selves; and all these persons, whom Kafka extracted with ecstatic and dolorous amusement from his heart, ended up loving each other, hating each other, attacking each other with desperate neurotic intensity. During those years no one had a more antagonistic soul than Kafka—the mildest of men. In the enchanting "Description of a Struggle," written between 1904 and 1910, which was born from these experiences, the story is a vertiginous play of mirrors, in which Kafka uninterruptedly depicts himself through ever new characters, and where even the words pronounced become invisible interlocutors. Among these figures there is no respite: now they hate each other and would like to attack and kill each other; now they embrace each other, kiss each other's faces, kiss each other's hands with tearful effusiveness. Undoubtedly Kafka realized that he risked being overwhelmed by the violence of his projections; and with a gesture that he repeated endlessly, he tried to transform friendship into a pure epistolary relationship. Was not perhaps the written word, of which he had been so doubtful, the perfect thing? Hearts open completely only when faces are distant, when presence does not imprison us and glances do not touch; but cold and impassioned hands cover the white paper with signs. Then we become light, and above us gleams the distant gaze of the moon.

The letters to Oskar Pollak are Kafka's first masterpieces. In them reign a contemplative passivity resigned to the inexorability of things; an exhaustion without reserve, which leads the young Kafka to become an echoing, empty place, in which the world comes to rest; and a sort of tranquil breakup of the self. "It is a singular stretch of time that I am spending here, you must have already noticed, and I needed so singular a period, a period in which I lie for hours on end on a vineyard wall and stare at the rain clouds that refuse to go away from here, or in vast fields which become even vaster when one has a rainbow in one's eyes, or when I sit in the orchard with the children . . . telling them stories or building sand castles or playing hide-and-seek or whittling small tables which—God is my witness—are never successful. A singular time, isn't it true? Or when I roam through the fields, all brown and melancholy now, with abandoned ploughs, which nevertheless send off silvery flashes when, despite everything, the sun makes its belated appearance and casts my long shadow onto the furrows (yes, my long shadow, who knows whether with it I might reach the heavenly kingdom?). Did you already notice how the shadows of late summer dance on the dark overturned earth, how bulkily they dance?" This is an undulating, melodic, florcal, suspended, cryptic, angelic prose: an unreal efflorescence of images which spring more from an overexcited imagination than from the mind, until the exhausted stylization of a gesture suddenly shatters it. As he said, it was "courteous" prose: written by one who did not wish to bear on himself the violent light of truth, the clarity of the great work of art. He lived in twilight and elusiveness; and if he had not dared to rip open this enchanting veil, he would have forever obtained, without anguish and laceration, the gift of fluency and lightness.

Often he wished to transform all of reality into a dream, into an aerial form suspended over his head. Once he imagined that the character in one of his novels lay in bed, in the shape of "a large bug, a stag beetle or cockchafer," with a dark yellow blanket stretched tightly over him, while he enjoyed the air flowing through the open window. He had not descended but rather ascended to the animal level: he had acquired the contemplative sovereignty of rocks and of the great divine-animal creatures; and from his bed, while a foolish and insignificant stand-in represented him in the world, he dominated the reality of life, which asked him for permission to exist. He did not often abandon himself to such dreams of narcissistic omnipotence. But rather he was filled with doubts about reality. He would have liked to know what reality was like before showing itself to him, before his fragile and dissolvent eye had come to rest upon it; and he believed that, to all others, it offered itself whole, compact, round, heavy, all-encompassing. For them, even a small glass of liquor stood firmly on the table, like a monument. As for himself, he was not at all certain that it was solid. The first mark of reality was that of being unreal. Everything was so fragile, uncertain, disjointed, full of cracks. "Why ever do you act as though you were real? Are you perhaps trying to make me believe that I am unreal, so comic on the green pavement? And yet much time has gone by since you, sky, were real, and you, city square, were never real." And then things began moving and vertiginously changed names: should not that poplar be called "tower of Babel" or "Noah, when he was drunk"? In that case, if the universe was only the illusionistic invention of a witty theatrical demiurge, he must continue that game, with image and word. Who could exclude that, with an act of magic, he might be able to create another universe, of cardboard, plaster and smoke? He closed his eyes, and behold, he made a mountain rise, widened the banks of the river, created a forest, made the stars ascend to heaven, erased the clouds, became smaller and smaller, with a head like an ant's egg and very long arms and legs: at his gesture the wind blew through the town square, lifting men and women into the sky; while his messengers— old servants in gray frock coats—climbed tall poles hoisting enormous gray sheets from the earth and spreading them out on high because their mistress wanted a misty morning.

He too, like all things, was unreal: only a silhouette cut from yellow tissue paper which rustled softly at each gesture and each step; only a shadow that made no noise, that no one saw, that hopped along the houses, disappearing at times in the panes of the shop windows, and could not expose itself to the light because it would have dissolved at the sky's first beam of light. If Peter Schlemihl had lost his shadow, he had not lost his body. He felt he was indistinct, had no contours, was lost in the atmosphere. If he suffered from unreality, he had but one path before him in order to exist. He must pretend, play-act ever new parts and characters on the great stage of the universe: even put on the stage the part of the man who prays, because only by playing the part could he achieve contact with transcendence. But in the end, all play-acting was useless. He had only one desire: to escape, fly away. Even as a young boy, when in the winter immediately after dinner it was necessary to light the lamp, he could not refrain from shouting; he got to his feet and lifted his arms to express his desire to fly away. He said to his friends: "Every day I hope that I shall move away from earth." He did not know how he would fly: he did not know whether he would open large white wings, like those of angels. "Is not, for example," he asked himself, "also an aptitude for flight a weakness, since it is a matter of vacillation, uncertainty and flapping about?"

He soon began to be aware of something more serious. He was not only an unreal phantom: the phantom was dismembered, torn to pieces, a heap of small bones and nerves that no one could hold together. "If I lacked," he wrote, "here an upper lip, there the pavilion of an ear, here a rib, there a finger, if on my head I had hairless patches and my face was pockmarked, this still would not be sufficient to match my inner imperfection." But even that was not enough: he must say everything. He was much less: an absence, a lacuna, a ditch that someone had excavated; something absolutely negative that an obscure god had imagined; an empty and restless form that was incapable of looking into the faces of strangers, that did not know how to answer questions, did not know how to think, speak, talk, eat, love, sleep as others do. He had neither foundations nor roots: he had no ground on which to rest, not even the little plot on which others set their feet and where they are buried;

he had neither country nor family nor heart nor feelings; and if he tried to think, all the ideas did not come to him from their roots but from some midway point. "So then try to hold on to them," he cried, "try to hold and cling to a blade of grass that begins to grow only halfway up its stem." His life was like that of one of those Japanese jugglers who climb a ladder that does not rest on the ground but on the upturned soles of a man lying on his back, and the ladder does not lean against the wall but rises straight up into the air. What could he do then but imitate those trapeze artists of the void who were the most faithful symbol of his art? And he too climb the rootless ladder? Thus, little by little, he learned his exercises. He walked along the beam, which led him over the watery abyss, without having any beam under his feet. He saw only his own image reflected in the water, and that projection became the ground on which to move; his unreal ego was at times so strong as to seem one of the five known continents, and it allowed him to keep the world united with his feet. He walked, walked, with his arms stretched out in the air, which for him replaced the tightrope walker's long pole.

Thus he began his delicate and funereal *clowneries*, which he resumed just before dying, as if he wished to salute his own adolescence for the last time. Now he was Baudelaire's clown, abstracted, inhuman, without a trace of emotion; now he evinced the buffoonish sentimentalism, the funambulism and brimming tears of Jules Laforgue's Pierrot; now he seemed a swaying, moving pole, on which was clumsily stuck a skull with yellow skin and black hair; now a bit-part vaudevillian, who petulantly kicked up his legs, joyfully making his joints crack; now he was a Hasidic fool, for whom four boards under his feet and a few colored rags were enough to recite unperturbed the role of the schnorrer who remained stretched out on the ground under any sort of pressure, crying with a dry face, but as soon as the pressure ceased lost all weight and immediately leaped into the air,

light as a feather; now he was a flat spool of thread, the clown
Odradek, thing and nonthing, incredibly mobile, infantile,
who lived in attics, along stairs and corridors, and laughed
like the rustle of dead leaves. . . . All these clowns played to
escape the monotony and boredom of time: they played with
nothingness and desolation, with a multitude of No One, the
ancestors of Beckett's clowns. The first fruit of these games
was "Description of a Struggle," a book of extremely subtle
intoxication, of continual euphoria, tender, ironic, whimsical, capricious, freakish, based on thematic leaps and dizzying changes in tone. Kafka could have stopped at this book,
like a writer without sin and without theology, if, during a
night in 1912, he had not been overwhelmed by the tide of
his unconscious, which swept away all the tenuous games of
his youth.

Self-analyzing passion was not enough for him: he realized that it led down a blind alley. With a furious imagination, a superabundant fantasy, which his ego continuously
fired in him, he formed for himself ever new figures, which
were at once concrete characters and allegorical images. He
knew that only transposition assures us of the truth. A few
years later, in several admirable pages of the *Diaries* and
Meditation, he depicted himself in the image of the Bachelor.
He "goes about with his jacket buttoned, his hands in his
high jacket pockets, elbows pointed, his hat pulled down
over his forehead, while a false smile by now innate must
protect his lips just as spectacles protect his eyes, and his
trousers are tighter around his skinny legs than is becoming."
With what truthful anguish did he describe the solitary
evenings of the old Bachelor, who begs for hospitality from
friends and strangers when he wishes to spend the evening in
company: his return home, alone, the "Good nights" before
the front door, his not being able to run up the stairs swiftly
together with a wife; the long illnesses in the lonely bed,
the contemplation for weeks on end of the empty room and
of the window, behind which glimmer uncertain forms; and

the side doors of his furnished room, which lead to the rooms of strangers.

Like Flaubert, he said that all those who have children were "*dans le vrai.*" He had only to see a table with two chairs and a smaller one to think that he would never occupy one of those chairs with wife and child, and to experience a desperate desire for that joy. He would have extolled the "infinite, warm, deep, redeeming happiness of being close to his child's crib, in the mother's presence." He imagined that only by having children can we forget our ego, dissolve "the anguish of the nerves," the effort and tension, abandon ourselves to that passive quietude and tender relaxation which the continuity of generations assures. Collaborating with others, at times, gave him the same happiness. He hoped that the dreadful burdens he carried on his shoulders would become, in secret, shared by all, and that everyone would rush to offer him help. "The few times that men give me joy," he will write to Felice, "I discern no limits to this joy, I can never touch them enough; although this may seem not quite decent, I like to go arm in arm with them. I release my arm and immediately slip it back, if I feel like it; I would always like to urge them to speak, to hear not what they want to tell me but rather what I want to hear."

The Bachelor was the last incarnation of the Stranger: the last form assumed in Western culture by Raskolnikov; this man who lives in closets, experiences a tormented detachment from people, from his own life, from anything at all, who is unable to see the created shapes of the universe, does not participate in any of his own actions and if he does speak or act "seems to be repeating a lesson learnt by heart." Also the Bachelor, like Kafka, had "been kicked out of the world." He was excluded. He had no center, protection, family, income, love: nothing on which to rely; and he lived only on himself, feeding on himself, sinking his teeth into himself, as though he knew no other flesh. He had no human contacts. He did not know how to live with his fellow man—because any man, even the dearest, loved and desired, was profoundly repugnant to him. If he was in a room, talking with friends, people who liked him, he was unable to open his mouth: the whole room made him shudder, and it seemed to him he was tied to the table. His gray-azure gaze descended upon the others, cold, icy, alien, as if it descended from another planet or rose from the tenebrous cellars of existence.

For some, solitude can be a pleasure, an ease or a respite, or a moment of quiet; but the Bachelor's and Kafka's solitude was the kind without gesture and speech of the condemned animal, which withdraws into its burrow and does not ever want to leave it again; the solitude of an object that lies in the attic of a house, and which no one will ever go upstairs to retrieve. What ravings in solitude, what hermetic and monkish dreams—the great cloistered monastery with no one living there, no one visiting, no one bringing him food, no one ringing the bell—filled the Bachelor's mind. If by chance or mistake he entered inhabited earth, he immediately turned back and withdrew into the borderland between solitude and community, the desert and Canaan, the snow-covered countryside and the Castle, where he had the impression of waiting for a message. He had no home, except for the gutters in the street. Or perhaps his true home was hotel rooms: the Stranger's residence, where the unknown objects do not offer us the affectionate complicity, the friendly familiarity of old sofas, desks crammed with papers in our rooms, wardrobes in which our clothes are gathered, armchairs which tenderly throw open their arms to us. The hotel room was closed in, restricted, limited: it was a jail; and it resembled a grave, his grave—what the Bachelor preferred over all else. "In a hotel room I feel particularly at my ease. . . . I have to myself the space of a hotel room with four clearly visible walls, and being able to lock it, knowing that my possessions, consisting of specific objects, are stored in specific points in the closets, tables and clothes racks, always gives me at least a breath of a feeling of a new existence, not yet consumed, destined for something better, possibly extensible, which actually is perhaps only desperation driven beyond itself and which has truly found its proper place in this cold grave of a hotel room."

The Bachelor, the Stranger, who was in Kafka, was disgusted with life: indeed, everyday existence, the existence that seems most touching and defenseless, aroused in him the Gnostic's tremendous hatred. He could not live in disorder and chaos: he could not tolerate his family's summer residence, where medical cotton lay next to a dish full of food, where nightshirts, clothes and sweaters were piled up on unmade beds, where his brother-in-law tenderly called his wife "darling" and "my everything," where the child defecated on the floor, where his father sang, shouted and clapped his hands to amuse his grandchild. "I'm bored with making conversation," Kafka said. "I'm bored with calling on people, the joys and sorrows of my relatives bore me to the depths of my soul. Conversation deprives everything that I think of its importance, seriousness, truth." But above all the Stranger hated loudness, uproar, the noise of life. He detested the slightest whisper, a cough, an infinitesimal susurration, the rustle that immediately vanishes in the air, the tenuous song of birds: because sound is the distinctive sign of life, that which differentiates it from silent death, and by means of sound someone had introduced sin into the terrestrial paradise. With lacerating hysterical tension, which almost seems on the point of breaking into madness, Kafka recorded all noises in his *Diaries* and letters, as though he were drawing up a musical score of the universe. At home there was the chatter of his sister and cousin, the card games of his father and brother-in-law, laughter, howls, shouts, the canary's dreadful twitter, noises as though of tree trunks behind the wall; the mechanism of the elevator which thundered through the empty attics, the maids' slippers on the floor above, which tapped against his cranial vault, and in the apartment below the cries and scamperings of children and nurses. What good were the plugs of Ohropax wrapped in cotton wool? They only muffled the noise.

But if he escaped from home to obtain silence, he again knew despair in the furnished room. The landlady volatilized until she became a shadow; the young man in the next room returned in the evening tired from work and immediately went to bed; he had stopped the pendulum of the clock in his room, but what did it matter? There was the noise of the door, the landlady's whisperings with the other tenant, the sound of the clock next door, the sound of the bell, two, perhaps three bursts of coughing, a sudden crash in the kitchen, a loud conversation coming from the floor below, and up there, in the attic, the mysterious, incessant rolling of a ball, as in a game of bowls. "I struggled a bit against the noise, then I threw myself onto the couch with almost lacerated nerves, after ten o'clock silence, but by now unable to work." Kafka knew the Stranger he carried within himself very well: he knew that he wanted silence because he desired death. "The deeper one digs one's grave, the more silence one achieves." And yet he continued to search for pure, immaculate silence: the silence that men violate, offend and lacerate with their voices, because they refuse to accept death. "I'm again going with Ottla [his sister], we went to two stupendous places I discovered recently," he wrote to Felice after a walk on the outskirts of Prague. "The first of these places is still covered with high grass, completely surrounded by low slopes, irregularly close and distant, and entirely exposed to a beatific sun. The other . . . is a deep valley, narrow, very varied. The two places are as silent as the earthly paradise after the expulsion of men. To break the quiet I read Plato to Ottla and she teaches me how to sing."

Thus, little by little, the Bachelor built his own prison. He suffered from it. He felt he was entirely imprisoned within himself, heard the faraway voices of men, friends, beloved women—and he desperately reached out his arms for them to free him. Life seemed to him terribly monotonous: it resembled the tasks schoolchildren are given when, in order to do penance for a misdeed, they must write the same sentence ten, a hundred, a thousand times. He felt oppressed by *die Enge*, "the tightness": his self, his home, Prague, the office, literature (this barrier of limits), the entire universe hemmed him in on all sides to the point of stifling him; and he thought that even the eternity he carried in his heart hemmed him in, just like the small bathroom blackened by smoke and with cobwebs in its corners with which he identified Svidrigailov's eternity in *Crime and Punishment*. He spoke openly about prison; as the years went by, the walls' barriers rose ever higher. Once, in writing to Milena, he recalled Casanova's prison in the Piombi: down in the cellar, in darkness, dampness, perched on a narrow board which almost touched the water, besieged by ferocious, amphibious rats which screeched and ripped and gnawed all night. Once he wrote: "Everything is fantasy: family, office, friends, the street; all fantasy, more distant or closer, the woman; but the closest truth is simply the fact that you are pushing your head against the wall of a cell without windows and without doors." He tried, attempted to escape from this prison; he fled into the open, uttered cries for help; perhaps literature was for him also a grand flight into the infinite, but did not his desire for marriage—Felice, Julie—represent in turn the desire for another, tighter incarceration? Thus, toward the end, he wrote: "My prison cell—my fortress." And in a stupendous aphorism he added that the prison in which he had lived had been a false prison. It was a cage; the bars were at a meter's distance from each other; through them entered the colors and sounds of the world, indifferent and imperious as though right at home; and, strictly speaking, he was free, he could participate in everything, nothing of what happened outside escaped him, he could even have left his cage. His dizzying claustrophobia had no use for this condition midway between freedom and prison. He wanted to be totally enclosed, bolted in, cut off, abandoned by the world; he wanted very high and impenetrable walls, like those of Gregor Samsa's room or of the cellar where he dreamt he could write.

If he thought about himself, the Bachelor recognized that he was, like the clown, the child of an original defeat, for which fact he found no words that would express it except the theological ones of sin and fall. Like the trapeze artist, he realized he had no ground under his feet—but if they both walked over the void, the trapeze artist at least had a safety net that protected his flights. While all other human beings possessed space, even if they spent their entire lives sick in bed—since besides their own they also had the space inhabited by their families—he possessed a space that gradually, with the passing of the years, grew smaller and smaller, and when he died, the coffin was exactly what suited him. While others had to be felled by death, because their robust relatives gave them strength, he became thinner, shrank, entrusted himself to death and died almost of his own volition, like Gregor Samsa, who dies of inanition and sacrifice. He did not even have time. Other people, immensely rich, possessed present, past and future. He, the Bachelor, had "nothing ahead of him and therefore nothing behind him": he had no prospects, dreams, future; and so he did not even have a past, since it is only the idea of the future that orders our memories. The whole enormous expanse of time, where as though in a highly mobile plot present, past and future alternate, was for him reduced to the moment, the fleeting instant. He felt he had nothing but this tiny treasure; and only with the passing of the years would he be able to transform the instants into time, dissolve the fugitive illuminations and shards into the consoling and uninterrupted fabric of a story. If he reflected further, he realized he did not even have a body—like his uncle, so slim, so weightless, so sweetly crazy, so aerial as to resemble one of those birds which barely interrupt nature's silence. "My blood," he was to write to Max Brod, "invites me to a new incarnation of my uncle, the country doctor whom at times (with all and the greatest affection) I call 'the chirper' because he has such an unhumanly subtle wit, that of a Bachelor, which issues from his narrow throat, a birdlike wit which never deserts him. And so he lives in the country, impossible to extirpate, as satisfied as one can be with subdued and rustling madness, which considers itself life's melody."

When the wind of depression blew most violently over his soul, his tender, anxious, molecular, tragic sensitivity suddenly turned him cold and motionless as a stone. He no longer felt anything. He was cold in all of his limbs; the blood curdled in his veins; he turned to stone; and he felt an icy breath strike him from within his being, carrying with it the taste of death. He felt he was a dead man who brings death, just as the corpse of a drowned man, borne to the surface by some current, drags with it into the abyss the sailors who try to save themselves from the shipwreck. At that time, he felt he was becoming a thing. He did not, like Flaubert, have the ecstatic desire to lose himself in objects: he did not stare at a drop of water, a stone, a shell, a hair until he had crept into them, penetrated them, was absorbed and swallowed by them, flowing like water, glimmering like light, descending deep into matter. He did not have the need to *become* matter: he sensed within himself—grim, menacing, irrefutable—the naked, bloodcurdling presence of the object, the mute eternity of the thing, and he was nothing but this absolute otherness. He felt the stone within himself: "I am the same as my gravestone. . . . Only a vague hope survives, no better than the inscriptions on gravestones." Or else he was a piece of wood, a dry stick severed from the trunk and shriveled by now, a coat rack hung in the middle of the room: "a useless stake encrusted with snow and hoarfrost, lightly and obliquely stuck in the ground, in a deeply torn-up field, at the edge of a vast plain, in a dark, wintry night"; or an iron gate or a moving pulley or a ball of thread; or an iron box into which someone had discharged a pistol shot. Even more atrocious must have been the moment in which he sensed in himself Odradek's presence; the star-shaped spool of thread, completely covered with frayed, knotted and tangled fragments of thread, from which protruded a small stick that was joined by another stick, to which another added itself at a right angle. That completely gratuitous object, without sense, without purpose, which laughed like the leaves, now mechanical, now almost human, which would survive all the generations—was none other than he.

Who could affirm that the Bachelor was weak and without intellectual knowledge? He had immense energy. Like Archimedes, he had discovered the lever with which to lift the world. But the world was no longer there: there was only he, who occupied the entire world; an Archimedes' lever was now used against him, to lift and detach him from his hinges. While the act of Archimedes was the triumph of the calculating mind that dominates things, the Bachelor's act only unhinged and destroyed his own ego. That was its only purpose. He lived and like everyone else tried to go down a path, but he had the impression that by the simple fact of living he blocked the road he was supposed to travel. There he was, on the road opened for him alone, like a felled trunk, like a stumbling block, an enormous boulder. The proof of life was not given to him by his condition as a man who breathed, moved, had a body, was free: it was given him simply by the fact of his blocking his own path, being his own stumbling block. On another occasion, in the later years of meditation during which he developed all the Stranger's thoughts, he expressed the same condition with a marvelous and almost mad aphoristic concentration, as if only by hammering at the language and challenging its meaning could he reach the truth. "His frontal bone blocks his path, he beats his forehead against his own forehead until he makes it bleed."

His was not a self: it was a battlefield on which innumerable adversaries confronted each other, all extracted from him, all fraternal, and ranged one against the other. Once he wrote that he had two adversaries. One pursued him from behind from the beginning: perhaps it was his destiny, the condition into which he had been forcibly placed. The second blocked the path before him: perhaps it was none other than himself, the way he lived. And besides there was his self which, on a second occasion, contained these two enemies. On the restricted field of his existence, the two enemies did not fight each other as he watched them, but both, simultaneously, fought him: one in front, the other at the back. Then there was the third enemy, the worst: his self: because it was possible to gain knowledge of the intentions of the two adversaries, but "who could know his intentions?" Depending on the circumstances, time, the passing of the hours, the light and the night, alliances were formed on the field: now the self struggled with the first adversary against the second, now the second against the first; these were alliances impossible to determine, which continually changed alignment, since one never knew whether in its heart the self favored the first or the second enemy. The Stranger knew that in the eternal struggle for his soul he could not hope for salvation to come from the victory of one or the other— because in fact he would have rushed to the assistance of the weaker adversary, who was almost drained of all blood. He had only one dream: in a night so dark as never had existed, he hoped to leave the line of combat "and because of his experience of struggle be called to judge his adversaries." Thus his salvation did not lie in a solution of the conflict: there was no possible solution for the war that had assumed the name of Kafka. The only hope was that the battlefield should become that of another, and that he should be able to watch the battle as one might watch a spectacle. Was this desire based on anything? Not in his lifetime: until the end, or almost the end, Kafka was torn by a struggle in which none of the bloody combatants perished. He found support only in literature, in the "undulating act" of writing, where impulses were represented by characters, where the perfect form of a narrative architecture, closed and ambiguous, was born—and he remained outside, identical with the totality of the book, and watched and looked and perhaps even judged.

His superhuman lucidity deepened his wounds—instead of soothing them with peace of mind. His gift of duplication allowed him at every moment to detach himself from his self and see his self from the outside and judge it with the meticulousness, coldness and hatred of the most involved and terrifying of Tribunals. All his offensive weapons, all the accusations he addressed to his father or anyone else, were instantaneously transformed, in his *Letter to His Father* or in the *Diaries*, into weapons against himself. He accused himself, tortured himself, wounded himself. "Every day I want at least one line pointed against me, just as today binoculars are pointed at comets." No matter what he did, he felt guilty: the great sinner, even when Felice, in Berlin, had a toothache or a cold; *masochism* seems too weak a word for this grandiose tragedy which takes place inside a room's four walls, and on small sheets of paper. "This morning for the first time after a long time the joy of imagining a knife twisted in my heart." "Continually the vision of a sausage maker's knife which through one side enters the body with great speed and mechanical regularity and cuts the thinnest slices, which, because of the speed, fly off almost rolled up." "I am being dragged toward the windows on the ground floor of a house by means of a rope around my neck, and I am lifted, bleeding and dismembered, without regard, as if by someone who is inattentive, through all the ceilings of the rooms, the furniture, walls and attics, until high above on the roof appears only the empty noose, as the shattering of the roof tiles has destroyed even my remains." "The most effective spot to deliver the blow seems to be the one between neck and chin. The chin must be raised and the knife pushed into the tensed muscles. One expects to see blood spurt out in torrents and to lacerate a tangle of tendons and tiny bones like those found in the thighs of roasted turkeys." Especially during his youth, the desire for suicide gave him no peace. Rarely was it the brutal violence of the pistol: almost always an impulse for flight, the rush toward the window, the shattering of wood and glass, straddling the sill, leaping into the void; or becoming liquid and pouring from the balcony, just as the pail of dirty water is emptied indifferently by the housewife over the windowsill.

In the depths of his soul he wanted much more. He wanted to suffer, sacrifice himself, be immolated: as the pile of straw is destined to be set afire in summer and burned; like Christ, like Georg Bendemann and Gregor Samsa, the two heroes of the stories of his youth, who by immolation reestablish nature's offended harmony. Then he would be happy. As he told Max Brod, he was certain that on his deathbed, if the pain were not too great, he would be "very satisfied." His heroes die unjustly: suffocated by Oedipal love, drowned in the river, dead of inanition or by a knife through the heart. But while they were dying, the Stranger carried on with them, inside them, a secret game. He was glad to die; and in those too-human laments he insinuated his hidden happiness, his lucid mind, his mild voice, his subtle feigning, his delicate *clownerie*, his metaphysical longing, everything that in him was supremely quiet—like the phoenix who lives alone in the Hindustan, without females or offspring, and when it is about to die, enveloped in a pile of palm fronds, pours from the hundred holes in its beak ever more tender, pure, heartbroken and lacerating sounds.

CHAPTER TWO

An August Evening,
on the Schalengasse . . .

Many were the memorable days in Kafka's life—marked with a white stone, as Lewis Carroll said, or instead with a black stone of misfortune. Certain days of his childhood remained intact in his memory, surrounded by their unspeakable horror: the night that his father put him on the bedroom balcony; the mornings when the maid took him to school threatening to report him to the teacher; the Sunday on which, a boy, he began to write a novel and was scorned by his uncle; the day on which he made a gift of a twenty-cent piece to the beggar woman on the Kleiner Ring. Those moments stood out, gigantically enlarged, isolated from all the rest of his life. But the most memorable of all was the evening of August 13, 1912, when he met Felice Bauer. He remembered her always, down to the most infinitesimal details. His amorous memory needed anxious and total completeness: he jealously wanted to possess all of the past, all the seconds of that evening, and he incessantly returned to that scene, interrogated it, knocked at the mind's doors, was able to resuscitate now a gesture, now a word that he thought forgotten, as though the past were an island that slowly surfaces from the gray sea of time. He did not select:

he did not wish to distinguish between important and casual, significant and insignificant; but he leveled gestures and words in the same presence-absence of significance, because behind all of them destiny could be hiding. He was never satisfied. He feared memory had lost something; and he turned to Felice's memory—perhaps as precise as his own—so that she might add one last color, one last shadow of the scene. "Completing it," he wrote to her two and a half months later, "would give me much greater joy than I was able to give you with this first collection of details."

That evening Kafka had an appointment with Max Brod in Brod's parents' home at No. 1 Schalengasse. He was supposed to review with Max the sequence of the small prose pieces of *Meditation*, which was about to be printed by the publisher Rowohlt. The appointment was for eight o'clock. As usual Kafka arrived late, perhaps after nine. These evening arrivals represented a threat for the Brod family, because as the hours passed Kafka's vivacity increased and often this meant loss of sleep for Max's brother, Otto, who liked to go to bed punctually: the entire family pushed Kafka affectionately out of the house as if he were a disturber of the peace. When he arrived, Kafka saw a girl, an unknown girl, sitting at the living room table: he found out later that her name was Felice Bauer, that she lived in Berlin, was twenty-five and worked as a department manager at the Lindstrom Company, which produced the Parlograph, a rival to the Dictaphone. She wore a white blouse, rather casual; on her feet she had Mrs. Brod's slippers (it was raining and her little boots had been set to dry); her gaze was polite but imperious. Before being introduced, Kafka offered her his hand even though she had not gotten up and perhaps had no desire to offer her hand to him. Then Kafka sat down and observed her attentively: with one of his alienating, implacable stares, which fixed things in space and in the memory and rendered them immobile, dead and absurd like stones. She looked like a maid. She had "a bony and empty face, which openly wore

its emptiness"; an almost broken nose, blond hair, a bit stiff
and unattractive, a strong chin. Her skin was dry and
blotched, almost repugnant, and the very many gold teeth,
which interrupted the grayish-yellow color of her filled teeth,
frightened him with their infernal sheen and compelled him
to look at them again and again, as though it couldn't be true.
But what was the meaning of that empty face? Was Felice
without a soul? Or was she without sin? Yet that empty,
absent face fired Kafka's furibund imagination in a way that
nothing else did.

The conversation began. Max Brod and Kafka handed
Felice the photographs of the trip they had taken to Weimar
the month before; Felice examined each image with great
seriousness, bent her head and each time brushed away the
hair from her forehead. Meanwhile the telephone rang and
she talked about the opening scene of an operetta, *The Girl
with the Car*, in which fifteen characters on stage hasten one
after the other to the phone in the hallway. Later on, the
conversation turned to the quarrels between brothers; Felice
said she had learned Hebrew and was a Zionist; Brod's
mother began to talk about her profession, about the very
efficient Parlograph manufactured by the Lindstrom Company and the fact that Felice had to go to Budapest to attend
her sister's wedding, for which she had made herself a
beautiful batiste gown. When the conversation broke off,
they all got up hastily and went into the next room to listen
to some music. Kafka accompanied Felice, who was still
wearing the slippers; they went through a room immersed in
darkness and she said, who knows why, that usually she
wore slippers with heels. While someone was playing the
piano, Kafka sat down behind the girl, sideways; she had
crossed her legs and several times touched that colorless, stiff
hair which was her constant preoccupation. At the close of
the short concert, Kafka began to talk about his manuscript:
somebody gave him advice on how to mail it; Felice said that
she loved to copy manuscripts on the typewriter and that she

would have gladly copied Max Brod's. There was talk about a trip to Palestine; Kafka asked her to go there with him, and she offered her hand to seal the promise. Afterward the company broke up; Brod's mother dozed off on the sofa; they spoke about Max's books *Arnold Beer* and *The Castle of Nornepygge*, which Felice had been unable to read to the end; old Brod brought out an illustrated volume of Goethe in the Propilei edition, "announcing that it would show Goethe in his underpants." Quoting a famous sentence, Felice said, "He remained a king even in his underpants"; and this sentence, because of its banal solemnity, was the girl's only utterance that displeased Kafka. There is only one thing we do not know about that tranquil bourgeois evening, the same as hundreds of thousands of others which during those hours took place throughout the world: When did Kafka decide on the sequence for the *Meditation* pieces: was it in the living room or the music room, at the beginning or toward the end? Everything happened rapidly, before Felice's inquisitive eyes; and at the last moment the dedication "For Max Brod" as fully written out became: "For M.B." so as to allude at least in the surname to Felice Bauer.

The evening came to a close. Felice hurried to put on her coat and boots, while Kafka leaning against a table languidly said, "I like her enough to make me sigh." The girl came back with her dry boots and a wide hat, white on top, black underneath, around which Kafka fantasized for days. They left to accompany the Berlin guest back to her hotel. Kafka was tired, confused, awkward; he sank into a half-wakeful state in which he accused himself of being good for nothing; and when they arrived at the Graben, out of desire, awkwardness and restlessness he stepped down several times from the sidewalk into the street. She asked him for his address; then she spoke about a gentleman from Lindstrom's Prague branch with whom she'd gone that afternoon in a carriage to the Hradčín; and she told him that whenever she came home from the theater, she would clap her hands from

the street and her mother would open the street door for her
(another detail which, for months, plunged Kafka into a
vortex of fantastications). Brod's father advised her about her
trip: there were certain stations where one could get good
lunch boxes; but like the modern industry department head
she was, Felice answered that she preferred to eat in the
dining car. They had arrived at the hotel. Kafka pushed into
the revolving door through which she had already entered
and almost crushed her toes. They were all gathered in front
of the elevator; Felice haughtily said a few words to the
waiter; the last good-byes were said, Kafka once more
maladroitly brought up the journey to Palestine—a trip no
one but he took seriously. He dreamt that Felice would grasp
his hand and say into his ear, without any consideration for
Dr. Brod: "You too come to Berlin, drop everything and
come." While the elevator flew up in the large, remote and
unattainable hotel, he got the idea of going to Franz Joseph
Station early in the morning, with a large bunch of flowers.
But it was too late. All the florists were closed.

On the evening of August 13, faced by that girl whom he
had described with the coldness of an entomologist and the
repugnance of an ascetic, Kafka felt irremediably caught. He
sensed a gash in his breast through which, for the first time,
the feeling of love entered and issued, sucking, without being
overwhelmed. He discovered that he belonged completely,
soul and body, to that woman of the lusterless hair, spoiled
teeth and empty expression who for five years he transformed
into his life's radiant heart. No erotic desire dominated him;
he felt calm and reassured by the fact that Eros did not rule
over their relationship. Immediately, at first sight, with an
unshakable decision, he saw his wife in Felice: the humble
and prudent mediator, who could introduce him into the
unknown city of men, the land of Canaan, to which he had
for so long wanted to be guided. Felice had all the qualities he
did not possess: she was active, sure, quick, practical,
realistic, tranquil, observant. She was masterful in the realm

of numbers and calculations from which he was excluded; she was solar while he was nocturnal; she regulated time, controlled the beat of clocks, while all his clocks were late or ran crazily fast. He could entrust himself to her completely, as one entrusts oneself to the creatures who live aloft, to Our Lady of the land of Canaan: she imparted calm, strength, quiet, certainty.

A month went by before Kafka decided to write to Berlin. He had not lost track of Felice; he had heard that at the end of August she was staying at Breslau, and he would have liked to send her flowers there with the help of a certain Dr. Schiller. He had gone "begging" for her address; first he found that of her company, then that of her home, without the street number, and finally also the number. He was afraid the address might be wrong: who indeed might that Immanuel Kirch be? "There is nothing sadder than sending a letter to an uncertain address, it is not a letter, it is more like a sigh." He was full of uncertainties and disquiet, anguish, anxieties and hopes: each new human encounter aroused the greatest tension. Slow, cautious, meticulous, full of scruples, he rested his hand for a long time on the knob before opening the door behind which was hidden the new human being, and then he opened it very slowly. Dozens of times he composed his first letter by heart, in the evening before falling asleep; but when he began to write, the flow was arrested, and before his eyes he saw only fragments and could not see either among them or beyond them. Finally, at the office, he sat down in front of the typewriter; if he could not compose with the full élan of his heart, he could at least write with "the tips of his fingers." He began: "My dear Fräulein. In the easily possible likelihood that you no longer remember me in the least, I introduce myself once more. My name is Franz Kafka, and I'm the person who met you for the first time in Prague that evening at the home of Director Brod, then handed you from across the table, one by one, the photographs of a trip to Thalia [Weimar], and finally with this hand which now taps the keys held yours when you confirmed the promise of going with him next year to Palestine." As was his habit, precisely while he introduced himself and should have affirmed his ego, he eclipsed himself and volatilized into the air like some sort of smoke. Perhaps Felice did not remember him, perhaps he did not exist, and besides, he was a very bad correspondent, incapable of punctuality in answering . . . he, of all people, the most precise, most punctual, most obsessive correspondent in the history of the world.

Felice did not answer his second letter, and Kafka, who lived only in expectation, let himself be gripped by anguish. He asked himself whether he had written something improper, or whether Felice's parents had disapproved of the correspondence between them. Then, desperate, he turned to Max Brod's sister and Felice's cousin, Sophie Friedman, so that she would act as mediator. Her letter had been lost. When at last Felice answered, Kafka was beside himself: anxiety and anguish still made him very restless; he could not become calm; he could not tolerate having lost all those weeks of his life without news; so exclusive and possessive was his curiosity that he could not bear not knowing what the lost letter contained. He went to the post office to try to find out, but in vain. He asked Felice to sum it up for him in ten words. Then, little by little, he calmed down and began his slow approach toward Felice's heart. He changed his salutation: "*Sehr geehrtes Fräulein*" (September 20), "*Verehrtes Fräulein*" (September 28), "*Gnädiges Fräulein*" (October 13), "*Liebes Fräulein Felice*" (November 2), "*Liebstes Fräulein Felice*" (November 7), "*Liebste, Liebste*" (November 14); he arrived at the intimate "*du*" and to kisses "on your beloved lips," even though "only in imagination." Locked up in his Prague prison, relieved only "by the undulating motion of writing," he crawled toward her heart like a mole that digs in its burrow until it is exhausted; and he tried to draw her into the net with his slow, meticulous, spiderlike wiles, holding her prisoner with words written at a distance of eight hundred kilometers.

Not much later, the precise Parlograph girl let herself be swept away by the enthusiasm of that strange bureaucratic angel who filled her days with his boundless letters. She must have been attracted by his defenseless tenderness, his weakness, his affectionate possessiveness and the incredible gift of imagination and metamorphosis, the burst of fire and mist which kept her stupefied until the end. Soon she too was writing a letter a day, telling him about her office life and her little Berlin tales. As for Kafka, from the "gash" in his breast issued a tumultuous torrent, in which fluctuated and whirled and collided, foaming, leaping beyond the rocks and the obstacles on the bottom, snatches of life, literary confessions—the treasure of his genius which had not yet been expressed in books. Despite her cautious warnings, he refused under any circumstances to be moderate. We continue to marvel that this man, so modest, so discreet, so elusive, should confide all without reserve, almost as though he had always known Felice; the ardent and unlimited élan of his heart, the gift of tenderness, the need for revelation, were put on paper without the slightest let or hindrance. He projected Felice outside himself, and he totally identified with his projection; he devoted himself to her, consecrated himself to her, as though it were Felice and not literature that gave meaning and value to his existence. "Write to you I must so that the last word written before falling asleep is written for you; and everything, wakefulness and sleep, acquires at the last moments that true meaning that it cannot draw from my scribblings." His diary had almost come to a halt: his lean, silent, hammered, fragmentary prose style had been transformed into the wave of a dialogue or mono-logue that nothing could contain. During those last months of 1912 he had confidence in himself—something that would never happen to him again. He was full of good humor; he arrived at the office singing, he walked quickly, he quickly wrote the long, handwritten letters; he was euphoric, dancing and Dionysiac. His life was going through a moment of expansion.

Thus, during the months between the end of 1912 and the beginning of 1913, from Kafka's hands was born the most beautiful poem on the "mail" that was ever written. Letters replaced everything—office, family, friends, at times even literature; all of life became a letter on its way to Berlin; the remote and the absent became magically close; and upon contact with the mails and the mail carriers reality was transformed into a cloud of smoke, a hilarious, aerial and meticulous bureaucratic comedy. He did not like to phone Felice, in part because phoning produced in him too intense an emotion and he avoided emotions, in part because "*les demoiselles du téléphone*" put us in touch, bringing together voices and souls, and he preferred epistolary distance. He waited an hour to obtain a connection, he hung on to his seat out of anxiety; then he would be called and ran to the phone, making everything shake, while the people around him, either too happy or too loquacious, watched him. He asked for her in a plaintive voice and out of anxiety could neither hear her voice nor answer her (meanwhile, behind him, a director bubbling with mirth suggested that he hold the phone to his lips instead of his eyes). Finally he emitted an "anguished sound," whereas Felice later wrote him that his voice had been "fearfully mean." But writing was a joy! He wrote to her from all places and at all hours: he wrote to her from the office, while the clerk was asking him for information about insurance for convicts and the typist dozed off and stretched lazily before him; he wrote to her from the boss's desk, and then he had to stop because department heads must not write letters to their girlfriends; he wrote to her in the afternoon, right after lunch; he wrote to her at night, after working on *Amerika* or "The Metamorphosis," when he was not distracted by life's noises, and often writing his "novel" was nothing but the repressed wish to write to her, and his letters expressed something of the exhaustion and inebriation of the solitary nights; and he even wrote to her when in a state of half-wakefulness which seemed to him populated by the light, insistent clatter of the keys. He wrote all the time, interminably, dozens of pages, reaching for the infinite, slowing down time: as though his hand's gesture were a kind of long, drawn-out lament, a slow and weary mewling. He bought envelopes and stamps, went to the post office, all the way to the central railroad station at night; he courted and pursued the mailmen who carried regular letters and registered letters, as well as the unattainable lords of the telegrams. The letters left every few hours, they seemed to pursue and dog each other's heels, one after the other, one on top of the other, as though he had reserved for himself alone all the postal traffic between Prague and Berlin.

Then began the waiting, the long, dreadful waiting for Felice's letter, which was coming down from Berlin: the symbol of all the waiting for something or someone, a message or a messenger, that fills Kafka's books to overflowing. Almost always Felice sent her letters to his office. He had given three of the employees orders to bring him her letters before the other correspondence. The first, the messenger Mergl, was humble and solicitous and shared his anxieties; but he almost always disappointed the hopes of Kafka, who began to dislike him intensely. The second messenger was the head of the clerical office, a certain Wottawa, an old, tiny bachelor with a wrinkled face covered with blotches of all colors, his face bristling with hair, who always smacked his damp lips while sucking on his Virginia cigar. But how divinely beautiful he was when, on the threshold, from his inner pocket he extracted Felice's letter and delivered it! The third hope was Fräulein Böhm. When she found the letter, she arrived radiant and handed it to Kafka as though in reality the letter concerned only the two of them; if the other two managed to get hold of it she almost felt like crying and resolved to be more attentive the next day. But Kafka was insatiable. At times thinking of the enormous incoming correspondence, he died of impatience, distrusted his three messengers, agitatedly roamed through the corridors, inspected the office boys' hands and finally went down himself to the Institute's mailroom. When the letter arrived, he took it with the usual tremor of his hands, read it, reread it, put it aside, went back to reading it, picked up a dossier, but he still only read the letter. He stood next to the typist to whom he was supposed to dictate, or to someone asking him for information, and again the letter passed through his hands, and he thought only about Felice enclosed on a sheet of paper. It seemed to him that the sheet and the postcard gave him calm and security; it was enough for him to put his hands in his pockets and feel with his hands her words. Once he dreamt that the mailman was bringing him two registered letters and was handing them to him, one in each hand, with a magnificently precise movement of the arms, which sprung out like the pistons of a steam engine. They were magical letters. The envelopes were never empty, just as from the hazelnut in the fairy tale streams meter upon meter of extremely white linen, billowing and tumultuous like the waves of the sea. Kafka would stand halfway up the stairs, read and drop on the steps the pages already read; continually new sheets filled the inexhaustible envelopes; the entire stairs from top to bottom were covered with thick layers of paper which gave off a loud rustle.

The speedy and scrupulous postal service of the Austro-Hungarian Empire was his best ally. All one had to do was write to Felice on Tuesday evening and she would receive the letter in Berlin at ten o'clock on the morning of the following day. This permitted a marvelous correspondence of tempos: "I write you only for myself, to experience tomorrow at ten o'clock the sensation of having arrived for one instant in your dear proximity which brings happiness." Subjected to the regular rhythms of the mail service, Kafka had the feeling that there existed somewhere the rhythmic regularity that some attribute to the gods and to Providence. He had an absolute need for this regularity: to soothe the anxiety of his heart, Felice's letters must arrange themselves in an uninterrupted sequence without hitches, without gaps, without absences. Every day, at the same hour, the mailman must arrive at the Institute's mailroom with a letter for him from Berlin: "It is precisely their regularity that does the heart good, always the same hour at which a letter arrives every day, that same hour which carries with it a sense of peace, fidelity, order, the impossibility of ugly surprises." To propitiate the benignity of the postal service he sent only registered letters and begged Felice to do the same. Thus, perhaps, he would be able to ward off the greatest of misfortunes: that a letter might lose its way forever in the dusty meanders of the offices, or be dropped mistakenly into a box in some town, some village. He had another postal dream. He was in his room, in Prague, and next to his bed a telegraphic apparatus communicated directly with Berlin; all one had to do was press a button and the immediate answer appeared on a sheet of paper. He was nervous; he was afraid to telegraph, but he must do so because of a strong apprehension and a burning desire to hear from Felice. His younger sister pushed the button. Immobilized by expectation, Kafka watched the tape which unrolled without marks; it was not possible to see them because no answer could arrive before Felice was called to the apparatus in Berlin. But how great was Kafka's joy when the first characters appeared on the tape! A true and proper letter followed, full of tender recriminations and affection, which dispersed in the labyrinths of his dream.

Despite precautions, sometimes the letters arrived irregularly or not at all. Kafka had the impression that at the center of the precise postal organization of the Austro-Hungarian Empire there was an employee who played perfidious games with their letters. He sent them off whenever he wished, and so they were delayed, kept one waiting for days and nights, slowing and hindering the flow of time—"because here the clocks strike only when a letter of yours arrives." Perhaps it wasn't an employee: it was some dark power which amused itself behind his back, just as it will amuse itself behind the backs of his characters; and Kafka felt that he did not have a relationship with Felice, but with an enigma, an ungraspable reality which sent him messages that could be lost. When a letter was delayed, he was full of anguish. He was alone in his office, in the presence of his typist, of clients who thought only about themselves, clerks who came to ask for information, and he asked himself: Did her mother torture her? Does her head hurt her? Or her teeth? Or is she too tired? He was no longer able to work, talk, get through his days; and he begged for the alms of two lines, a greeting, an envelope, a postcard, "Felice on a bit of paper." When letters were lost, it was a tragedy. What to do? Give them up forever? That would have been reasonable. But he would have liked to go hunting through the Empire's post offices, searching for them in the pouches of all mailmen, in cellars where perhaps some distracted person tossed lost messages—perhaps they contained marvelous statements, unique truths that could save him from despair.

We go through this immense correspondence with a kind of terror, so great is the intellectual and spiritual tension it reveals in every line. We must devote to these letters the same attention devoted to "The Metamorphosis" and *The Castle*, because they have the same dramatic concentration, the same symbolic charge; and our wonder is continually renewed by this fantastic wealth in the pure state, such as the German world had not known since the times of the young Goethe and the young Hölderlin. Like the great lovers of life and literature, Kafka questioned. Interrogated. He wanted to know everything that concerned Felice, even the facts that to another would have seemed remote and indifferent; at a distance of eight hundred kilometers, condemned by his own

wish to separation, he wanted to discern all the intimate
details of her life and possess them with his maniacal gaze.
He asked at what time she went to the office, what she ate for
lunch, what were the names of her girlfriends, how was she
dressed, what she saw from her office window, to what
theater she had been and where she had sat and what her
mood was and why. And what was the street where she lived
like—quiet, hidden, far from Berlin's noise? And where was
she as she wrote? Was she resting the paper on her knees, and
did she have to bend over? The streetcars in Berlin were
slow, isn't that true? In long files, one after the other? And in
the morning did she walk to the office? And in what boxes
did she drop her letters? And what were the guests at the
summer pension like? And whom had she met on the train?
And could he have a photograph of her office? Nothing could
ward off Kafka's total curiosity. After he knew her present,
he wanted to know her past, right down to the very first
images of her childhood. He tried to meet people to whom
Felice wrote; he waited for them to pronounce her name; and
he resumed his inexhaustible questions. Even though he did
not wish to possess her body, he was jealous of every glance
that grazed her, every thought directed at her, every greeting
placed at her feet. "So then I am jealous of all the people in
your letter, mentioned and not mentioned by name, men and
boys, business people and writers (of course, especially the
latter). I am jealous of the Warsaw representative. . . . I am
jealous of those who offer you better jobs, I am jealous of
Fräulein Lindner. . . . I am jealous of Werfel, Sophocles,
Ricarda Huch, Lagerlöf, Jacobsen. . . . But in your letters
there are also other persons with whom I would like to pick
a fight. . . ."

Felice had sent him her photograph as a little girl, and
then a photograph as an adult. Kafka kept the two images
side by side: Felice had split into two different persons, and
he was divided and wooed them both—the terribly serious
little girl, the young miss who inspired respect. He had

realized two dreams in one: to live a love composed only of images; to love a person in two different forms—but he sensed that the two images had a tendency to fuse, the little girl led him to the grown miss and recommended him to her. Then, from Berlin arrived a wallet with a photograph inside. Desire gripped him at the throat; he continually opened the wallet and contemplated the figure with an insatiable gaze— "in the light of street lamps, along the streets, in front of illuminated shop windows, at my desk at the office, at a sudden stop in the hallways, close to my typist as he dozes off, at the living room window, while behind my back a large crowd of acquaintances and relatives filled the room . . ." And then all the other photographs that came down from Berlin! They surrounded him on all sides; he looked at them, scrutinized them, questioned them obsessively with his eyes so as to grasp the mystery of that life so far from him. He called her by name, kissed her tenderly before falling asleep, felt he belonged to her entirely. At moments the distance seemed canceled: Felice was there at his side, imprisoned in a photograph; but if he looked more attentively, with the multiplied tension of his feelings, he realized that Felice's gaze, from the wall or his desk, refused to dwell on him, did not stare at him and lost itself beyond the window. . . . "I turn your picture every which way, but you still find a way to look elsewhere and do so with calm and almost with deliberate intention." Now the closeness he had dreamt of was shown to be illusory. He too sent to Berlin a photograph of himself as a child, before becoming "his parents' monkey"; and a photograph of two or three years before, with a high collar and the eyes of a visionary dazzled by the magnesium flash. Felice put the picture in a locket; and he was jealous of his own portrait, wanted to go to Berlin, tear it out of the locket and keep Felice's gaze for himself alone, as though he felt that many Franz Kafkas roamed the earth, in reality or image, hostile to one another.

He thought about her all the time. Felice had become the

single obsession of his life: a tumult of ideas, feelings, images and fantasies bore her name and assailed him from all sides. This obsession occupied his mind, heart and body, not allowing anything else to dwell inside him. "It is as though the entire world had precipitated into you. . . . The love you grant me becomes blood that runs through my heart, I have no other." "I would like you not to be in the world but entirely in me, or better yet, that I should not be in the world, but entirely in you, I feel that one of the two is too many, the division into two persons is insufferable." With all the power of his intelligence, he exasperated sensations: the slightest facts took on an infinite resonance. His emotions, which seemed to possess a physical quality, rose every day in tone. His nervous tension grew, the emotional violence became intolerable, an obscure flame drove his spirit to a kind of fury. He would not, could not, stop. He could not endure the rhythm of the daily letters. When he answered, he did not distribute his emotions tidily in separate sentences but "vomited" all of himself into one long sentence, in a terrible tension that seemed to want to kill him, as though the words sprang from an unfathomable biological depth. This was not love but a battle. With ardor, tenacity and despair, he fought for her, against her, for himself, against himself, against all possible and imaginary enemies; it seemed to him that the world was too small to contain the fantastic riches of his love.

No one could doubt the tragic truth of Kafka's passion. But this correspondence is also fiction. This long love, celebrated in hundreds of letters, is a theatrical performance before a mirror, in which Kafka plays all the parts. He wrote and answered himself all by himself. He spoke and was the echo that repeated the last syllables. He loved and loved himself, hated and hated himself, or tried to damn and save himself at the same instant. Only someone who does not, by experience, know the power of imagination can believe that such a performance is less authentic than the love between two "real" persons. If Kafka pushed his performance to the extreme, it was not without reason. He complained, aroused in himself imaginary passions and sorrows, deliriously play-acted death and destruction; and all along, his mind remained free, lucid, detached from all that which, desperately moved, mouth and heart cried out. Thus he achieved a superior tranquility: a limpid quiet within the heart of true and feigned tragedy; that "smile of the dying man" happy to die which imbues his pages with a luminous tenderness.

During five years of correspondence, Kafka lived with Felice only for very few days. With every excuse and pretext, he avoided taking the train to Berlin and joining her. He did not spend his vacations with her, did not share with her the crowded or solitary railroad compartments. He understood the risk "of having attached himself to a living person"; and he told her that he remained in Prague so as to remain closer to her. With extreme clarity, almost with cruelty, he explained to her that he could love a woman only from a distance, protected by the twofold distance of space and literature. He pursued the dream of a love that never existed, a love that completely excluded proximity, daily sharing and community, and he entrusted himself to the soundless words of letters and photographs. He was the one who "received messages" from a remote point in space, where a hand would incessantly write for him, as he would write to her without interruption. But what a strange distance! The sheet of paper palped and clutched in his hand was supposed to reveal to him, as by a procedure of "high magic," what Felice was doing in Berlin: whether she was healthy or sick, gay or sad, whether she suffered from a toothache or nostalgia. "We must organize ourselves," he added, only apparently in jest, "in such a way that at the very instant in which one asks something of the other, the mailman will enter at a run at any hour of day or night."

Without seeing her and speaking to her, Kafka made every effort to realize this magical communication and affinity of souls. In the evening, unimpeded by the day's din and by work, he tried to see her as she chatted with her mother; at night he tried to dream about her. He sent his magic vibrations in the direction of Berlin, and he had reserved a place for her in his office, which she could inhabit like a silent shadow, while like a shadow he would inhabit the Parlograph offices. What did places and spaces matter? Together, in Berlin and Prague, like the magnetic needles of the same compass, they formed "a single great reality" of which they would always be certain; one of them would think something in a low or loud voice, and the other, at a distance of hundreds of kilometers, would answer, without even having been questioned. Consciously or unconsciously, Kafka had in mind the magical power of attraction that utterly binds Ottilie and Eduard in the last chapters of *Elective Affinities*. Thus distance would be turned into absolute closeness. They would write continuously, until their pens and papers would come close, almost merge, one would read the other's letters, finding himself in the end in the other's arms. "Yes, yes, we ought to stop writing letters, but we ought to be so close to each other as to exclude the need to write; not only that, but so as not to have, due to excessive proximity, even the need to talk." At such a moment their relationship would reveal its secret law. Theirs was not a human love, based on communication and words, but a magnetic love, like that which bound Ottilie and Eduard and can bring two stones, two great stars in the firmament close together.

Kafka was too whole a man to be satisfied by these tragic spiderwebs woven over the chasms of distance. On certain days, at moments with terrible intensity, he was assailed by the sensation that their exchange of letters was a vain and delusive thing, which rendered the distance even more irremediable. "Actually, if we were separated by continents and you were somewhere in Asia, we could not be more distant than this. . . . This time too I do not give an answer, answers are given by word of mouth; by writing we do not understand each other, we can at most have a presentiment of happiness." He experienced the desolate anguish of distance. When he was alone in the office, before his untidy and paper-covered desk, next to Felice's silent shadow, he thought that he would not be able to live with her and felt like overturning tables, shattering the cabinets' glass doors, insulting his office director. He had an almost animal need for closeness and affection; he had the desire to grasp those distant hands. "How is it possible to hold on to a person only with written words, one holds with hands. . . . I stop now, it is already late. . . . A strange way to act, using one's hands to write letters when they are made for something else and want nothing else than to hold you tightly." At least when he was finished writing to her, he would have liked to look into her eyes. He dreamed of taking walks with her along the avenues of Berlin. He offered her his arm, like a fiancé, but their shoulders touched closely, their arms adhered for their entire length, like those of Joseph K. and his assassins. So, disappointed by both distance and closeness, he became convinced that he would spend all his life before a closed door, before the servant's entrance of Felice's house, waiting in silence to hear whether from beyond that door would come a word, a sound, an echo of laughter, an incomprehensible mutter. He could wait for a long time, without impatience, for eternity, because his capacity for waiting was immense, and because he knew that the door would never be flung open to his timid knocks. Or, perhaps, who is to say, one day the door would open: Felice would appear in the light of day—a shape glimpsed a few years before, a shape glimpsed in a dream and by now unrecognizable—getting into the carriage that waited for her. He would stand in the dust, the mud, the gutter: humble and humiliated like a dog, or like one of those abject parasites that he—the Stranger— carried within him. At that instant he would throw himself at her feet and kiss her hand. "I will confine myself to kissing

like a madly faithful dog your absentmindedly dangling
hand, and it will not be a sign of love, but only a sign of the
despair of the animal condemned to silence and eternal
separation. . . ." Then he would run after her carriage,
through great whirling traffic, without losing sight of her,
without letting himself be deflected by any obstacle. This
was the only thing he knew how to do. There would be
nothing else: until the end of time he would remain the one
excluded, rejected, deserted, alien. This was the principal
figure of his life: the countryman's waiting before the divine
law, the waiting of all the Chinese for the emperor's message,
the waiting for the angel, the waiting at the Castle populated
by gods: a waiting destined to remain eternally disappointed.
It was not the intuition of God and the notion of transcendence
that generated Kafka's waiting, but rather this sense of waiting, which coincided with the very fact of living, that generated Kafka's idea of God and his theology.

    At the beginning of 1913, the impulse of exaltation, folly
and euphoria that had sustained him during the writing of
"The Judgment," *Amerika* and "The Metamorphosis," and
which had allowed him to write to Felice, came to a halt.
When Karl Rossmann was about to be lost in the American
slums, he abandoned *Amerika*. Depression once more dominated him. He was exhausted, desolate, defeated; he spent
hours on end, "gloomy and dazed," in the bed where Gregor
Samsa had awakened on his back, hard as armor; he took
lonely walks, spoke to neither his parents, his sister nor his
friends; and he walked like a somnambulist, stumbling
through the streets, his heart reduced to a flickering muscle.
Before himself he saw nothing but despair, absolute, absolute
despair that no rational thought could ward off or alleviate,
despair as the sole content of his life. Around him rose the
waters of a dark destiny. There was nothing but misfortune,
unknowable, without name or face, which every day hurled
its threats at him. No improvement was possible, because he
had only the strength given him at birth and no succor would

come from some obscure reserve. Like every Stranger, he did not know the future: "Naturally I haven't any plan or any foresight. I cannot enter the future, but I can fling myself into the future, wallow in the future, stumble into the future, and more than anything else I can lie down on the ground." As for his love for Felice, it had been a disaster from the very beginning. It was an obscure necessity—a magnetic force, which attracted him and made him rotate in the distance, but only to his ruination.

He wrote to Felice at the beginning of March, asking her to chase him away. There were three possibilities. "Either you have only pity for me . . . or you do not have exclusive pity for me, but have been deceived for six months, do not have an exact vision of my miserable nature, overlook my confessions and without being conscious of it prevent yourself from believing them." Or "it may be that you do not have exclusively pity for me and also you understand my present state, but believe that one day I might still become a useful man with whom a regular, tranquil, living dialogue is possible. If you believe this, you are terribly deceived. . . . Do not give way, Felice, to such illusions. You could not live at my side even for two days." Despite this, on March 22 he left for Berlin, stopping at the Askanischer Hof. He wanted only to prove to her that he was unworthy of her. "Presence is irrefutable."

CHAPTER THREE

The Writer as Animal

Even in the years of his youth, Kafka experienced poetic inspiration as a flow: as a tide or very strong wind that filled his mind and his body and could have carried him far out to sea, where the currents of great poetic creations run. This wind arose in him particularly at night, leaving him sleepless or at war with his own dreams; it was a liberating force but also a fury that tore him limb from limb, a revolt that rose from the outskirts, the abysses of his soul, the unconscious darkness of his spirit. Something inside him, he did not know where, resisted this tide, "contained it, oppressed it," did not give free rein to the unconscious and precisely because of this could not guide it. Thus Kafka had the impression that, in him, instead of a majestically vivacious harmony there was an uproar. He sensed the hostility of words: "My entire body puts me on guard against every word, before letting itself be written down by me every word looks around it on all sides"; and his mind did not as yet impose on things that irresistible fluency which would be the gift of his great novels. At each line he had to begin all over again, as if he were composing laborious mosaics. On his desk, everything looked to him dry, distorted, immobile, embarrassed by all that surrounded it, shy and above all full of gaps. Only truncated beginnings rose to the surface; every fragment scurried about homeless and rushed in opposite directions. "Almost none of the words I write is suited to the others, I feel as though the consonants grate against each other with a tinny sound and the vowels accompany them with song like Negroes at the exposition. My doubts stand in a circle around each word and I see them before I see the word." The words scattered and he was not able to gather them into a complex sentence; and between one phrase and the next crevices opened up that were so large he could push both of his hands into them, or one sentence had a high tone and another a low, or a sentence rubbed against its neighbor as the tongue scrapes against a rotten tooth. To Max Brod he described the first draft of *Amerika* (a book that would turn out to be tumultuously rich) as an ensemble of "brief pieces set side by side rather than entwined with one another."

Finally, liberation came. It was a Sunday—September 22, 1912, approximately a month after he had met Felice. He had spent the afternoon in a tedious family occupation: his brother-in-law's relatives had for the first time come to visit him. he never opened his mouth and would have liked to howl from boredom and despair. After supper, around ten o'clock, he sat down at his desk. He had intended to describe a war. From a window a young man saw a crowd approach; at that his pen, almost unbeknown to him, began to write "The Judgment"—a story of fathers and sons, tacit usurpation and condemnation, cruelty and sacrifice—which for the first time mirrored his own Oedipus complex. He immediately had the impression that it was no longer a matter of "playing with one's fingertips," as at the time of "Description of a Struggle." This story was written with all his energies: with mind, soul and body. It was a true and proper birth, "covered with filth and mucus." The powers of his unconscious, which until then he had contained and repressed, had suddenly come to light, breaking down the barriers that had stood in their way.

He wrote all night without ever interrupting himself, without sleeping, his legs stiff from sitting at the desk; he slid over the surface of events and things—no psychology, no apparent explanation—while he brought to light the enormous richness of what he had stirred up. If he had halted for an instant, if he had moved or opened a book or been distracted, he would have blocked access to the until then unspoken truths. Writing was exactly this irresistible tide: it had the unlimited, undefined and uninterrupted quality of water, and at the same time it seemed a navigation on water, as though successive masses were being superimposed one on top of the other in the ocean's unity. Clinging to the desk as to a rock or grave, he could not lift his hand from the page, for otherwise the story would have lost its élan, its impetus, its natural and continuous development—the magic fluidity of breathing to which he had so long aspired. He understood that one must write in a single breath, not only short stories but also long novels like *The Sentimental Education*, which he dreamt of reading in a single session to his audience: "*Only like this* is it possible to write, only in connectedness of this kind, with a complete opening up of body and soul." At two he consulted the clock for the last time. His tiredness vanished. A few hours later, outside the window the air gradually turned blue; a cart rolled by; two men crossed the bridge. He turned off the lamp in the day's brightness. At six, when the maid crossed the foyer for the first time, he was writing the last paragraph. He pushed back the chair, rose from his desk, left the room and stretched in front of the maid, saying: "I've been writing till now." Trembling, he entered his sister's room and read the story, whose meaning he still did not know. He felt his eyes were bright. Then, exhausted and happy, he went to bed, "with slight pains around his heart and twitchings in the muscles of his abdomen."

In those few hours between ten in the evening and six in the morning, Kafka established once and for all his conception of literature and his idea of poetic inspiration—the most grandiose after Plato and Goethe. He was certain that somewhere there was a "supreme power" that made use of his hand. It did not matter who it was: whether an unknown god, or the devil, or demons, or simply the sea of darkness he always bore within himself and of which he was aware as a supremely objective force. He must obey it, follow its hints, open himself to its word, transform his life, his mind and his body into a "precisely articulated" instrument to secrete literature as the great writers whom he admired had done. It was a tremendous task! It meant continued labor, full of doubts and waits! He was not content to obey; he must destroy many things inside and outside himself, and with atrocious asceticism, with frightful avarice he must save and economize on everything that regarded his existence. So many things must be forgotten: family, friends, nature, women, travel, Felice, children, conversation, music. It was a kind of alchemy: to abolish life within oneself and transform it into that pure, translucent, absent and empty substance called literature. If he did not do this, if he was not burnt and sacrificed at the foot of the paper altar, the god of literature would prevent him from living. "Tomorrow I will resume writing, I want to throw myself into it with all my strength, I feel that if I do not write there is an inflexible hand that expels me from life." If he had stopped writing, he would have become the prisoner of the slightest gust of wind: slow, turbid, incapable of understanding; alone like the stone or piece of wood he sensed he was at his own origin. If he wrote, there was—perhaps—some hope. He would be able to stand up to the world; and the god of literature would have brought him the gift of Felice.

He knew that at night good men sleep, enclosed in their sleep like children, protected by a celestial hand against the assaults of nightmares. Sleep is the purest and most innocent of divinities: a mild blessing, which descends only on the eyelids of pure beings. Sleepless men are guilty, because they do not know the quiet of the soul and are tortured by obsession. Like all guilty men, he suffered from insomnia. In the evening he fell asleep, but after an hour he woke up as though he had placed his head in the wrong hole. He was perfectly awake, had the impression of not having slept at all or having slept covered by a very thin skin, and he still had ahead of him the effort of falling asleep. Then he fell asleep again; his body slept alongside itself, while his self thrashed about and struggled with dreams. Around five, the last traces of sleep were consumed; and the dreams were much more fatiguing than being awake. When he awoke completely, all his dreams were clustered around him and watched him with silent, frightening eyes. But he understood that insomnia—his sin—was also his strength. Anyone who slept in such a restless and agitated way lived in a close relationship to the spirit of the night, the demons and powers that nest in darkness, the powers that crowded his unconscious; and he must evoke it, as on the night that he wrote "The Judgment," at the cost of never sleeping again.

In a *History of the Devil* he had read that among present-day Caribbeans "he who works at night" is considered a creator of the world. He did not have the strength to create or re-create the world; but if he were to stay awake at night he would be able to bring to light what his unknown god had revealed to him. So he imposed this discipline on himself: he sat down at his desk at ten o'clock in the evening and got up at three, sometimes at six. He wrote in the dark, silence, solitude and isolation while all the others—Felice, whom he did not wish to see; his mother and father, with whom he exchanged very few words; and his friends—slept; and it seemed to him that he still did not have enough silence and that "the night was still not night enough." He would have liked to cancel day and summer, dawn and sunset, prolong the night beyond its brief confines, transforming it into an interminable winter. Around him there was the most profound immobility, and it seemed the world had forgotten him.

The night alone was not enough for him. Since his inspiration came not from above but from the abyss, he too must descend ever lower, toward the depths of the earth, and once arrived down there, lock himself up like the prisoner he was in the depths of his soul. "I already thought more than once that my best way of life would be that of living with what was needed to write and a lamp in the innermost room of a vast, closed cellar. I would be brought food; it would always be placed behind the cellar's farthest door. The distance to go in my robe and fetch my meal, passing beneath the cellar's vaults, would be my only walk. Then I would return to my desk, eat slowly and moderately, and immediately resume writing. Who can say what things I would write! From what depths I would draw them!" But not even this image was enough: some noise might perhaps reach all the way to the segregated cellar; perhaps someone—his unknown companion, Felice, friends would surmount the obstacles and come to disturb him in his solitude. He wanted something more than a hermitage, the profound sleep of death, the imperturbable peace of the grave, where all human contact is done away with. So, having become a recluse and a dead man, Kafka found at last the proper conditions for writing. Without the bother of the office, or human contacts, or marriage, all of time was at his disposal: an infinite stretch of time, because an inspiration boundless as the sea must not be confined. Shut within the profundity of night, he drew close to the core of his being, concentrated without effort and difficulty: yet at the same time "he expanded," "he poured out," issuing from the body's straits into the infinity of writing; he liberated all that was hidden or rigidified inside him, and so obtained that great fervency and happiness that warmed his icy hands and shivering heart.

As soon as he went to his desk in the evening, the tumult,

the violence, the splendid recitation of his letters to Felice deserted him. There was no mirror there, nor other human beings, nor he himself, to be convinced. Above the neurosis, hysteria and anguish that tortured him during the day, he found a superhuman corner of peace: that serenity of the mind, from which descend his accents of almost Taoist quiet. Down there he—the tortured one—never wrote a broken or disjointed line: the terrible tranquility, the light, discreet touch are not violated even when Gregor Samsa and Joseph K. are taken to their deaths. The story was the place where everything was placated and set onto "the right path." Meanwhile, precisely in the nocturnal place, the complete transformation of darkness occurred. He knew very well that his immersion in the unconscious involved tremendous dangers: he risked never coming back from his journey of exploration, or coming back with the madman's distorted features. But he also knew that if he brought darkness before the eyes of reason, transforming it into a daring intellectual game as Poe had done, his work would have been in vain. So during those nights, the miracle took place that makes Kafka unique among modern writers. Darkness lost none of its disquieting power, its viscosity, its irradiation; the unconscious assumed a shape but remained unconscious; reason never interposed its mediation; and yet the whole unknown archipelago came to light, with not a single shadow or an undefined stroke, as though it were a creature of the day. We receive a unique impression: we are immersed simultaneously in the unconscious and in a vortex of light.

His great novels are of an extreme complexity: a thousand relationships and internal connections run through them; an impression or an event is corrected, at a distance of hundreds of pages; every figure has only one meaning when counterposed to all the other figures; every sentence can be understood only if we set out from the totality of the book. So we would tend to believe that he laboriously drew up plans, projects, work schemes, or corrected and continually rearranged his book like Dostoevsky and Tolstoy. None of this is true. Down there, in the cellar, writing *Amerika* or *The Trial* or *The Castle*, Kafka did not even draft an outline or sketch: for him the problem of narrative architecture did not exist. Like a man possessed, he surrendered himself to the illimitable, wavelike imagination that flowed through him at night; and this nocturnal inspiration was endowed with all the structural knowledge he needed. The text was a great lava flow not divided by chapters, paragraphs, punctuation marks—which were added at a later stage. He corrected very, very little. Those months in the fall of 1912 were the decisive moment in Kafka's life. After the cobwebs and *clowneries* of "Description of a Struggle" and *Meditation*, he discovered that he was not at all the exquisite and tenuous writer he had thought. The shadows of the unconscious had invaded him; and while he was writing letters to Felice, "The Metamorphosis" and *Amerika*—an immense correspondence, a story of incommensurable significance and a novel that could have continued into infinity—he realized that he possessed a torrential imaginative wealth. Everything seemed to be in his hands. Had he wanted to, he could have become another Dostoevsky: author of a work that could compete only with nature. I find it hard to say with how much awareness Kafka rejected this. As he said in a few illuminating lines, he sent "the great masses" of his imagination down "narrow roads" within "narrow limits." Down there, in the shut-in cellar, he must concentrate, renounce all desire for expansion, all variation, all dilation. He must tend to the heart. Prison: this was the source of Kafka's greatness. No one knew, as he did, this dreadful desire for self-limitation, which led him to restrict his circle more and more, check whether, by chance, he were not hiding somewhere beyond the confines that had been assigned to him. Because, as he said, "only a limited circle is pure." He could not do otherwise. But for all his life he had the regret of having committed a sin, rejecting the possibility the unknown god had offered him.

He had other doubts. It was enough for him to stall before an obstacle, and for two days he would quit writing, because he feared that he had forever lost his talent. He of all people, who like no one else had an almost animal-like gift for writing, felt this gift to be a fragile, rarefied thing, liable to vanish at the first breath of wind. He did not trust his inspiration: he felt he was "vacillating," flying without interruption toward the peak of the mountain, but unable to stay up there even for an instant. In part these doubts were understandable: he was not one of those writers who sit down every morning before their worktable—inspiration came and went; it could fall silent and abandon him for years, plunging him into bitter despair. And besides, what if everything were an illusion of his? If no superior power intended to utilize him for its ends? And if, finally, the act of writing, the gesture of shutting himself up in the cellar, were the most terrible of sins? What if he had rejected the Law? He adored literature, but he was the opposite of an aesthete. He had always believed that man's most sublime act was the act dictated by *caritas*, like Gregor Samsa who immolates himself for his family.

Throughout his life, Kafka—the most spiritual of men—was obsessed by his body. The body that someone had attributed to him by chance or hatred when he was born, that hindered him, sabotaged him, impeded his intellectual and spiritual development: together with it, he would never know anything but a miserable future. It was too long, angular and pointy; it did not grow in a straight line, like the beautiful youthful bodies he admired, but forced him to bend and fall; it robbed him of all spontaneity and naturalness. The weak heart which now and then attacked him with painful twinges could not succeed in pushing the blood along the entire length of his limbs, which remained cold and stiff. He had no internal fire, nor that minimum of fat on which the spirit might feed. Quite soon he understood the reason for this thinness. All his energies had become concentrated on literature; he had suppressed the forces that, in others, induce one to eat, drink, listen to music, write about philosophy, and his body had grown unnaturally thin, keeping him young like an ephebe, immutable through the passing of the years. The most serious thing was that this body was alien to him, the most estranged among the elements that composed his nature as the Bachelor. What hostile divinity had imprisoned him in it, as though inside a hard bark? Now it was turned against him and plotted who knows what traps. "All that I possess is against me, what is against me is no longer in my possession. If, for example, my stomach hurts me, it no longer is really my stomach but something that essentially is no different from some extraneous person who wants to give me a beating. And everything is like this, my entire being is made of barbs which pierce me, and if I try to defend myself by using force, all I do is push them in deeper." What was there inside his body? Perhaps a ball of thread that rapidly unrolled, with an infinite number of ends? And wasn't there a danger that it would be overrun by enemy forces, coming from the world's alien vastness? So until the years of his illness, Kafka decided to appropriate and tame his body. He walked for hours, swam, did calisthenics, exposed himself half naked to the open air, hoping the elements would reconcile him with himself.

He sensed an animal within him. Again and again, composing with the figures of his unconscious a bestiary just as immense as a medieval one, he felt within him a beetle or a hibernating cockchafer; a mole that dug tunnels through the ground; a mouse that fled the moment man arrived; a slithering snake; a worm squashed by a human foot; a fluttering bat; a parasitic insect that fed on our blood; a sylvan beast

that lay desperate in a filthy ditch or in its den; a crow gray
as ashes, with atrophied wings; a dog that snarled and bared
its teeth at anyone who disturbed him, or barked nervously
running around a statue; a twofold animal with the body of
a lamb, the head and claws of a cat, the soft pelt and wild,
flaming eyes of both; or one of those despicable, sinister
and parasitic men he depicted in the last part of *Amerika*.
He was horrified by many animals. When, at Zürau, he
lived among the mice, he was frightened by the silent, insidious, bestial force that he felt was lying in ambush; but at the
same time he felt that those very beasts were hidden inside
of him. He was horrified by them precisely because he sensed
the unknown potential beast that inhabited him and, with
terror and desire, waited for it to reveal itself suddenly, for
his limbs to become covered with hair and his voice to begin
chittering, as he had read in Ovid's *Metamorphoses*. He
knew that in that way he would descend below the human
level, into the unknown darkness that yawns beneath our
consciousness; but he was not afraid of it, because the descent would also be an ascent in rank, the conquest of a
light and a music of which until then men had only a presentiment. Then he understood the meaning of his sensations.
The animal that inhabited him, bug or weasel or mole, was
indeed nothing but his soul and his writer's body, which
every night and every winter shut itself away in the cellar,
obeying the voice of inspiration, as certain animals spend
the winter hibernating in their nocturnal dens.

On the morning of November 17, 1912, he lay in bed, shut
up in his room. It was Sunday. The night before, while
writing *Amerika*, he had not been satisfied: it seemed to him
that the novel had gotten worse; then he dreamed that a
fantastic mailman handed him two magical, inexhaustible
letters from Felice. Now, in bed, he waited for the real mailman with Felice's real letters. He waited until a quarter to
twelve; and during those two hours of dreadful waiting, he was
assailed by his recurring anguish—the anguish of being ex-

pelled from the world like a parasitic animal that men can squash or kick about. He must have gone through moments of total hallucination and delirium, almost completely losing his human dimension; and he conceived a brief story which pressed inside him and wanted to be released in words. As always, possessed by the formidable speed of his inspiration, he did not waste time. That very evening he began to write it, putting aside the writing of *Amerika;* immediately the story lengthened in his hands: it no longer was an apologue but a story that expanded, broadened on all sides and embraced the fantastic complexity of his life and that of all men; and he would have liked to have before him an interminable night, in which to unravel it in its entirety, and then sleep forever. He finished it on December 7. It was "The Metamorphosis."

During those days in the small room in Niklasstrasse a twofold transformation took place. Writing in his nocturnal den, Kafka descended ever more deeply underground, where no explorer of the abyss had ever penetrated before him. Like all creators, he revealed the gift of taking on all shapes and changing into all species: in the space of almost a month in cold delirium he assumed another body; and with exceedingly attentive and sensual eyes he followed the transformation of his character, as though he too, as he was covering the sheets of paper with signs denser than those vibrating little legs, was slowly turning into an *Ungeziefer*, an enormous parasitic insect. Tolstoy also became insect, horse and bird, transforming himself into the vastness of the living universe; Kafka, however, transformed himself only in order to discover the depths in himself. For one thing, he transposed the apartment on Niklasstrasse where he lived with his parents into Gregor Samsa's apartment. Everything matched: the closet filled with clothes, the desk and couch, the hospital outside the window, the street lights reflected on the upper part of the room, the doors, the arrangement of the other rooms in the apartment. So, for one month, his room became the theater of a tragedy that lasted through the winter.

When we begin the story, the metamorphosis has already taken place. In the evening, Gregor Samsa was an ordinary traveling salesman; that night he had troubled dreams; in the morning—a winter morning like the night on which Kafka was writing—his back is hard as armor, his abdomen is arched, brown and divided by curved ridges, while innumerable small, pitifully thin legs tremble and vibrate with painful excitation before his eyes. All around, everything is the same: the small old room, the fabric sample book on the table, the female portrait cut out of an illustrated magazine, the melancholy rain which falls from a darkling sky. How great is the participation with which we share the emotions of the new *Ungeziefer:* like Gregor, we feel our back hard as armor; slightly raising our heads we examine our arched abdomen and the thousand little quivering legs; we feel a slight, dull pain in one side, an itch on the abdomen, dampness, cold; we are astonished when an unrestrainable and painful peep mingles with our voice, and when those little legs which stir frenetically do not let us get off the bed. No bestial metamorphosis—neither in Ovid nor in Dante—has ever been so meticulous, so lenticular, so capable of involving us irremediably. But Gregor Samsa seems much less involved than we are. He is not amazed, he is not stricken; it would seem that for him the metamorphosis is an obvious natural fact, like catching the train at seven in the morning. Consciously or unconsciously, he minimizes everything that has happened to him; he attaches no weight to it, considers it revocable, almost as though he were incapable of tragically living the absurd tragedy of his fate. With pathetic goodwill, he tries to impart order to what has happened to him and so both the incommensurable and the terrible become normal. Kafka had recourse to one of his best-loved narrative techniques, "restriction of the field," which deprives us of some elements of Gregor's consciousness (as, later on, the consciousnesses of Karl, Joseph K. and K.). Thus, without any narrative intervention, he was able to represent with lacerating simplicity the terrible atony, the painful acceptance of life which makes Gregor the last and greatest of Flaubertian heroes.

The metamorphosis takes place before our eyes. At first Gregor Samsa feels that he is the prisoner of a body that does not belong to him and that he can neither direct nor dominate with the same naturalness with which he directed his old limbs. When he opens his mouth to talk, he hears that unrestrainable and painful peep come up from below and mingle with his words, and become so confused in the echo as to make him doubt he has heard them. He realizes that his body is "incredibly wide." When he tries to get out of bed, he no longer has hands and arms but only tiny legs; if he tries to bend one of them, he must stretch, and when he finally manages to bend it, all the other little legs move, without his moving them, with extreme and painful excitation. His bestial nature soon progresses: his voice, half human and half animal, becomes completely animal, and he clearly recognizes the new words that before seemed obscure to him. He begins to adapt to his new body and make it his own: the innumerable twirling little legs no longer terrorize him; when he touches the floor, he feels that they fully obey him, that they can transport him wherever he wishes, like his old legs, and he experiences a sense of physical well-being and joy as though he had just entered his true limbs. He begins to use his antennae. When he immerses his head in the milk, which he once adored, it now disgusts him: now, as an insect, he loves withered, almost rotten vegetables, spoiled cheese, putrefied food. The very-high-ceilinged room frightens him; bestial instinct leads him to hide under the couch and wander through garbage and refuse.

As Kafka follows him with his implacable eye, Gregor gradually loses all his old human senses, which had articulated the shapes of the world for him. At first he still has sight and hearing. Like many wretches, sight had been his liberation. Many were the hours he passed at the window of his room looking *out*, and that sight had given him the hope of losing himself in the elsewhere. Now, if he pushes a chair to the window, climbs onto the sill and looks out, he distinguishes objects with less and less clarity: he can no longer discern the hospital across the way; if he didn't know he lived on Charlottenstrasse, he could believe that he was looking into the desert, where gray sky and earth joined indistinguishably. Nothing is left but his hearing; and great is the anguish with which, closed in his room, he listens to the apartment's noises and voices—the voices that no one thinks he understands. But he has not lost human emotions: dreams, a few seizures of megalomania, a few absurd hopes, memories—about his job, his trips as a traveling salesman, some fleeting love affair, his narrow and enclosed life. So the metamorphosis is not as complete as Ovid's. Gregor Samsa has not become a bug or cockroach: he is a divided creature, split, a halfway creature, something that oscillates between animal and man, that could become completely animal or return to being man and does not have the strength for a complete metamorphosis.

The external world is erased in the fog. All the immense "outside" is reduced to the rain on the windowpanes, which imparts rhythm to the step of the winter, the fog, the electric light from the street lamp, which reflects on the ceiling and on the upper parts of the furniture. In the room there is no other light: closet, desk and couch which once enjoyed the triumph of electric illumination know only those pallid twilit irradiations; and down below, where Gregor Samsa is, there is darkness. The door, which is locked with a key, almost never opens. The room is a prison, in which the insect leads his life as a recluse, just as Kafka's claustrophobia had dreamt of so many times. Space has become concentrated. Time is completely lost. The alarm clock, which in the beginning scanned the hours and minutes, reminding Gregor of train schedules and the vastness of the distant world, has vanished. Someone has taken it away. In the dark room, no one marks off the divisions of time any longer: the hours are confused in an atemporal twilight. Gregor has lost the memory of duration; and halfway through the story, he no longer knows whether Christmas is already past or still to come.

After a few weeks, having gained familiarity with his new body, Gregor learns to crawl to and fro on walls and ceiling. Clinging up there on high, far from the earth where men live as prisoners of weight, he breathes more freely; a subtle vibration of well-being traverses his body, and with happy forgetfulness he begins to play, letting himself fall onto the floor. Although he has lost his sight, the highest of human senses, he has attained a condition superior to the human one: the ability to rise, the sovereign levity of birds and angels, an almost physical and spiritual happiness, the incomparable gift of playfulness, contemplative joy. In his incarnation as a traveling salesman, he had never known so blissful a life. If these animal games had continued, Gregor would have completed his transformation. Closed in his room cleansed of all human memory, without any more sight, memory or hearing, free from the sensations and thoughts that still bound him to our world, he would have known the terrible happiness of silence, solitude and lightness, becoming entirely an insect. Every day his sister would come to bring him food, comforting him with her mute presence, and his animal metamorphosis—this horror, this tragedy—would have become an incomparable bliss, saving him from his Oedipal destiny. Begun under atrocious auspices, dreamt in an anguished morning, the story would end radiantly, in pure animal glorification. Kafka dreamt of no other fate. To live in a dark cellar, spacious and locked, with a lamp, a table and some sheets of paper, in a den, like an animal, without seeing anyone, talking to anyone, just barely grazed by the vague and distant breath of a sister-mistress. Down there, he too could forget the thoughts of men. He could write for whole months, day and night, concentrated, without effort, drawing his material from the darkness of his body, with the same supernatural lightness with which the insect happily vibrating climbs along the ceiling of his room.

Gregor Samsa has a younger sister, for whom he harbors feelings that are at once paternal and incestuous. Grete plays the violin; before his metamorphosis, he had thought of sending her to the conservatory to perfect her musical talent. Her brother's metamorphosis devastates Grete; she cannot bear the intense animal odor, the monstrous sight, and does not dare touch the food bowl with her hands. Despite this repugnance, brother and sister are still bound by their old amorous relationship. Between them an unspoken convention is established; as soon as he hears the sound of the key in the lock, Gregor hides under the couch and covers himself with the sheet, and his sister thanks him for his humble attention with a look of gratitude. Grete is jealous of him: she wants to be the only one to take care of him, and when the mother cleans the room, she is offended and cries. While Gregor indulges in animal games, Grete understands his wishes; and she thinks of removing from the room the chest of drawers and desk laden with the past and family memories, so that he will be able to crawl about and fall freely from the walls. Her unconfessed dream is that Gregor should become completely animal, that he should play in the empty den, and that between them should exist that pure magnetic love Kafka dreamt of having with Felice. The mother does not agree: she does not want the inhabited room to change into a den; and she hopes that the pieces of furniture, with their ballast of affection, will keep Gregor from leaving men's existence.

So Gregor stands at a crossroads. But immediately, denying his own desires, he accepts his mother's thoughts: he will never renounce the warmth of those objects and the past, his old room "warm and furnished so comfortably with the old [family] furniture," as in a nineteenth-century novel. He does not have the strength to descend into the animal's vertiginous world, without memory, without thoughts, without speech, without friends and relatives, renouncing his human past and his Oedipal conflict—assisted only by games of supernatural lightness. Should we accuse him of weakness? Should we demand from the humble traveling salesman an act of courage that no man ever performed? This descent into the bestial could be accomplished only by Kafka, when in his imagination he went down into the dark cellar and there wrote not like an animal but like a dead man.

The women had already removed the chest of drawers. The desk was still in the room, and on the wall a woman's portrait that Gregor had cut from an illustrated magazine, showing a seated woman who wore a cap and a fur boa and raised toward the observer a heavy muff into which her forearm disappeared. On his melancholy evenings as a traveling salesman, Gregor had decorated the portrait with a frame carved from wood and covered with a thin layer of gold leaf. Like a meticulous and silent Flaubertian symbol, the portrait gathers all the repressed erotic desires of his youth, his unrealized dreams of love, perhaps his unconfessed fetishism. With an act of aggressiveness, Gregor rebels: "They were emptying his room: taking everything that was dear to him: the chest, which contained his fretsaw and other tools, had already been carried away; now they took apart his desk, so firmly planted on the floor, on which he had once written his homework when he was a student at the Commercial Institute, in high school and even in grammar school. . . ." After a moment's uncertainty, he rapidly crawls up to where the picture of the woman with the fur hangs from the almost bare wall: he climbs hastily and with his big body covers the glass, which gives pleasure to his warm abdomen. "This picture, at least . . . nobody was going to take it away." Gregor has made his choice. Hoisting the image of the woman in her fur, the symbol of his previous existence, his artisan manias and his sentimental fantasies, he rejects the dream of the silent and dark life *à deux* his sister had proposed to him. The process of animal metamorphosis is arrested.

Before his son's metamorphosis, the father had seemed

worn out: in the evening when Gregor returned from work, he welcomed him sitting in his armchair, dressed in his robe, unable to rise to his feet; during their walks together—two Sundays a year—he dragged himself more and more slowly, wrapped in his old cape, propping himself up with a sort of crutch. Now, since his son has been shut away speechless in the den-room and no longer threatens his vitality, he has blossomed anew: he has sucked the blood, robbed him of the human lymph that, at one time, the son had taken from him. A short time before, he resumed working in a bank. He sits quite erect in his tightly fitting blue uniform adorned with gold buttons; over the high, stiff collar of his tunic protrudes his large double chin; from his thick eyebrows the gaze of his black eyes darts out, vivacious and attentive; his white, untidy hair is combed flat, with a precise and shiny part under the cap with its gold monogram. The struggle between them is a struggle for survival: if the son had consciously tried to kill the father, the father now consciously wants to kill the son. Gregor's metamorphosis is a misdeed, a sin, a caprice that must be punished with ferocious severity.

One evening, when the father returns home, the mother lies in a faint and Gregor, full of despair, is stretched out on the living room table. As soon as he sees him, the father lifts his foot and the son is struck by the "gigantic size of the sole of his boot," as though he were the ogre in a fairy tale. The father chases him through the room with his huge shoes, and he starts to gasp, terrorized and with his eyes closed. If he had wanted to escape the paternal violence, he could have climbed the walls, high up amid the furniture and pictures, taking refuge in his intact animal world and forever abandoning the Oedipal world of men, where fathers kill their sons and sons are forced to kill their fathers. But he has renounced becoming an insect: he prefers to be a sacrificed son instead of a free insect. And so his painful race through the living room continues. The father removes some small red apples from the bowl on the cupboard and begins to bombard him with them:

the first apples roll as if electrified along the pavement; then one apple grazes Gregor's body and another drives violently into his back, while his mother, her gown unbuttoned, begs the father to spare him. Gregor stretches out full length on the floor, in a total confusion of his senses. What a grotesque and terrifying scene, in which Isaac's sacrifice by Abraham is finally accomplished, in which we feel the shudder of the sacred and both the violation and fulfillment of the Law.

Gregor suffers for over a month from the wound. He lives in his room—no longer a man, not yet an animal; wounded animal, degraded man. That apple embedded in his body is his incurable wound, which no female hand will ever be able to alleviate, the visible memory of his father's hatred, the sign of his martyrdom. Now he is unable to climb freely on the walls; he is locked in the human world; he will never again be able to flee; and almost as recompense, pardon and reconciliation, he is reabsorbed into family life. Every evening the living room door opens: "so as to allow him, buried in the darkness of his room and invisible from the living room, to see the entire family around the lit-up table and listen to their conversation with every one's consent. . . ." Even though mute, he is re-admitted to the world of speech. But at that contact which rises from darkness, the family's life declines, and it becomes a degraded repetition of its earlier existence. No longer are there the animated conversations of happy times; his uniform worn and stained, the father falls asleep at table every night, the mother sews in silence, ruining her eyes, the sister studies stenography and French, the maid is discharged and the family jewels are sold. There is nothing sadder than these silent evenings glimpsed from the dark room, while the women work and the father sleeps. Then a further descent: three boarders are taken in; the family eats dinner in the kitchen; from his den Gregor hears the noise made by the masticating boarders and senses his family's humiliation—his parents do not dare sit down; the father stands by the table, cap in hand like a beggar, and bows. Gregor's existence is also degraded. Mother and sister consider him with the intolerance one has for a relation or family member struck by an incurable disease, the intolerance that his wife and children feel for Ivan Ilyich. Love is extinguished: what remains is the incapacity to bear a superhuman misfortune. The sister, who once prepared his food with great love, now with great haste pushes any sort of food into his room with her foot, unconcerned whether Gregor touches it. She no longer cleans, and she prevents the others from cleaning; on the floor lie clumps of dust and garbage, piles of filth stretch along the walls. Unneeded furniture is thrown into the room, together with junk, the ash can and garbage pail. Gregor had rejected an empty den, where he could give way to his pleasures and his pure animal games; now, almost in contraposition, the den becomes a lumber room, where humanity collects its refuse. Like a cockroach, he begins to wander about among the household goods: all dirty, repulsive, covered with lint, dust, hairs, leftover scraps of food, which he drags about on his back and sides.

Some time goes by. One evening, surrounded by the boarders in the living room, Grete plays the violin, standing in front of the music stand; her face is bent to one side and her eyes follow the lines of notes with attention and sadness; her imprisoned soul yearns for its country. The boarders do not understand; they had expected an amusing piece, and now they smoke their cigars nervously and with indifference. Gregor hears the violin's beautiful, sad sound; filthy with dust and covered with lint and hair, he crawls, leaves his room, advances into the living room and keeps his head close to the floor to intercept his sister's glances; deprived of speech, communication with his eyes is the only kind left him.

In the past, when he was a man, he did not like music. Now that he has descended and ascended toward the beast, music moves him, and it seems to open a path "to the desired and unknown nourishment." We have reached the heart of Kafka's work: "desired and unknown nourishment" is the great Platonic theme; the soul's aspiration toward the unknown archetype; the Flaubertian character's excited drive toward unrealized and unrealizable hopes. When he lived as a man, in his life as a repressed and obedient son, in his fatiguing journeys as a traveling salesman, Gregor had not discovered his profound aspiration. Upon becoming an animal his soul had at last opened to the superhuman music. Only now, a parasitic insect, a wounded beast, filthy, covered with dust and leftover foods, he understands that his soul's profound voice is an indefinable, inexpressible desire, which cannot be represented, which leads him to a goal beyond the division between human and bestial.

Without realizing it, Gregor revives the two archetypal conditions of the fable: the dragon which jealously guards the treasure; and the Prince transformed into a Beast, who lives at the side of Beauty and hopes to marry her and become a man again. But unlike the Beast, Gregor does not wish to become a man again; he understands that, as his sister suggested to him, the animal condition is the only one that suits him. He would like only to venture out as far as his sister, tug her by the skirt, induce her to come into his room with her violin, because nobody appreciates her music as he does. He would lock her up in his room, barricading the doors, holding off assailants, as the dragon kept the Princess locked up, as Kafka locked himself up in the cellar so as to write: because happiness can be attained only where walls enclose and imprison us: in jail. Now, finally, Gregor understands the incestuous theme that his sister had proposed and he had rejected. His sister would sit down on the couch and bend toward him on the floor, so that he might be able to confide his plan in her ear (speaking with the chirp of an insect, or with some sort of sound? He no longer had a voice): he had meant to send her to the conservatory and, if his misfortune had not occurred, he would have announced this to everyone last Christmas. "After his explanation, his sister would have burst into heart-felt tears and Gregor would have raised himself up to her shoulder and would have kissed her on the neck, which now, since she started going to the office, she left uncovered without scarf or collar."

But precisely now that Gregor thinks he is close to the "desired and unknown nourishment," Grete denies her brother. She, who had wanted to live in the den together with the Gregor-animal and had been rejected, refuses the incestuous dream he offers her. She takes her revenge: whenever she sees him, she denies that that "monster" is still her brother, and in the presence of father and mother she sentences him to death, with the cruelty of youth. "You perhaps do not understand him: I do. I don't want to pronounce my brother's name before this monster, and so I say only: We must try to get rid of it." Beauty kills the Beast. Gregor starts to turn around to go back into his room. Nothing could be more laborious: his body is enfeebled by starvation, his head rigidified; he is unable to understand how he could have covered that distance; and little by little, helping himself with his head, striking it against the floor, breathing heavily because of the effort, resting now and then amid the deadly silence of the family, he crawls back into his den. As soon as he is inside, Grete slams the door furiously, turns the key and cries: "At last!" At this point for Gregor, in the dark of the room, which no gleam from the street illumines, there is nothing left to do but die. He dies of starvation: he has gone without eating for too long. But his death is also a sacrifice: he accepts, bows his head to his death sentence, thinks back to his family with deep emotion and love. As Walter Sokel writes, he is a "scapegoat" who takes upon himself the sins of those dear to him: he is the Christ who dies, to save all human beings. The supreme value is no longer the dream of mute bestial levity, or the expectation of the "desired and unknown nourishment," or the incestuous life with his sister, the act of writing without lifting his hand from the page in the cellar's silence, but it is sacrifice, *caritas*. Before dying, Gregor receives the gift that perhaps one can obtain only before death: the quiet of the empty and contemplative mind. For a last time he listens to the clock of the tower strike three in the morning. He sees the sky brighten outside the window. Then his head droops, and the last breath weakly leaves his nostrils. He lives in darkness but dies in the light.

Gregor's sacrifice has a cosmic echo: it announces the end of winter, the arrival of spring. If Gregor had not sacrificed himself, perhaps nature would have been rigidified forever, in its dead wintry forms, "dry" like the corpse of the large insect. Now lymph can again flow through nature's veins, and the universal metamorphosis resumes its cycle. The sad months of winter and rain which have battered Gregor's window give way to the first warmth of spring, under the light of the March sun, which shines above city and countryside. The family casts off its wintry degradation, the father retrieves his lost dignity and expels the boarders, the sister's face becomes animated and flushed, mother embraces daughter. All together shed tears over the sacrificed one, moved and reconciled.

But we mustn't believe in nature's goodness. No one buries Gregor's body: the task of his burial—in who knows what way—is entrusted to the coarse, rude maid, the only person, however, to have had a true relationship with the "old cockroach." Gregor's metamorphosis—this capital event in the history of the universe, which has allowed us to understand other worlds, to attain things and dreams that have remained hidden, to take part in the life of literature seems by now last winter's nightmare. We have the strange impression that it never happened. Father, mother and daughter go into the countryside by tram, and talk animatedly about the future. The prospects are attractive: the three jobs are very promising, they must look for a new place to live, better situated than the present one, and think about Grete's marriage. The girl rises to her feet and stretches her young body, with the triumphant cruelty of life toward all sorrows and all deaths. Gregor has saved the perennial nature of existence. But unlike Christ, he has not redeemed it. Life continues as it always has been, with its horrors and egoisms, and no one any longer craves our soul's "unknown nourishment."

CHAPTER FOUR

Amerika

Kafka began writing *Amerika* at the end of September 1912, a few days after inspiration had reawakened in him as he was writing "The Judgment." We can follow him almost day by day through his letters to Felice: we come to know his fervor, his enthusiasm, his doubts, his despair; we know at what page, what line of the manuscript, he stopped on October 18, or at what line he resumed on December 24, and when he thought he was stopping forever. Never have we been this close to the secrets of creation. He wrote rapidly, "in ecstasy," as Max Brod noted, in a state of exceptional creative felicity such as he had never experienced before. "After having written well on the night between Sunday and Monday—I could have written all night and day and again night and day, and finally flown away. . . ." It appeared that the book resembled him; in it he felt safe, as had never happened to him when he wrote "Description of a Struggle" and *Meditation:* something or someone protected him; all sensations and feelings and suggestions, from wherever they might originate, were placated and set on the "right path." Once, he who never wept, wept over his book, and was afraid that he might awaken his parents in the next room with those sobs he could not restrain. What sort of tears were these? Of sorrow? Distress? Pity for himself and for everyone? Or, on the contrary, of happiness over his book? Deep emotion? Or were these the infinitely tender tears that bring about catharsis?

Perhaps there is no moment more extraordinary in Kafka's work than these last months of 1912, when he embarked on two such opposite experiences as those of *Amerika* and "The Metamorphosis": pushing to their extreme on the one hand the forces of expansion, dilation and distance and on the other the forces of concentration, weight and profundity. The man who wrote *Amerika* belongs to the family of the great novelists: he possesses the gaiety of time, the pleasure of storytelling, the joy of movement, at times a Dickensian euphoria and caprice, and a levity and fluency which allow us to glide over events without encountering anything that jars or disturbs us. Whereas in "The Metamorphosis" he transformed himself into himself, in *Amerika* he transforms himself into all the persons in the world, drawing them from his generous womb: with sovereign aplomb he surrenders himself to reality, moves and skitters about among things, ventures beyond all limits, full of sympathy for parasites and crooks, such as Robinson and Delamarche. There everything took place in a room, *his* room: here lives the excitement of adventure in the great American spaces which Kafka knew only from books. There existed a great symbolic concentration: every page was layered like a cosmos; here meaning and allusions assail us with less intensity and do not form such a close-meshed net.

Amerika is an encyclopedia of literary genres entwined and harmonized with each other. It is not entirely impossible that Kafka, at least at the beginning, intended to write a family saga: some say that he himself, like Karl Rossmann, was seduced by a governess when he was sixteen; young Robert Kafka, his cousin, certainly did have a son from his parents' cook in 1896. Furthermore, Otto, Robert's older

brother, emigrated in 1906 to the United States, where he
had adventures similar to those of Karl and then later became
a powerful businessman like his uncle Jacob. Three years
later, another younger brother of Otto's, Frank, emigrated to
America, also at sixteen. With what great ease Kafka ex-
ploited the resources of literature! As Marthe Robert points
out, *Amerika* is a realistic novel about modern cities: an
adventure novel (the boy who finds his American uncle); a
serial novel (the young man who is thrown out of his home);
a picaresque novel (life at the bottom with Robinson and
Delamarche); a fairy tale (the uncle who punishes Karl-
Cinderella at the stroke of midnight; Karl-Pinocchio explores
Pollunder's dark house with a candle; Green and the doorman
as ogres); an educational book (Karl–diligent boy); a myth
(the lost paradise); a utopia (the Oklahoma Theater); perhaps
a theological novel (the triple original sin).

No book appears richer, more robust, better able to
expand ad infinitum. And yet "The Metamorphosis," the
story that had interrupted its writing from November to
December, probably irremediably undermined it. The descent into the abyss of animal life, the discovery of literature's
heart in the place where beetles and cockroaches lightly
climb along walls and ceilings, prevented Kafka from going
back to live in the open air, where so-called real life unfolds.
From December, his letters to Felice are full of ill humor, as
though the book no longer enchanted him. On the night of
December 23 he wrote, "How will it end if I will no longer
be able to write? It would seem that the moment has come:
it is a week and more that I'm not accomplishing anything, in
the course of the last ten nights . . . I've been carried away
only once and that was all. I'm continually tired." He
claimed that he worked by joining and patching together
small passages, because inspiration had deserted him. On
January 26 he declared himself defeated and gave up the
book: he thought that it had taken flight and moved away

from him, leaving him once again alone in the desolate desert of his existence.

When he told Karl Rossmann's adventures, Kafka's mind was traversed by a gleam of hope. He knew he was condemned. Any story or novel that took its departure from a person like himself—the Stranger—could end only in defeat: a suicide in the waters of the river, or a death sentence, with a butcher's knife plunged deep into the heart. But what if he were to narrate the adventures of *another*? Of someone who possessed all qualities contrary to his own? Someone who had in common with him only the childlike gaze? Someone blessed by grace? And so he told the story of Karl Rossmann, cast out by his family, flung into a strange country, a country of insomnia and maelstroms. For some time Kafka hoped to save him, because together with Karl he would have saved himself; and perhaps he imagined his comic redemption, during the very same days in which he told the story of Joseph K.'s irremediable sentence in *The Trial*.

I believe that Kafka never loved a character as much as he loved Karl Rossmann. What love could he have for Joseph K., or for K., or for the lord of the burrow, or even for poor Gregor Samsa? Throughout the book, before Karl sets foot on American soil, or as he sinks into abjection, or when he observes the angels of the Oklahoma Theater, Kafka follows him with such tender affection that it recalls Tolstoy's and Stevenson's tenderness as they contemplated their beloved creations Nikolai Rostov and Jim Hawkins. Like them, Karl possesses "natural grace": the most precious gift in a human creature, which attracts the affection of others and perhaps that of God, a gift Kafka feared he did not possess and which he did not attribute to any other of his characters. Karl is vital, joyous, naive; his father's horrible punishment, being driven at fifteen across the ocean, has not cracked his childlike confidence and faith in life. He has not yet been disillusioned. His "marveling gaze" rejoices at the sight of the world's beauty and dwells on all of reality's spectacles. He cares not for the past: he loves the present, the labile and fugitive moment in which he lives, as though there were nothing else, even to the point of forgetting everything—his umbrella, his suitcase, his hat—with a vagueness that charms us. Often he is the victim of circumstances. He does not make plans, does not set himself goals, does not build his life as adults do, even though the future seems to reveal to his gaze a treasure of desirable things. Like all people attached to life, he has the gift of transforming himself and changing, so much as to become the succubus of things and others. There is nothing more delightful than the scene in which, in a short time, he becomes a perfect elevator operator. He had studied in high school; for one month he had been his uncle's favorite nephew; and here he is in his handsome suit, with his profound bows, his artistry in accepting tips, his small chivalries toward the ladies, his agility in summoning a carriage —as though he had been an elevator boy all his life.

According to an all-too-famous phrase, literature cannot depict "good sentiments." Karl Rossmann proves the contrary; the entire treasure of love, of affection, of impulses for the good, of naive ideals, tender convictions and trust that ever crossed men's spirits is to be found gathered in the quiet lake of his heart. It is easy for us to imagine his childhood. He was an obedient and loving son, devoted and extremely diligent: an Isaac ready to be immolated by his father's ax; and even now, when he is sixteen, we perceive in his voice, as Musil said, "the sense of excited childish prayers," "something of the restless zeal that goes with diligent homework." Those who do not love him claim that he is only the ideal boy to be found in textbooks. Despite the horror he has experienced at home, he has faith in the world's goodness: he believes in good causes and ideals—with the candor, lightheartedness, simplicity and lack of analysis that have always distinguished pure goodness. No one is more honest, diligent and scrupulous than he, in whatever situation he finds himself. He has one illusion: that the world is rational, that everything can be explained, that good words and good sentiments are enough to change the universe. The others mock him, deride him, rob him. And yet at the end of every illusion, sore in the flesh and wounded in the spirit, he cannot stop himself from going to meet others with an impulse of love and devotion, of sympathy and trust. He needs friendship, affection and the sound of a human voice like a dog, and if he is injured once again, he forgives.

Some critics have described him as a small Don Quixote, a young Idiot, nourished on German books. Karl would not understand this. He does not know the madness of vagabonds and saints. He would never fight with windmills; he would never sacrifice himself to save another creature and reestablish the world's harmony. He is a "normal" boy, accustomed to believing in the normal values of life: devotion to one's parents, respect for the law and society's conventions, friendship for one's comrades, an honest wish to ascend the social ladder and become a perfect employee. Tragedy decrees that these values no longer exist in the contaminated Eden, protected by the angel's sword, which is to be found across the Atlantic. Karl never ate from the tree of knowledge, as Gregor Samsa did without wishing to; and all the truths about the body, the animal, incest and literature that the poor employee has learned through his metamorphosis are absolutely foreign to him. Now here he is in America, the realm of great spaces: no adventurous desire to cross them animates him; the word *freedom* says nothing to him; his one dream is to find a refuge—no matter where, in a stoker's cabin, the room of a head cook—and plunge his head in the lap of a father or mother. Kafka wrote that "there exists only one capital sin: impatience." If this is true, Karl does not know what sin is. No character in a novel is more patient than he. With his exceedingly sweet childish stoicism he accepts what destiny or chance offers; he believes everything, hopes everything, tolerates everything, endures everything,

as St. Paul said; and in whatever situation he happens to live,
he meekly bows his head.

But Kafka did not wish or was unable to keep Karl
Rossmann completely distant from himself; and he injected
his own poison in him, as though he could not help but
contaminate him with what was perhaps a disease, perhaps a
sign of election. Just as Kafka remained a pure adolescent
until maturity, so Karl refuses to grow up. Without knowing
it, he refuses to take the step that will leave him defenseless
to the vice of maturity; he remains unchanged and candid
through all his experiences—since experience is *horror;* and
he preserves and hardens in his mind his inviolate childhood.
This is the ultimate secret of his charm: that which moves
and enchants us to the point of tears.

Seen with the eyes of childhood, adults eat and copulate.
To avoid becoming an adult, Karl will eat little and copulate
not at all. All the great and sanguine eaters who traverse the
book gobble with inexhaustible greed squabs, sausages,
sardines and chocolate creams, smearing their faces and
hands with grease; Dickens would have found them picturesque and adorable; Karl (and Kafka) finds them disgusting.
When he meets Clara in Pollunder's immense house, dark as
a castle in a fairy tale, Karl perceives the fascination of that
flushed face and young athletic body, tensed beneath the
clinging dresses. But it is barely the shadow of a temptation,
like the one he experienced with Brunelda; he unconsciously
removes them from his mind. The sexual act continues to
seem repugnant to him. The sole sexual experience of his life
has forever left in his mind the remembrance of a sinister
combination of possessive desire, physical overpowering,
heat, grease, hysteria, incest, servility, sentimental falsity,
alienation from his self, humiliation and misery. The last
Kafkian trait we encounter in Karl is the most unmistakable:
nostalgia. When he sings his beloved soldier's song, trying to
find a new song in the old song, he reveals his striving toward
the indefinite, the impossible, the unattainable. Like Gregor

Samsa, he dreams of his soul's "desired and unknown nourishment."

When he is fifteen years and nine months old, Karl is cast off by his father, like a cat who has dirtied the floor and is flung out into the street: shut in the lowest class of a ship that takes him to New York, with an old suitcase, an old suit, a few shirts and a piece of salami; expelled into a desert of solitude and uncertainty. Why this vengefulness? Why this biblical ferocity against an innocent? Why this brandished sword? Karl is a loving son; he's been seduced—guiltless—by a maid much older than he. In "The Judgment" we heard the father's reproaches against his son. Here, with one of those omissions of which he is a master, Kafka does not let us hear the voice of the father's Law. We must suppose that the Law does not tolerate excuses. Despite the protest of innocence on the part of the accused, it does not consider their feelings, their general behavior or their heart's uncontaminated innocence. Karl has sinned against the form of the Law. When the form is offended—even in a slight detail, which some judge has perhaps already forgotten—the Law condemns without mercy. Karl has allowed himself to be seduced by the maid, in his house's lumber room. He did not commit an erotic sin (the Law is not moralistic), but he has violated the pact of fidelity and exclusive belongingness that bound him to the family. If for one instant he dissolved the bond, the bond flings him away with the violence of a sling.

We can imagine how dreadful for Karl must have been the evening on which he was informed that he would be expelled from the family. But he does not remember that evening: he has removed it from his consciousness, erasing the wound's unbearable violence, the sorrow over the offense and the desire for revenge. When his memory harks back to his German childhood, it summons up scenes of a family idyll enclosed within itself: tranquil evenings, when his mother locked the door of the house and sewed with her needle, his father read the paper or did his accounts, and he did his homework, seated at the table with his parents. Karl is neither the brother nor the heir of Georg Bendemann or Gregor Samsa, the Oedipal sons who have tried to kill the father or take his place in the family. He accepts his father's authority, defends him and would like to regain his esteem and love. The feeling he has for him is that solid affection made up of habits lived in close proximity, that very sweet and painful physical tenderness which sons experience living every day with the father, taking breakfast in the morning in bed with him, strolling around the apartment in pajamas or doing homework at the same table. There is no page more anguishing—the Kafkian anguish, lacerating like a knife—than the one in which, chased away by his uncle, lost in a dark American inn, Karl picks up his parents' photograph—his father standing upright with his fist clenched, not looking at him, his mother with her hand dangling from her chair's armrest, so close he could have kissed it—rests his face on it, feels its cool against his cheek and falls asleep with this sensation of peace and quiet.

As soon as his ship docks in New York Harbor, Karl loses suitcase and umbrella: Flaubertian objects, to which Kafka attributes an intense symbolic charge, which takes the place of a long psychological analysis, as does the female portrait in Gregor Samsa's room. He does not lose them by chance: he *wants* to lose them because they are the signs of his laceration, of the journey, of the wandering into which he is forced; they will disappear in the pauses, when he will have found a home, and they will all reappear together, with his cap, as soon as he is seized again by exile and uprooting. Meanwhile, Karl already finds a first home abroad, in the stoker's cabin, where he feels at ease and rests and almost sleeps, calm and pacified, as will never again happen in the novel. With one of those emotional impulses of which he alone is capable, he feels he belongs to the stoker: he chooses him as a father, a son, an older brother.

We wonder what would have happened if at the end Karl had adopted the stoker as a father—this amiable brother-father, who is unacquainted with the rigors and exquisite ferocity of the Law. He might have forever eluded the world of the Law, of the father, of Oedipus, of God. Like a picaresque vagabond, together with the stoker, Karl would have passed through all the ports and cities of America, coming to know its streets, adventures, its open air, the flavor of its rivers, its clouds, grass and skies; and *Amerika* would have become a kind of new *Adventures of Huckleberry Finn*, written by a clown and a Stranger who had escaped condemnation. How much we would have gained! How much we would have lost! This is Kafka's second great refusal—after the refusal to represent Gregor's life as a pure animal—and I believe that he always loved "The Stoker" (the title of the first chapter in *Amerika*) so passionately because in it the Law does not appear. But destiny demanded that Kafka live within the Law and depict it alone. So Karl is forced to leave the stoker; and with dismay, tenderness, the hidden knowledge that his life is forever deflected, with sympathy for the fate of all the defeated, he seizes the rough, almost dead hand, kisses it and weeps, pressing it to his cheek like a treasure he must give up forever.

When the ship enters New York Harbor, Karl catches sight of the Statue of Liberty immersed in a suddenly more vivid light. America, the land looked forward to by immigrants, the land of Karl's hopes, seems to be the space of light. That splendor illuminates a strange spectacle: Liberty's arm brandishes not a torch but a sword—the same flashing sword with which the cherubs, after Adam's fall, kept men away from "the path to the tree of life" (Genesis 3:24). So Karl goes down a road in the opposite direction from Adam's: he leaves old Europe, where without wishing to he ate the apple and where he was cursed by the Father-God, crosses the ocean and returns to Eden, out of which the first man was driven. Everything has remained as it was then: the old angel is still there, his sword raised, and allows him to enter the land, where, perhaps, the tree of life stands.

Some time later, Karl arrives in the city of Rameses. The name is not new to us: we have already encountered it in Exodus, where the Jews, fallen into slavery, are forced by the Egyptians to build the treasure cities of Pithom and Ramses and where "they made their lives bitter with hard labors in the preparation of the mortar and bricks" (1:11–14). Eden is therefore false, the angel a purely human image: fleeing toward paradise, Karl has landed in the New Egypt, where men are enslaved. It is precisely in the hotel at Rameses that Karl is told the story of Therese's mother, one of the masterpieces by that Dickensian-Dostoevskian Kafka for whom we feel such regret. The mother, consumptive and starving, has no bed in which to sleep with her daughter; she wanders all night through a New York struck by a blizzard, dragging along the little girl; she enters houses, squats gasping on the steps, goes again and again through narrow labyrinths and freezing hallways which lead to the top floors, knocks at random on doors. Here and there the inferno of the underground opens up, releasing a smoky mist of unbreathable air; strangers and drunks climb the stairs stomping their feet heavily or spitting, until in the morning the mother climbs up the ladder of a construction site—surrounded by the same scaffoldings, beams and bricks of the old Rameses—and plunges into the void. This is the inferno of America, which at the end of the book Karl will know with his own eyes. And yet we must not forget what his uncle tells us. While Europe is a land of pure appearances, the "signs and miracles" of the Old Testament are still alive in America, as the novel *Amerika* will prove, full as it is of "signs and miracles," right down to the incomplete miracle of the Nature Theater of Oklahoma.

Uncle's house, where Karl lives in New York, has six stories, besides being over three cellars, and his room is located on the sixth, surrounded by a narrow balcony which overlooks the street. Fascinated and bewitched by the sight, Karl spends hours looking at the traffic which flows in a very long straight avenue between two rows of houses which vanish in the mist, where the enormous shapes of a cathedral rise. His gaze possesses a unique gift. From up there he goes down into the street and looks at things from below, as though he were set at the lowest level of things; and he sees also what nobody is able to see, noises and smells. Things mix with and contaminate each other in an incessant movement: down below, a mixture of contorted human figures and the tops of vehicles; above, a new mixture, even more complicated and tumultuous, of sounds, dust and smells— and above it all, a final stratum composed of light. It is a potent and full-bodied light that is dispersed and carried away by the mass of objects and then quickly gathers again; and it seems to the eye that a scintillating slab of glass which covers everything is at every instant shattered with great force above the street. These are Karl's impressions: in America everything is visible, also the invisible; nothing is pure, everything is mixed and contaminated; everything is physical, even light, the most spiritual of objects.

Later on, Karl understands that the essence of American life is automatism. The first encounter is a prodigy of mechanical engineering, which attracts his childlike spirit. His uncle has left in his room a typical American writing desk, with a hundred compartments of all sizes, which could have contained even the papers of the president of the United States. On the side of the desk there is a regulator; by turning a handle, depending on need or whim, the most diverse changes and adjustments can be obtained. It is enough to turn the handle, and the thin dividing partitions descend, slowly or with prodigious speed, to form the base and ceiling of new compartments. Also his uncle's house is a kind of enormous desk, a mechanical toy. Outside it is iron; the inner walls are glass. A special elevator can lift a concert piano or an entire truckload of furniture as high as the sixth floor. Karl goes up on the regular elevator and, deftly maneuvering a lever, stops level with the freight elevator so as to stare through the glass panes at the beautiful piano his uncle has given him. In the immense offices automatism stages a grandiose and absurd puppet comedy. In every telephone booth there is an employee, indifferent to the enormous racket: a steel clamp grips his head and presses the phone against his ears; his only task is to transcribe as exactly as possible the incoming conversation; his fingers vibrate with a regularity and speed that is somehow inhuman, while another two employees simultaneously record the same conversation. Thus all error is excluded from the great American machine, which operates above and outside man. But the telephone-employee cannot lift his head or talk or answer the voices that reach him from afar, not even if he must present serious objections or communicate a decisive piece of information.

In the open air, automobiles swarm through America: they advance and overtake each other swift and light; and it seems that from one end of the horizon always come the same number of vehicles, while at the other end the exact same number are expected. As he watches them, Karl thinks he is contemplating an admirable universal automatism, a perfect order, that is governed not by any human person but by the very force of the machinery. He cannot make out whether anyone sits at the steering wheels. The cars accelerate or slow down all at the same time, almost as though regulated by a single set of gears; they never stop, and no passenger descends from those phantomatic shapes. Above them there is not a trace of dust—the dust that abounds where the weight of nature and soil dominates. All contrasts and individual tensions are annulled; an impression of calm and quiet is born, as though America were the realm of universal harmony, obtained without man's participation. But does this machinery really exist? Is America real? Or is it not rather a dream of the mind, an illusion of specters? When

Karl sees New York from above, the harbor and the long narrow bridge over the East River, he does not see anything: on the bridge there does not appear to be any movement, the ships seem motionless, the sea smooth and inanimate, everything is empty and without purpose. Perhaps, down there, in the invisible depths of the streets, life continues, automobiles move, men walk, live and die; but farther up one sees only a light mist which effortlessly dissolves.

American automatism reaches its peak in the enormous lobby of the enormous Occidental Hotel. Behind the slabs of glass, two assistant desk clerks recite their information to the patrons like litanies, attaching one answer to the next without interruption: they look neither at the desk nor into the face of those with whom they talk, but straight ahead, into empty space, to conserve and gather their strength. They talk into their beards, now German, now French, now Italian, now who knows what foreign language issues from their automaton's lips, always distorted by a strong American accent. The patrons understand almost nothing. They stand there, openmouthed, barely grasping a few pieces of information, without realizing when the answer addressed to each of them is completed. The laborious effort is overwhelming for all of them, assistant desk clerks, messenger boys, patrons, subjected to this flood of senseless words. As soon as the clock marks the hour, a bell rings. Immediately from a side door enter two new automatons, two new assistant clerks, each followed by a messenger boy; they place themselves at the window, lightly tap the shoulder of the first assistant clerks and take their place, with a speed that astonishes and frightens the patrons standing before the slab of glass. So continues the endless game of answers, while the first assistant clerks sit down in a corner of the reception office, stretch their arms and pour water from a basin over their heads burning with fatigue.

Toward the end of the book, from the top of Brunelda, Robinson and Delamarche's house, we witness an election rally. It is evening. At the end of the street, trumpet peals, drum rolls, dense ranks of drummers and trumpeters, and shouts from the houses. On the sidewalk young men march with long strides, their arms flung wide, their caps raised and in their hands long poles on which sway lanterns surrounded by yellowish smoke. Then, at the center of this massed escort, a gigantic man appears. On his shoulders sits a gentleman; from the high balcony where Karl is, one can make out only his bald, shiny head—and the top hat that he holds raised in a continuous salute. The crowd claps its hands and shouts a short, incomprehensible word, perhaps the name of the gentleman with the top hat. Some people arrive with very powerful automobile headlights, lighting up the houses on both sides of the street. The crowd stops in front of a tavern. A man signals with his hands. The bald gentleman tries unsuccessfully to stand upright on the gigantic man's shoulders; he straightens up, but falls back to a sitting position, and then he delivers an equally incomprehensible speech, waving the top hat in front of him with the speed of a windmill, while all the headlights of the cars turn toward him, make him the center of a luminous star. On the balconies, the people are dressed for the night: many have thrown a coat over their shoulders, the women are wrapped in large black clothes, the children, no longer tended to, climb frighteningly about on the railings. The people shout. On the balconies occupied by the bald man's supporters, they all sing his name in unison and mechanically clap their hands; on the other balconies, occupied by his adversaries, they shout other names, whistle, play phonographs, fling objects. When the racket becomes excessive, drummers and trumpeters again blow the trumpets and beat the drums, and a tremendous clamor drowns out the voices. Suddenly the noise ceases abruptly; and the crowd of people in the street, which hold up the bald gentleman, exploit the moment of silence to begin howling their party slogan, their gaping mouths illuminated by the headlights. The great scene, described by Kafka with an extraordinary sensitivity to the interplay of masses of people, lights and sounds, derives its effectiveness from an omission. High up on his balcony, Karl does not understand a thing: neither the candidate's name nor his speech nor the howls of his opponents nor the words shouted by Delamarche; so the scene seems a pantomime at once silent and deafening, and America becomes a slapstick farce, absurd and abstract, as in the *clowneries* of Kafka's youth.

When he looks out from his uncle's house, contemplating the traffic of automobiles below, Karl is stricken by the first American disease: the disease of the gaze. Confronted by that vortex of bodies, noises, smells and lights, confronted by that visual excess, confronted by the desks, telephones, vehicles, reception offices, the American election rallies in which automatism triumphs, Karl's gaze is spellbound, enchained and benumbed, like the gaze of someone who has stared for too long into a vortex and can no longer take his eyes away from it. Some immigrants spend entire days on the balcony, staring at the street below, like lost sheep. The uncle, who knows more about this danger than anyone, tries to help his nephew overcome the disease of the gaze; he advises detachment, coldness, care not to pass hasty judgments that might introduce confusion into all his future opinions. But there is another American disease, of which the uncle is completely a prisoner: insomnia. With its perennial tension and agitation, its continuous visual provocation, the enormity of its spectacles, America is, as Macbeth says, the country that "murders sleep." So it is a country not of innocents but of culprits. Even though he is innocent, Karl never sleeps: he does not sleep on the ship that takes him to America, he does not sleep enough in his uncle's house, in the first hotel, the second hotel, he dozes a bit in Pollunder's car; and like him the young elevator boy does not sleep, Therese and her mother do not sleep in the New York night, nor does the student who during the day works as a salesman in a department store and at night, in the open air, reads his medical textbooks.

From the very beginning, Karl confusedly senses these dangers. When his uncle gives him the piano, he puts it in front of the window thrown open to the noises of the street; and he plays a soldier's song from his native country—one of those songs that soldiers sing of an evening, sitting on the sills of the barracks windows, looking into the dark square—in the childlike hope that music might have an influence on American life, restoring harmony where he had seen only a cruel mixup of sights and sounds. But Karl fails. Nothing changes, in the street and in life. For him reality remains alien and impenetrable, like the traffic that nobody directs: an immense cycle, a great circle that incessantly rotates before him, just as again and again the mixup of vehicles, people, noises, smells keeps ever forming anew, compenetrated by the full-bodied light. There is only one possibility of salvation. To arrest the great cycle, he must come to know all the forces that keep it in motion: all the sensations, sentiments, impulses, tensions, violences and insomnias of American life. Naive Karl will not even attempt this cognitive task. The person who will try to know the great cycle in all of its parts is his older brother, Franz Kafka, in the densely articulated complexity of his novel.

On seeing the American desk, Karl is reminded of a mechanical crèche he had admired during the Christmas festivities of his childhood: an old man who turned a handle, the three Magi who advanced jerkily, the star that lit up, the child in the holy stable, the tiny rabbit in the grass rising on its hind legs and dashing away. American inventions re-awaken in him a childish pleasure in ingenious contraptions that encourage fantasies. This is another road that Kafka offers us, through Karl, to save ourselves from modern life. The only way is to transform everything that casts a spell and renders our gaze sleepless—the desk, the glass-enclosed elevator, his uncle's telephone, the automobile traffic, the reception office's information, the rally, the great cycle of sounds and lights—transform it all into a playful spectacle that consoles our childlike soul. This is what Kafka did, madly amused by his bureaucratic-automatic inventions and carrying them into the absurd, with a fresh, joyous laughter that one does not hear in any of his other novels. No one can say how he would have written the conclusion of this book. But the Oklahoma Theater is also a mechanical prodigy, a mobile automaton, a providential game, like the desk with its hundred compartments. Perhaps grace, while descending to save Karl, would with childish enjoyment play with those jerkily advancing Magi, those twinkling stars, those small fleeing rabbits, with all the great inventions of the American machine.

When he leaves the ship together with his uncle, Karl bursts into a flood of tears, he cannot bear to have abandoned and betrayed the stoker—his humble brother-father. Uncle Jacob puts a hand under his chin, hugs him against his body and caresses him; and tightly embraced he descends the ship's gangway with him, stepping onto the boat that takes them to shore. Karl accepts his second father in silence. At first he feels a strange distrust of him: when his uncle embraces him he remains cold and suspicious. Then he seeks the only relationship with him that, for the time being, is possible: he looks into his eyes—but the uncle's eyes avoid his, just as in the family photograph the son cannot catch the first father's eyes, and stare at the waves that rock the boat. Wrapped in their numinous omnipotence and their tenebrous blindness, the father-gods, the great custodians of the Law, do not grant the light of their gaze to those who seek it. Arrived in New York, in the iron and glass house, Karl's first impression is tempered. His uncle is a man of rigid principles in both public and private life: a concentration of ego and puritanical self-control. He does not bestow on Karl the fatherly tenderness that he desperately desires, but he cares for him. He tolerates his little whims, his passion for the desk

and piano; and he tries to give him the austere manly
upbringing that will prepare him to confront without too
much danger the maelstrom of lights and sounds that constitutes American life.

Sometime later, in the false American Eden the great
event of the Temptation, Fall and Sentence occurs a second
time; now that Karl has entered the house of the Law,
nothing can prevent the inexorable mechanism of Prohibition
and Sin from striking him. This time the serpent is not a poor
hysterical maid, but three people: Mack (a friend of Karl's),
Mr. Pollunder and his daughter, Clara: now too Karl yields
to Temptation; and the American Jehovah is his second
father, his uncle Jacob. Hidden in the semidarkness of the
room like a disgruntled god, the uncle does not like his
nephew to be invited to the Pollunder house in the suburbs
of New York: this visit upsets the regular rhythm of the
English and horseback-riding lessons which regulate Karl's
existence. But he does not clearly declare his will. Does it
matter? What difference does it make if the Law is not
pronounced? If no one puts into words the prohibition of
eating from the tree of good and evil? The new Law, which
during these months has begun to dominate in Kafka's world,
does not need to be promulgated. We—its sons and slaves—
must intuit it, know it, read it, come to meet it, bow our
heads to it, perform it, even if no father-god has formulated it.

Despite the uncle's displeasure, Karl yields to the small
temptation. In the evening, the car reaches the country
house, surrounded by the soughing and fragrance of big
chestnut trees, while Karl has dozed off. When he opens his
eyes, he realizes that he has penetrated into America's night;
whereas his uncle's glass house coruscates with light, Pollunder's unfinished villa is the realm of darkness—interminable
dark passageways, atriums, galleries, chapels, empty rooms
that only the weak flame of the candle illuminates, as in a
fairy tale about ghosts. It is the abode of the Disquieting and

the Labyrinthine: it is traversed by terrible drafts, which
scurry down the passageways and blow out the light; it looks
like a papier-mâché cathedral in which actor-automatons run
about; and Green's hand blocks all the doors, imprisons Karl
in those old walls and deprives him of the open air, the
perfume of the trees, and the full moon. The villa is a
continuation of his uncle's empire: a perfectly specular
couple is at his service: Green with his odious vitality and
Pollunder with his unctuous sentimentality. Green could be
one of those gobblers of food who enchant us in Dickens's
novels: he voraciously gulps down his soup, quarters the
squabs with great slashes of his knife, seizes the food with a
leap of the tongue, desires women as though they were food,
contaminates the dining room with smoke, rummages in his
enormous wallet as though it were his stomach. But what in
Dickens is candid, sparkling and rosy here is gloomy conta-
gion. Pollunder too could descend from the procession of
Dickensian hypocrites. Unhealthily fat, his back curved, his
abdomen flabby and drooping, his face pale and tortured, his
gestures repetitive and coerced, he continually buttons and
unbuttons his jacket, then wipes his face with his handkerchief and noisily blows his nose. When he talks he is
ceremonious, tortuous, full of qualifications and concessions
to the same extent that Green is abrupt and violent; he
pretends that he has a tender heart, and continually touches
Karl, puts an arm around his waist, hugs him, pulls him onto
his knees, like an old homosexual.

Karl is steeped in malaise. He fears that he has been
remiss with his uncle, by not respecting his wishes. In the air
of the dark house, everything seems to announce sinister
events; and his affection for his second father, stifled for a
few hours, grips his heart and makes him suffer with a kind
of tender sorrow. The next morning, in New York, he would
go to his uncle's bedroom, where he's never been until now;
he would surprise him in his nightshirt, perhaps have
breakfast with him; and this breakfast together would become

an infinitely affectionate habit. The house oppresses him: Green and Pollunder detain him with all sorts of excuses; the road that must lead him to his uncle, through the French door, down the flight of steps, along the driveway and country road, calls him in a loud voice. Time passes. The clocks mark eleven, quarter past eleven, half past eleven, eleven forty-five. To Karl, who wants to get out of the house, it seems that time runs slowly, while for us those indications of hours and minutes seem the ticking of a very fast infernal machine that leads to catastrophe. Finally a bell tolls twelve times, almost without interval: each toll strikes while the preceding one is still resounding. The dark empty house is filled with this menacing presence, and Karl feels upon his cheeks the air stirred by the movement of the bells. It is midnight: Green hands Karl his uncle's letter. It is the second sentence, as definitive as the first.

Thus, hidden among the events of an adventure novel, Kafka has discovered the great edifice of Paternal Law, which from then on never stopped obsessing him throughout his life. As Karl will say, the Law's most evident characteristic is that of not having any "good will." For the Law there are no innocents, but only the guilty: the most innocuous things are seen in the most sinister light, and the guilt, as he will comment in "The Penal Colony," is always "beyond discussion." Thus the Law initiates an interminable trial against us, which lasts longer than our lives. What are the charges against us? Let us not confuse Paternal Law with human law, which charges us only with acts and ignores our unconscious. Karl has not violated any prohibition; he has yielded to an innocent, childish whim, a slight infidelity to the paternal home, and the Law, here as in "The Judgment," accuses him precisely of these small desires and unconscious rebellions, as though they were capital crimes.

Any defense attorney, actuated by the spirit of good sense and tolerance, could stand up before the prosecution and maintain that Karl is a good and affectionate nephew, just as later on, at the Occidental Hotel, he will be an excellent elevator boy. Even if his small infidelity were a crime, Karl repented that very evening; he missed his uncle and did everything to return home. The great accuser would smile, or snicker like Green. The Law does not recognize extenuating circumstances, repentances, states of mind, good intentions, tender devotions, regrets. It ignores psychology; when it wishes, it neglects the unconscious, leaves this mined field to men—even though, afterward, it demands that men make use of psychology and venture into the unconscious, when they are expected to intuit by a kind of telepathic communication the prohibitions that the Father-God does not promulgate. The Law—the prosecution might continue —is an exact science. For it there exist only admissible or mistaken actions, prescribed by a rigid norm. Karl should not have left his New York home (even though no one ever issued a prohibition), or returned there at the twelve strokes of midnight (although this was materially impossible for him).

What could Karl's defense attorney answer? Probably he would keep quiet, like Karl, who withdraws into the most obstinate silence. But he would have forgotten one thing. The Law, which boasts so much of being an exact science, is, however, when it so pleases, the most inexact of moralities. Green and Pollunder, those arms of the Law, use every trick to prevent Karl from returning to New York: they tell him there is no car, no chauffeur, that the trolley stop is far away, that he must say good-bye to Clara and wait for a letter. . . . But men rarely notice the Law's insidious, hidden activities. Like Karl, they invest it with good sense, rationality, reasonableness, understanding, a readiness to compromise. Paternal Law possesses none of these very human qualities; and it is precisely because of this that we—blinded by the dark violence of its light—worship it.

The event of the Temptation, Fall and Sentence is repeated for a third time at the Occidental Hotel: Karl is thrown out into the streets of Rameses. By now he has reached the place from which there is no return. Just before, he had lost his parents' photograph—upon which he had fallen asleep and which for him represented family, native country and hope of return—and although he does not open his mouth, we cannot forget the tragic intensity of his sorrow. He is alone, in the vastness of America. Then he loses his suitcase, so hated and loved, the symbol of his expulsion and his journey; his jacket, which he leaves in the hands of the Occidental Hotel's desk clerk; his money; the address of the Brenner rooming house, where the cook had prepared a refuge for him; and the documents of which he was so proud, which he displayed with so much trust to the ship's authorities, as though it were so terribly important to possess proof of one's own name. The situation in which he finds himself can be compared only to the terrifying scene that shows David Copperfield fleeing down English roads, threatened by the horrible creatures of the abyss. But at the end of his road, David has Betsey and Uncle Dick waiting for him. Karl has nobody. With two of the most inspired omissions of his art, Kafka prevents us from knowing what he feels in his heart when his uncle Jacob and the headwaiter at the hotel throw him out into the street. If we watch his face, we understand how much he has changed. There are no longer the enthusiasms, outbursts, dreams, hopes and tendernesses that made him so enchanting at the beginning of the book. He is silent, and he bows his head before the irreparable. Naked, stripped, with an empty mind, an empty heart, he contemplates reality with petrified eyes and observes his degradation with sublime stoicism.

Coming out of the Occidental Hotel with Karl, Kafka left behind him the reign of the Law, where we live only to be sentenced. No more fathers, or father substitutes; nor mothers, all victims of the paternal will. Now Karl lives in the lap of reality, where he could have lost himself if he had fled with the stoker on the riverboats or over the plains of America.

But this reality is not all of reality: it is not the rosy, dizzying world of food and love, adventure and fantasy, beer and sex, rivers and streets, taverns and kitchens, laughter and madness, idiocy and euphoria—the "savage and completely inexplicable world, the best of impossible worlds," in which Dickens lived. With a significant restriction, reality for Kafka is only the louche, the equivocal, the abject: the Dostoevskian "underground" where Brunelda, Delamarche and Robinson perform like coarse ham actors. To discover this underground, Kafka had no need to look very far from himself, either in the crowd that went down the alleyways of Prague or in the streets of his imaginary America; he carried it within himself, because he, the purest spirit of his time, was the Stranger—and the Stranger was also a parasite, like the parasites in Jacob Gordin's Yiddish plays.

At the time of *The Trial*, Kafka would have seen degraded forms of the gods reflected in abasement. But in *Amerika* the underground did not yet have a metaphysical value. He could describe it without tremors and without anguish, with an immense storytelling pleasure, an airiness of the hand that perhaps he never again found. Guided by the allied spirits of amusement and levity, he overcame all inner defenses and described America as a country that spends the night in the open air, at windows and on balconies, amid the sound of phonographs, while in the street the electoral pantomime runs wild.

The house of Brunelda, Delamarche and Robinson is the gigantic labyrinth-house Kafka had recently learned to love in Dostoevsky. There are atriums, smaller and larger passageways, crowded and almost deserted courtyards, whole series of apartments; and the stairs, the terrible dark stairs which at every landing widen and continue to climb without apparently ever coming to a halt—symbol of the cloistral and of the vertigo of the infinite. Instead of at the bottom of the stairs, the underground is found at the top of the stairs: here and in *The Trial* the experience of the den-burrow becomes that of the attic. High up there, where one should experience openness and light, one is enclosed as in a prison. A curtain reaching down to the floor prevents the sun's rays from penetrating; closets and hanging clothes clutter the stifling, dusty room; unwashed dishes with remnants of food are piled up on the chairs; on the floor are burrows formed by clothes, blankets and drapes; under the sofa are balls of dust and women's hairs, big boxes and smaller ones; and from the drawers flows an irresistible lava of dead things—old novels, bundles of sheet music, small medicine and ointment bottles, powder puffs, jars of rouge, hairbrushes, curls, letters, needles, scraps and lint compacted like felt.

The queen of this lowest of spaces, dusty and shut in, this burrow built on the rooftops, is Brunelda. The name recalls Wagner. If we are to believe the legend told by Leporello-Robinson, she was in the past a great opera singer, a lithe and beautiful woman completely dressed in white and with a small red parasol; but we never hear her sing, and all that remains of this gilded legend are a cape, a few laces and a pair of opera glasses with which one can inspect the street. In her attic, Brunelda is degraded. She wears a small bonnet over her unkempt hair, several skirts pulled on one over the other, dirty yellowish underwear; and coarse thick white wool stockings reach almost up to her knees and make her look like a shepherdess. She no longer even resembles a human creature but a soft animal, swollen and fat, a seal or a she-elephant, which from its lips extracts a heavy, red tongue. During the day she lies stretched out on the sofa, sleeps or snoozes; at night she snores and is racked by bestial night-mares. She ingurgitates sex like an animal or an enormous pas-sive plant; and she will end up in a whorehouse, as a kind of sacred prostitute. She's always hot, almost as if she were burnt by an erotic fire or incessant hysteria, and she must extin-guish it, continually bathing in a small washtub. Robinson, gasping, carries up the water, Delamarche, surrounded by a thousand splatters and splashes, washes and rubs the soft body of the huge she-elephant whose head protrudes above the closets.

Up there, among the rooftops, in the enclosure of her dusty den, protected by the lowered curtains, Brunelda carries out her erotic mission. She does not know the excitement and fire of desire—but rather eros as enslavement, abasement, degradation. Delamarche waits on her like a servant, dresses her, cleans her, combs her, bathes her; he dominates her sexually and is supported by her. Her deserted husband pays Robinson to obtain news about her; and he would pay a lot of money just to be able to stand on the balcony, from which he hopes to watch the couplings of Delamarche and his wife. But degradation reaches its nadir in the figure of Robinson, who is a man transformed into a dog and who loves to be treated like a dog; he lives stretched out on the balcony, where he quarrels with the cats, is summoned by a bell, beaten on the snout with a whip. Kafka amuses himself, playing with his vertiginously profound theme. Robinson is not a debased Dostoevskian character pretending to live the life of the soul and weeping over his degradation; he is not a Kafkian animal, which finds again in its darkness a truth that man ignores; and his depravity is not even like Block's, a path toward the sacred. In this part of the novel there wafts the aroma and breath of comic opera: an eighteenth-century atmosphere that will never again be expressed in Kafka's books. Robinson is a Harlequin or Leporello, lazy, foolish, idle, sentimental, boastful and megalomaniac, who tries to infect Karl with his canine physiology. There he is, on the balcony, stretched out like a dog, chattering on and on. He eats a piece of black sausage, hard as a rock, dips bread in a can of sardines which drips oil from all sides, and dries his hands on one of Brunelda's shawls; then he soaks the bread in the hollow of his hands full of oil, chews a mass of squashed and glued-together chocolate creams, and talks again and again about Brunelda, would like to touch her, lick her, see her copulate with Delamarche, munch on that fat seal or she-elephant flesh, as though coitus were only a prolongation of his canine meal.

Karl works as a servant in this aerial den, surrounded by the cat-Delamarche, the dog-Robinson and the seal-Brunelda, works scrupulously, as he always does everything; he is an excellent servant, just as he was an excellent son and an excellent nephew and an excellent elevator boy at the hotel. The preparation of breakfast at four in the afternoon—in the kitchen are piled up the tenants' still unwashed dishes, jugs with a bit of coffee-milk and coffee, tiny dishes with dabs of butter, biscuits spilled from a tin, and Karl transforms these disgusting leftovers into a presentable breakfast, cleaning the tray, pouring together the dregs of coffee and milk, scraping up the pieces of butter, cleaning knives and spoons, trimming the nibbled rolls—is a masterpiece of craftsmanship. Then he sinks even lower: errand boy in the whorehouse, where he takes Brunelda in a little cart, and perhaps handyman for a band of gangsters where he is called Negro, if Hartmut Binder's hypothesis (unverifiable) is correct. Whatever happens to him, his nature does not change. He lives in debasement, sinks into debasement: without repugnance, one might say. And yet he is not even grazed by debasement; he slides untouched through the experiences that are imposed on him, preserving the immaculate soul of his childhood.

At this point, or just before, at the end of January 1913, Kafka stopped writing *Amerika*. For more than a year he wrote nothing; then came his engagement to Felice Bauer, the breaking off of the engagement and the beginning of *The Trial*. He asked for a leave from the insurance institute from October 5 to October 18, 1914. He would begin writing after dinner and stay at his desk until five or half past seven in the morning, and when the first lights and first noises visited him, he abandoned the sheets on which he had written a chapter of *The Trial* or "In the Penal Colony" and the penultimate and then the last chapter of *Amerika*, which Max Brod entitled "The Nature Theater of Oklahoma." We would like to know everything—the color of the sky, the bright or stormy clouds, the position of his desk, the quality of his writing paper, the furniture in the room, the number of nocturnal passersby—about those fourteen exceedingly dense days during which Kafka wrote three works so profoundly different from one another. Today almost all scholars are of the opinion that *Amerika*, like *The Trial* and "In the Penal Colony," was supposed to conclude with a condemnation. To me this seems impossible. I believe that during those fourteen days, dividing and lacerating himself within himself, grandiosely proceeding through the realm of possibilities, transforming himself into a vortex of antitheses, Kafka kept open before him two opposed theological and narrative hypotheses. On the one hand, at the end of *Amerika*, the divine world as grace, welcome, acceptance, refusal of the written Law; on the other, in *The Trial* and "In the Penal Colony," the divine world as the Law of the father, scripture and condemnation. No great artist was ever woven of a single fabric; and no one more than Kafka was inhabited by the tragic game of simultaneously trying out all the extreme hypotheses, all the polar contradictions of the universe.

We do not know how long after his imprisonment in the whorehouse Karl sees on the street corner a poster with the notice. "Today from six in the morning until midnight, at the Clayton Hippodrome, job applications will be accepted for the Oklahoma Theater! The great Oklahoma Theater calls you! Calls you only today, and only once. Those who miss this opportunity, miss it forever. . . . Everyone is welcome! We are the Theater that serves everyone, everyone at his rightful place! We offer this welcome to those who decide in our favor! But hurry, so that you can be admitted before midnight! At midnight everything will be closed down, never to be opened again! Cursed be those who do not believe us!" With irony, Kafka concocted this poster in two diametrically opposed languages. On the one hand, the advertising language of a Luna Park in Chicago, which he had found in a German book: "What formalities must one observe, before being admitted here? What papers, passports, legitimizations, tax receipts, christening certificates, labor permits must one produce to be admitted? Why! Nothing at all!* Our astonished American answers. . . . Everyone's welcome. . . . No one has to show papers, have his name registered in a book, neither his true nor his false one. Everyone is welcome. . . ." On the other hand, in the style of the notice, we hear the evangelical parable of the ten virgins who at midnight go to meet their bridegroom; and that appeal to the Kingdom of God, that dramatic sense of imminence which vibrates in the words of Matthew and Mark. "The time is fulfilled, and the kingdom of God is at hand: repent ye, and believe the gospel" (Mark 1:15). "When you shall see all these things, know that it is near, even at the doors. Verily I say unto you, This generation shall not pass, till all these things be fulfilled. Heaven and earth shall pass away, but my words shall not pass away" (Matthew 24:33–5). The Kingdom of God has already come with the word of Christ. The Gospels' voice summons everyone to the last roll call, everyone, the innocent and the guilty; summons them at a moment defined in time, at *this* moment, because afterward the summons will not be repeated.

The Oklahoma Theater is not a simple theater, although it can mount grandiose performances, which even the president of the United States attends. The Oklahoma Theater is one of those "prodigies," those "signs and miracles," which by now, the uncle says, exist only in America: a realized utopia, a *Theatrum mundi*, as vast as the universe, not unlike the utopias with which old Goethe played in the *Wanderjahre*. It can gather together all professions and human proclivities, all men, since "the number of seats is unlimited": engineers, mechanics, European high school students, elevator boys and even ex–whorehouse errand boys, if Karl had the courage

---

* "Why! Nothing at all!" appears in English in the original.—Trans.

to declare himself. It welcomes all professions, and tries to discover each man's true vocation and set him on the road to it. Whereas according to the Law "all, also the innocent, are guilty," according to the Theater all—also the guilty, or those who have no merits or lie or hide their real name, like Karl—are welcome and are elected. On the hippodrome's podiums, the Law of the Father—which continues to rage in "The Penal Colony" and *The Trial*—no longer exists. Here grace speaks. As Matthew says: "Ask, and it shall be given you; seek, and you shall find; knock, and it shall be opened unto you. For everyone that asketh receiveth; and to him who knocketh it shall be opened" (7:7–8).

As in the Gospels, Kafka seized upon a theological wisdom both ancient and subtle. But with lightheartedness and enchanting gaiety, he played: shoved onto the stage parodistic and comical images in which the form is degraded and inadequate in respect to its symbolic content. He knew no other way to compel transcendence to appear in the pages of a novel. The burlesque anticipation of the Kingdom of Heaven takes place in the hippodrome. Hundreds of women are dressed as angels in flowing white robes, loose hair flying and great wings on their shoulders. They seem gigantic figures because they stand on pedestals, some over two meters high, which are hidden by the flowing robes that flutter in the wind, so that the angels seem to have extremely small heads and too short, almost absurd-looking hair. As in the Annunciation and the Last Judgment, as in the paintings of Simone Martini and Melozzo da Forli, they blow into gleaming golden trumpets, but nobody pays any attention to the beauty of the choreography and the harmony of the song. The giant angels sound their trumpets all at the same time, producing a confusing uproar: now they play louder, now they fall silent; and the visitors can climb up on the pedestals, grasp a golden trumpet and begin to play a song heard in some tavern, without anyone's protesting. The hippodrome's betting booths are changed into the offices of the Kingdom of

God; and the signs with the names of the winning horses
proclaim the announcements of Election: "Shopkeeper Kalla
with wife and child," "Negro, mechanic."

As had happened to Christ's message nineteen centuries
before, the notice of the Oklahoma Theater—that urgent,
definitive summons which ends at midnight—is understood
by only a few. It does not mention pay; and how could it
speak of this when it offered nothing less than salvation? Few
believe the words of the Annunciation, and those few are
once again the "indigent and suspect," the earth's derelicts,
the homeless people without a country, those to whom the
Oklahoma Theater addresses itself, just as the Gospel once
addressed them. Karl accepts immediately, without doubts
or second thoughts. His journey to America has meant, for
him, the progressive loss of illusions; he lost many of them
when he left the stoker, others yet when he was thrown out
by his uncle, still others when he was discharged by the
Occidental Hotel and then, after being the servant of two
parasites, descended into a whorehouse. But hidden under
disappointment and ashes, his childlike soul is not dead: still
ready to believe, to delude itself, to devote itself completely
to something or someone. So when he reads the poster, he
feels forgiven, loved, welcomed with open arms. "For Karl
. . . there was in the notice something that strongly attracted
him." "Everyone is welcome!" it read. Everyone, therefore
also Karl. All that he had done up until now was forgotten,
no one would reproach him any longer. He was given the
chance to do work that was not shameful, for which in fact
one could be summoned publicly! . . . Even if the bombastic
words in the notice were a lie, even if the great Oklahoma
Theater was a small traveling circus, the fact that it wanted
to summon people was enough for him. He did not read
the notice a second time but fastened on the sentence:
"Everyone is welcome!" He enters the hippodrome's circle,
and his past—which with so much distress he was forced to
give up—returns. In a few minutes he again sees, disguised

as an angel, a girl, Fanny, whom he had met during a phase
of his adventures unknown to us; an office manager of the
theater reminds him of a professor at the German high school
where he was a pupil; and while at the table of the elect he
again runs into Giacomo, the elevator boy he knew at the
Occidental Hotel.

In its selection of personnel, the Theater seems to follow
the same procedure as the offices, organizations, institutions
and factories that form the painful fabric of human history. It
requires "identity papers." Karl has lost his passport at the
Occidental Hotel, and also his very name, by sinking into
depravity. Now his name is Negro. So when he declares that
he has no documents, the Theater's office manager, just like
any other bureaucrat on earth, says to him that "this is an
incomprehensible negligence." But here the new Gospel of
the Theater shows up. Just as the office manager is about to
ask Karl the most important questions, his underling—the
scribe—quickly states that Karl is hired. Immediately after
that, the same thing is repeated. When the office manager
asks him his name, Karl is ashamed to announce his real
name, and so he gives his false name: "Negro." The office
manager understands that this is a false name; he would
prefer not to put this name in his register and hire Karl, but
the scribe writes "Negro" and informs him for the second
time that he has been hired by the Oklahoma Theater. The
written Law—the Law of the Father, of documents, of name
and sentence—has been affirmed for an instant, only to be
torn up publicly. In the Oklahoma Theater it is the oral law
that triumphs, in accordance with which, despite sins and
lies, *"jeder ist willkommen,"* "everyone is welcome." While this
reversal takes place in the hippodrome, we witness another of
no less importance. The authorities are overturned. The
office manager is derided; the scribe, his underling—who,
ironically, tears up the written law—decides in his stead. As
in the Gospels, the Last have become the First.

On the hippodrome's tribune is set up a long table

covered with a white cloth. The elect dine: servants bring in
big chickens, such as Karl had never seen, with many forks
stuck into the roasted, crackling meat, and pour red wine into
the glasses. All the elect are merry and excited, many stand
up, glass in hand; one toasts the leader of the tenth recruiting
company, whom he calls "the father of the unemployed."
But the heads of the Theater take no notice, perhaps they do
not wish to notice the toast of the poor people, the humble
elect in the Kingdom of God, who are here consuming their
first feast in the land of Cockaigne. Karl sits down last at the
banquet, the last of the last; perhaps, therefore, the first of
the first, as Luke says: "And they shall come from the east,
and from the west, and from the north, and from the south,
and shall sit down in the kingdom of God. And, behold,
there are last which shall be first, and there are first which
shall be last" (13:29–30). Pictures of the Oklahoma Theater
are handed around among the people dining. No one looks at
them. Into Karl's hands comes the picture that depicts the
immense box of the president of the United States. Its
parapet of solid gold is broad and grandiose; between the
columns are set medallions bearing portraits of past presi-
dents ranged in a series. Toward the box, from the sides and
above, descend beams of soft white light which completely
disclose its front section; red velvet curtains, whose color
changes with the movement of their folds, fall over the
parapet; and the back of the box looks "like an empty, dark
space aglitter with feeble red reflections." As Karl gazes at
these colored images, we have reached the culmination of the
novel. The president of the United States is not to be seen.
God, or whatever we wish to call the Prime Principle of this
world of grace and election, does not appear. High up there,
an empty, dark space remains: his darkness, his absence. Did
perhaps Karl, the last of the last, having reached Oklahoma,
have the ultimate revelation? Or would the box remain
forever empty? Or would some obscure menace come from

that pomp, that gloom, capable of wiping out everything that Karl seems to have attained?

We do not know how the book—which is interrupted in the middle of a journey that seems serene, among high mountains, dark and jagged valleys, broad streams which make one shiver with their fresh, cold breath—was supposed to end. Should we trust Brod, who said: "With enigmatic words Kafka smilingly hinted that 'in the almost limitless theater' his young hero would, as by a paradisial enchantment, find again a profession, freedom, support—and even his native country and parents"? For some time the hypothesis of the Oklahoma Theater still occupied Kafka's mind. Then he reached the conclusion that, for his most beloved boy, diligent and scrupulous as in the school primers, there was no hope of salvation—and if there wasn't any for Karl, so much the less would there be for him. He imagined that Grace would be changed back into the Law; and that someone, in the Theater, or the Theater's entire prodigious machine, would prepare some horrible deception. Almost a year later, on September 30, 1915, he wrote in his *Diaries* the famous passage in which Karl Rossmann, the innocent, is condemned to death like Joseph K., although "with a gentler hand, more pushed aside than struck down." The innocent too must be sacrificed to the wrathful god to whom Kafka had consecrated his art.

With "The Judgment," "The Metamorphosis" and above all *Amerika*, Kafka elaborated and fixed once and for all his narrative method, which rests on a few very simple principles. The first of these principles, as everyone has observed, is the almost complete death of the figure of the Narrator: this great Ego, who in the novel of every epoch exhibits his fabulistic and histrionic qualities, insists on his exclusive relationship with the public, chatters volubly and comments on events, knows all occurrences, past, present and future, and penetrates without resistance into the characters' souls. In place of the Narrator there is an immense void, and we still perceive the anguish that this death has created in the world. With "The Judgment," Kafka began to narrate events from the viewpoint of a single character: Georg Bendemann, Gregor Samsa, Joseph K., K. and the animal without a name in "The Burrow." As Martin Walser has recognized, this carries with it a narrative impoverishment that Kafka chose deliberately. With a single gesture he condemned all those marvelous narrative games that a novelist obtains by bringing together the figure of the Narrator and the viewpoints of many characters, one of whom often speaks through the voice of another: alternating omnipresence and absence, omniscience and ignorance, vision and omission, light and darkness. Kafka did not seek multiplicity but concentration, clausure, suffocation, stylistic compactness—all of which the characters' viewpoint guaranteed for him. Occasionally, time passes more swiftly: Kafka condenses in one chapter (a "summary") what happens in three months, or a character recounts his mother's death or the vicissitudes of a family excluded from the life of the village. But this happens rarely. Like Tolstoy, but for opposite reasons, Kafka did not like foreshortened or reiterated time; he accumulated direct scenes, in the present, which the character-narrator experiences minute by minute.

In some modern novels, the character-narrator possesses the same knowledge as the Narrator and helps us interpret the confused and manifold tangle of events. Kafka's character-narrator never orients us: he knows only what he sees; he does not know what happens in other places, does not know the thoughts and intentions of the other characters, leaves certain capital events in the dark, dwells on minor ones, or, simply, *does not understand* what is happening. We, who are reading, entrusted to a guide so uncertain and so little worthy of faith, understand less than he does. A most

obscure tangle of events, woven by men and gods, becomes
an Enigma—which we cannot illuminate, so long as we are
unable to coincide with the books' living complexity. When,
at the beginning of The Trial, we read: "Someone must have
slandered Joseph K., for without having done anything
wrong, one morning he was arrested," we ask ourselves:
"Who is speaking? Who is telling us that Joseph K. did
nothing wrong?" At first sight, it can be only the Narrator,
who establishes an incontrovertible fact by the authority of
his voice. In reality, it is not the Narrator who is speaking:
Joseph K. is thinking, through a Narrator's voice, and a naive
reader will find it hard to understand that he is not at all
innocent. Kafka therefore is not satisfied to omit what the
character does not know, but intentionally deceives us,
putting us on the wrong track. The art of trickery, which he
knew as did few others, contributes to the Enigma.

We imagine that, in Kafka's books, the character is
speaking in the first person. Is it not perhaps an "I" that
colors the story with its own eyes, its own knowledge and
experiences? But, if we look for it among the great stories,
the "I" comes to meet us only in two instances: "Investigations of a Dog" and "The Burrow," two stories of his last
years. As for the novels, they are all written in the third
person: after a few days of writing, the "I" of The Castle was
changed into a "he." Only in "The Metamorphosis" is this
"he" colored by a sort of affectionate familiarity with the
character. Beginning with The Trial, Kafka adopted the
paradoxical condition of totally accepting the character's
viewpoint—but at the same time, he inserted a glass wall
between himself and Joseph K. and K., transforming that
"I-he" into something radically extraneous. This condition
becomes even more paradoxical because of yet another fact.
If one supposes that Kafka is narrating in accordance with the
viewpoint of Gregor Samsa, Karl Rossmann and Joseph K.,
it should follow from this that we know all their thoughts and
feelings, as though a mirror were following their conscious-

ness at every instant. Instead, Kafka systematically has recourse to restriction of the field. When he is supposed to tell the capital events in Gregor's or Karl's life—how they react to metamorphosis into an animal or to being thrown out by the uncle or by the Occidental Hotel—he says nothing. An impenetrable silence descends on the page. The more tragic events are, the stronger becomes the reticence and omission: every time another writer would pour out with abundance, he offers us the frightening absence of the void.

Without the help of the Narrator, without interpretations, subjected to omissions, absences, tricks, reticences and restrictions of the field, we journey through Kafka's great books as we would through the very body of Enigma. When shall we ever be able to understand? When shall we be able to choose among the thousand contradictory opinions? When shall we be able to know the truth without shadows? A final paradox decrees that Kafka's books are among literature's least difficult. There is nothing subjective, arbitrary or doubtful in them: *Amerika* is not the truth according to Karl, or *The Trial* the truth according to Joseph K. Dickens is hard to understand, not Kafka. We have only to keep in mind all the events and characters of *Amerika* or *The Trial* or *The Castle;* establish a living relationship among them, a plot without end among all the words Kafka has left on paper. Only this is needed: an art of patience. If all the threads are really pulled tight, the truth of *Amerika* or *The Trial* or *The Castle*—a truth that stands far above or lies much deeper than Karl, Joseph K., K. and Kafka—will burst forth by itself, dazzlingly.

CHAPTER FIVE

1913–1914

In his masterpiece *Stages on Life's Way*, Kierkegaard wrote a page that perhaps Kafka never read: "Should a soldier on the frontier be married? At the frontier of the spirit can he marry when day and night he struggles at the advance posts not against Tartars and Scythians but against the savage hordes of an essential melancholy? Can he get married at this advanced post? Even though he does not fight day and night and enjoys long enough respites, he never knows when the war will start again because he cannot mistake this lull for an armistice."

Kafka too was a soldier on the desolate frontiers of the spirit: he too struggled with attacks of melancholy, the temptations of nothingness, the anguish of the possible and unthinkable; and like Kierkegaard, he thought that marriage was "the magnificent central point of life and existence," the "fullness of time," something totally divine and totally human. He could not bear solitude. Alone, he feared he would not be able to endure the assaults of his life, the traps of time and age, the vague impulse of a desire to write, insomnia, the proximity of madness. He wanted to get married, to enter the longed-for land of Canaan. During those first months of 1913, the thought of marriage assailed him and greatly upset him, forcing him into contradictions, which nevertheless always led him to the same conclusion. He thought up always new objections to his marriage—always more arduous, difficult and unendurable—and he ended by hoping that marriage would descend on him as a celestial grace. He insisted that for Felice and for him there was no future; they must leave each other: "That would absolutely be the right solution. What I will suffer, what she will suffer—is not comparable to the common suffering that would result from marriage." But when Felice spoke of marriage, he dared not resist, even though his love was suffocated by anguish. He would have liked to tie his right wrist indissolubly to Felice's left wrist. He knew that in this way, as he had read in a book about the French Revolution, they would have gone together all the way to the scaffold, but he preferred this scaffold-marriage to the absence of marriage. Whatever his objections and reactions might be, the conclusion was the same. If he did not marry Felice, he would be ruined. "If we shall not be together soon, my love for you, which does not tolerate the vicinity of any other thought in my mind, turns toward an idea, toward a spirit, toward something absolutely unreachable, without which I cannot absolutely ever be—and this thought could tear me out of this world." Marriage with her was death—but the only death that forced him to remain on this earth.

Sometimes his anguished thoughts took another path. He thought about Felice, what she would lose by marrying him: "I would lose my loneliness which is for the most part frightening and acquire you, whom I love above all creatures. You, instead, would lose the life you've led till now, with which you were almost completely satisfied, would lose Berlin, an office you like, your girl friends, your small amusements, the hope of marrying a healthy, cheerful, good man, of having beautiful, healthy children whom, if you think about it, you ardently desire. In exchange for this certainly not negligible loss, you would acquire a sick, weak, not very sociable, taciturn, sad, rigid, almost desperate man, whose single virtue perhaps consists in loving you." Then he would express his repugnance, which lurked in his dark animal's abyss: "I am greedy for solitude, the idea of a wedding trip horrifies me, all couples on their honeymoon, whether I relate to them or not, seem repugnant to me, and when I want to feel nauseated, I have only to imagine putting an arm around a woman's thighs." A bond as tight as marriage would have ended by dissolving his vague and nebulous form in the air. Literature rebelled against conjugal life; and it seemed to him that marriage was a region completely covered by his father's gigantic body, or an aim too high for him—the prisoner, the outcast—to be able to aspire to. He loved Felice with the boundless force of imagination, anguish and a sense of guilt; for her he had created an altar in his soul—and precisely because of this he feared that by marrying her he would violate "a command of heaven," a sexual-religious taboo erected by someone, perhaps the ancient shadow of incest. "I have the precise sensation that I am going to ruin with this marriage, with this *bond, with the dissolution* of this nothing that I am, and not only I but also my wife, and the more I love her all the more swiftly and dreadfully will it happen. Now you tell me, what should we do?"

Then, once more, his resistances were swept away. He decided to marry Felice. He was not marrying her for love, even though he loved her very much; he was marrying her out of obligation to the sacred idea of matrimony—like "the soldier at the frontier," who has come home on a brief furlough—out of duty toward her, toward himself, toward the torture he had imposed on himself and imposed on her. It was a tragic choice, formulated on the brink of suicide, where a thread separated total happiness from total misery. On August 14, he wrote in his *Diaries:* "Coitus as punishment for the happiness of being together. To live possibly as an

ascetic, more ascetic than a bachelor, this for me is the only
possible way to endure marriage. But what about her?" So,
rigid, mechanical, linear, in the letters that reached Berlin
terrorizing Felice, he began to plan an ascetic, monastic
marriage. With an exasperation that seemed meant to destroy
the longed-for life in common, he depicted their ménage.
The husband would return from the office at half past two or
three; would eat, lie down, sleep until seven or eight, hastily
eat something, go for an hour's walk, sit down to write and
remain at his desk until two at night or dawn. "Would you be
able to put up with such a life? Knowing nothing about your
husband save that he is in his room writing? And spend fall
and winter in this way? And around about spring welcome
him half dead on the study's threshold, and watch him
through spring and summer as he tries to regain his health for
the fall? Is such a life possible? Perhaps, perhaps it is even
possible, but you must think it over down to the last shadow
of a doubt." His wife would lead a cloistered life. Cut off
from parents and relatives, deprived of all contacts, with the
door of the house closed even to the best of friends, she
would spend only one hour of the day "at the side of a *vexed,
sad, taciturn, discontented, sickly man* . . . tied with invisible
chains to an invisible literature." During that hour they
would not converse, because he detested the wastefulness
and futility of conversation; they would remain mute, in
silence, fascinated by their obscure magnetic affinity, like
Ottilie and Eduard in *Elective Affinities*, and would communicate only with little notes, as now between Prague and
Berlin.

During the last month of 1913, the tension between
Kafka and Felice became so violent that it led them to put
some distance between each other. Felice had the idea of
sending a friend of hers from Vienna, Grete Bloch, to
Prague, with the mission of "mediator"; and like all Kafkian
mediators, she managed to complicate the situation she was
supposed to simplify. Kafka expected a "rather middle-aged

spinster with maternal feelings, who, I do not exactly know
why, would be big and robust"; instead, coming to meet him
he saw a young girl, delicate, a bit frail. He felt sorry for her.
"In some way it is also true that I feel sorry for all young
girls. . . . I still haven't figured out where this pity comes
from. Perhaps I pity them because of the transformation into
womanhood that they must undergo." With Grete, the
epistolary magic of the previous year was reborn: Kafka
began to confide on paper; he talked about Felice, told stories
about Felice—but meanwhile he asked the usual tender
questions: "Have you already gotten a good place to stay?"
He told her his dreams, enveloped her in his exquisite
gallantry, asked her to send him photographs, wanted to
meet her alone. He needed the tenderness that Grete gave
him: not even a spark reached him from the absent Berlin
fire; above all, he needed to pour over her the stream of
tenderness that remained, dissatisfied, unexhausted, unused,
in his heart.

Grete soon developed scruples: it seemed to her that she
was betraying her friend by carrying on such an intimate
correspondence with her fiancé; she tried to break it off and
get her letters back. Perhaps she had fallen in love with
Kafka. Kafka wouldn't let her break it off: "You have already tried often enough to free yourself from the noose,
which however is not really a noose, but only . . . well, in
any case, I will try to hold tight to this noose with tooth and
nail, if you should try to untie it. But this is unthinkable.
And what about the letters? Obviously you can do as you
wish with those in the past (not those in the future!), but why
don't you want to leave them in my hands? Why introduce
even the slightest change?" He proposed that they go to
Berlin together for his official engagement to Felice; as they
sat facing each other in the same compartment she would tell
him something amusing, and he would nod and shake his
head, squeezing her hand tightly as a sign of acceptance.
When he and Felice would for the first time enter the house

they would share, she must be there to bless them, and even spend together with them the first period of their married life. Despite the vulgarity of the formula, Kafka was thinking of a sort of *mariage à trois*. His relationship with Felice remained unshakable and symbolic as before. A soldier at the frontier, grappling with Tartars and melancholy, was trying to enter the land of Canaan through her; no Grete would lead him there, but the fragrance of affection and gallantry, with which he had in the past surrounded Felice, had become exhausted and arid. His delicate soul needed it and had found it with that modest Viennese typist. Thus, at the feet of this great, austere matrimony that would consecrate him as a man of the community would be born this small, tender matrimony, nourished by the soul's superficial emotions.

Meanwhile, under that mild influence, his tragic and austere moralism seemed to thaw out a bit. Writing to Felice, with intense words he condemned Friedrich Hebbel, the men of "conscience," and rational control over one's actions. "No aspect of his character is nuanced, he does not tremble. . . . Whenever he speaks of something he's done, he can always begin with the words: 'If a tranquil conscience is the test of action . . .' How far I am from such men! If I wanted to make this test of consciousness even only once, I should have to spend all of life contemplating the oscillations of this conscience. So I prefer to detach myself. I don't want to hear about controls. . . ." He now rejected active analytical observation of oneself: the habit of continually checking one's existence, attributing one emotion to this motive, a second emotion to that motive, judging the circumstances that are at play at every moment. The self-analytical life—he observed—leads to an artificial existence, where every feeling aims at a goal and makes one forget all the rest; whereas true life is the life of him who surrenders himself, spontaneously, passively, without checking on himself, without judging, without acting. So he violently condemned all the psychological "constructions" that had passed through his mind during the spring and summer to the point of deafening his ears. All his debates about marriage and asceticism, with which he had made Felice and himself suffer, now seemed utter nonsense.

Having abolished the clamor of reason, he lived in silence and mental quiet. He wanted to marry Felice simply because he loved her, even if she felt for him nothing more than "a very tepid affection." He accepted her as she was, with what there was in her of the good and not so good, with her bourgeois common sense, aridity, pedantry, calculating spirit, inability to understand him. When Felice asked whether she would find in him "the support that she absolutely needed," with the purest impulse he answered: "If you ask me now, I can say only: I love you, F., to the exhaustion of all my strength, on this you can trust me completely. But for the rest, F., I do not know myself well enough. I suffer surprises and disappointments in an interminable series. These surprises and disappointments will continue, I believe, only for me; I shall employ all my energies so that only the good, the best surprises of my nature will reach you; this I can guarantee; I cannot, however, guarantee that I shall always succeed. . . . To your last question, whether it is possible for me to take you as though nothing had happened, I can only answer that it is not possible for me. But it is possible and even necessary for me to take you together with all that has happened and keep you to the point of madness." He dreamt he was going to visit her in Berlin. He arrived in Berlin and stopped at a pension where there were only Polish Jews. He searched for a street map of the city to find Felice's house. But he could not find one. One day, in the hands of one of the boarders he saw a book resembling a map; when he had it in his hand, he realized that it contained a list of Berlin schools, tax statistics or something of the sort. Then one morning he set out on foot toward her house, with a feeling of calm and happiness and the certainty of arriving there. The streets followed one

after the other; a white house displayed the sign THE SUMP-
TUOUS HALLS OF THE NORTH. He questioned an old, amiable
policeman with a red nose; he received useful advice about
trams, the subway, and was even directed to the railing
around a small grassy carpet in the distance, to which he
could hold on for greater safety. He asked: "It'll be half an
hour away, won't it?" In the dream the old man answered: "I
get there in six minutes." What joy! As he walked toward
Felice's house, someone—a friend, a shadow, he couldn't say
who it was—accompanied his every step.

Kafka never reached that house on the Immanuel Kirch-
strasse. For a few days he thought he had arrived there, and
set foot in it; and then he realized that the street map had
given him the wrong directions. On April 12 and 13, the
ceremony of the unofficial engagement took place in Berlin.
During the ceremony Kafka and Felice were never alone; he
wasn't even able to kiss her; he had the impression of
performing the comedy of a matrimony without the matrimony, to amuse the others. He suffered horribly because of
this—and yet he wrote that never in all his life had he done
"anything so good and absolutely necessary." The *Berliner
Tageblatt* published an announcement of the forthcoming
marriage. The announcement upset him: the invitation to the
reception gave him the impression it had said that on
Pentecost Sunday Franz Kafka would execute a descent on
the slide at the vaudeville theater—but their two names,
Franz and Felice, went well together. He could no longer
bear the separation: "When one kisses from afar, one falls
with one's well-intentioned kiss into darkness and the absurd
instead of touching the dear distant mouth."

He began to look for an apartment in Prague. On April 28
he saw one in the center of the city, one of those houses one
inhabits in anxiety-laden dreams: the stairs full of smells,
crying children, bedbugs waiting in their holes for the night.
"Here—the house seemed to say—one doesn't work, one
works elsewhere, here no sins are committed, they are

committed elsewhere, here one wants to live and just barely manages." On May 1 Felice came to Prague and took an apartment on the Langengasse: "three rooms, sun in the morning, in the center of town, gas, electric light, a room for the maid, a room for working, 1,300 kronen." He didn't like the apartment: it was hemmed in by buildings, the street was noisy, no greenery was visible from the window. And he liked the furniture bought in Berlin even less: heavy pieces, too solid, mausoleums, funerary monuments to a clerk's life—which oppressed his soul. "If during our visit in the rear of the furniture warehouse we had heard the toll of a funeral bell, nothing would have been more appropriate." That apartment was not made for him; it was just right for satiated people, for whom marriage was merely "the last big thick mouthful," whereas he had not founded any businesses, he did not need a definitive residence: he wanted only a less substantial house. He had labored so much, had worn himself out, exhausted himself and had not attained his ultimate dream. "Up to now," he wrote to Grete, "I've obtained everything I wanted, but not right away, never without being sidetracked, indeed for the most part on the way back, always with the last effort, and, so far as it is possible to judge, almost at the last instant. Not too late, but almost too late, it was always at the heart's last beat. And I have never completely attained what I wanted. . . ."

On May 30, at half past ten in the evening, he arrived in Berlin for the official engagement, accompanied by his father, instead of the tender, loving Grete. He was ill or imagined he was. "My baggage will consist of insomnia, heaviness in the stomach, twinges in the head, pains in my left foot." Then came the ceremony, at the Hotel Askanischer Hof: Felice wore a very beautiful sky-blue dress and gave him the engagement kiss—but he felt in prison, shackled like a criminal. "If with real chains they had put me in a corner with gendarmes beside me and had allowed the others to look at me just like that, it could not have been worse." His doubts multiplied as soon as he arrived in Prague: it seemed to him that his marriage was a lopsided edifice that would soon collapse, in its fall tearing out also its foundations. At night he slept barely two or three hours; and in the morning, as he lay exhausted on his bed, the strokes from the clóck tower punctually reminded him that time passes and that after the appalling night comes the appalling morning. He tried to cheer himself up by taking swimming lessons, doing calisthenics and drinking sour milk in a milk bar. In the evening he went to Chotek Park, like the old married couples who sat there at dusk, enjoying the carpet of grass, watching the sparrows and admiring the children's magnificent clamor; and he would write a letter to Grete. Writing to her soothed him, but then anguish attacked him again. It seemed to him that all the sufferings of his existence were only mirages, behind which there awaited him the true core of his truest misfortune, which he did not yet know directly, but only through its threats. Seeking comfort he opened the Bible and came upon these words: "Because in His hand is that which lies beneath the earth and His are also the summits of heaven." But they seemed to him words almost devoid of meaning.

On July 12 there was another meeting in Berlin, with Felice, her sister, Grete and Ernst Weiss. When Kafka reported the scene in his *Diaries*, he recorded only irrelevant details: Felice running her hands through her hair, cleaning her nose with her hand and yawning. That day, moved by jealousy or sorry for having advised the marriage, Grete played the role of accuser: from the letters Kafka had written to her she read certain passages underlined in red. Felice delivered the prosecution's charge. Kafka said nothing, or mumbled insignificant words. He had nothing to say. He had understood that all was lost and that the court judging him was only appearance. The true court was he, Franz Kafka; and he performed all of its roles—public prosecutor, chief judge, the court, the accused, the defense attorney who in fact reinforced the charge. The letter sent to Felice's parents seemed to him "an allocution from the scaffold." He returned to his hotel, visited her parents, in the evening sat under the linden trees, ate at a restaurant with Felice's sister, went to the swimming school on the banks of the Strahlau, traveled to Lübeck, Travemünde and Marienlyst, like an automaton repeating a lesson learned by heart. In his diary, he was silent about the thoughts that during those days crowded his mind. He recorded only the external gestures of life: "A man drinking wine observes me as I'm trying to cut a small unripe peach with my knife. I couldn't manage it. Ashamed under the man's eyes, I give up the peach and leaf ten times through the *Fliegende Blätter*. I'm waiting for him to decide to look somewhere else. Finally I gather courage and despite him bite into the juiceless, expensive peach." At Marienlyst he went back to eating meat; until then he was nauseated by it: in the morning in bed, after having slept badly with his mouth open, he felt his body "profaned and punished like some extraneous filth." Now that he had given up Felice, from whose laws he had defended himself by alimentary asceticism, he had also given up the prohibition of eating meat.

At the end of July, he returned to Prague, and took rooms in the Bilekgasse, later in the Nerudagasse, in his sister's empty house. In the beginning he regretted what hadn't happened: marriage, Felice's embrace, his silent entrance into the unattainable land of Canaan. Surrounding him there was perfect solitude: returning home he thought "no desired wife" opened the door to him. He had suffered deeply; and it seemed to him that sleep, memory, the ability to think, the strength to resist worries had been incurably weakened in him, almost as though he had lived for many years in prison. But soon he began to live without thinking about Felice, as though nothing had ever happened between them and he had never met the person who "had come closer to him than any other person." He lived under constant, tragic tension. When he thought about himself, it seemed to him he was the bedbug he had just squashed against the wall: he was the tortured bedbug and the contorted hand that had pressed and held the bedbug; he shifted his gaze back and forth between insect and hand, merging in himself the figures of tortured and torturer. What immense energies he wasted in these cruel exercises! But meanwhile, there he was, squashed, *upright* against the wall, maintained there with superhuman strength without dropping to the floor. He felt like an empty vase, still whole and already surrounded by its shards, or already a shard and still among the vases. It seemed to him that he had been wrong in everything. His ability to describe his own "dreaming inner life" had atrophied and would continue to atrophy for all the rest of his existence: the ability to live, think, love, travel, listen to music. And now, perhaps, also his literary gift—his Archimedean point—had disappeared. He was finished as a writer.

He lived absolutely alone, somewhat disturbed by the chatter of his neighbors, strange noises and rumbles over his head, and by whistles that every now and then broke the silence. He loved to walk in Chotek Park, looking at the leaves on the trees and listening, partly abstracted and partly amazed, to the twitter and warble of the birds. His was a crazy life, a bachelor's life. "I withdraw from men into my den not because I want to live a quiet life, but because I want to perish quietly." It seemed to him he was a stone, unable to think, observe, remember, talk, have experiences together with others; or a stake stuck into the ground, in a profoundly chopped-up field on a dark winter night; or a ghost that fluttered around his desk. He vacillated, flying without pause toward a mountain peak, and arrived up there, in the place of vertigo, fell and got up again, collapsed and again began to climb, suffering at every instant death's eternal torture. He was writing in the desert, in the provisory, without earth, without roots, suspended like the Kalda railway clerk in his wooden hut besieged by rats. If we are to believe this story, solitude cured him of past misfortunes; gave him strength and again pushed him out among men, to converse with them. But perhaps he was only driven by both misfortune and solitude. And it seemed to him that his life was like the Kalda railroad project: an ambitious project that someone, who knows who, had drawn up a long time before and which had remained only half finished, an abandoned and useless ruin.

Toward the middle of August, he began to write *The Trial*—under the sign of the "tremendous Strindberg," recalling his "rage, his pages won by fighting with his fists." He was thinking about the end of 1912, when he had burrowed into the work like a rat and had felt completely secure; and an impetuous novel, a great symbolic tale, an immense correspondence had sprung up from his imagination's élan. Now he was colder. But now too his empty, mad, bachelor's life disclosed a reason and a justification. He was no longer staring into darkness and an absolute void. He was no longer a ghost or a bat fluttering around the writing desk. After two years, he had again found the succor of writing; and he hoped that literature would impart reality, wholeness and freedom to his destiny. Tense, febrile but extremely lucid as he was, it seemed to him that in those months his "battle for self-preservation" was beginning. He was approaching the theme he bore locked in his body and mind and had not yet expressed with words. For almost six months he was unable to stop. He wrote until late at night, sometimes until the morning, as long as his strength—which already seemed to him enfeebled and corroded—permitted it. He spent seven, eight, ten hours tied to his desk. Often he wrote almost in a state of unconsciousness: "enraptured," "completely enraptured" by the continuous and desperate effort of writing which carried him away like a current of water. He had found his tone: a long, monotonous modulation, a stifled lament, a slow loss of blood, a fastidious chinoiserie, without ever permitting his voice to vibrate, or an image to disturb its marvelous uniformity. As he wrote, he descended ever deeper into the depths; he dug down and down—which for him was the only way to fly with firm, secure wings around the unattainable mountaintops. On November 1, he sensed certain "subtle obstacles" that he had to shatter in order to proceed; then he had the impression that he had reached the "final limit," where he would perhaps be halted for years, "perhaps then to begin a new story which will again end by remaining unfinished." In January 1915 he stopped definitively.

Some months before, at the end of June, he had entrusted to the *Diaries* a story two pages long. The protagonist was, like himself, a bachelor, who from morning to night paced about in a room, surveying the walls with his eyes, following down to its final ramifications the design of the wallpaper and its traces of old age. Why did he stare so? What was he staring at with such intensity? Did he perhaps want to produce a laceration, an opening in the ceiling? One evening, for the first time, seated on the windowsill, he looked at the room, pacified. At that instant, the ceiling began to move: from its borders, around which ran a light plaster molding, small pieces of plaster broke off and fell to the floor with sharp taps. Soon the cracks widened. The center of the ceiling began to emanate a radiant white, above the puny light bulb: farther to one side a bluish purple blended in, and the color or perhaps the light continually spread toward the border, which grew darker. Golden yellow colors crept into the purple. It wasn't only a color: it seemed that behind the ceiling objects hovered and tried to burst through it, and soon an arm stretched out, a silver sword rose and fell.

The bachelor knew he had not prepared this apparition: a nameless reality was descending into the room and soon would free him from the chains of everyday life. He leaped onto the table, ripped out the light bulb and flung it on the floor, pushed the table against the wall. At that moment, the ceiling opened up. From a great height, into the semidarkness, an angel dressed in a bluish-purple robe girt by thick gold cords slowly descended on large white wings that had a silken sheen, brandishing the sword horizontally in his hand. "So then, an angel," he thought. "He has been flying toward me all day long and I, skeptic that I am, did not know it. Now he will speak to me." When he lowered his eyes, the ceiling had closed up again, and the angel hovering in midair was only a figurehead of painted wood from a ship's prow, whose sword hilt served as a chandelier, like those one sees on the ceilings of sailors' taverns. What an ironic transcendence, what a delusive apparition! No one had descended to earth to free him. Night had fallen. The light bulb was ripped out. The bachelor, not wanting to remain in the dark, climbed up on a chair, stuck a candle into the sword's hilt and lit it. Thus he spent the entire night "beneath the angel's tenuous light." What did it matter that the angel was only a ship's figurehead and the transcendence delusive? The candle stuck into the hilt cast the same gentle, tranquil light that the gods bring to men when they descend to free them.

Kafka did not imagine that *The Trial* would plunge into his room like the tavern's figurehead-angel. During the years of his youth, he had been indifferent to the gods, or their names concealed literary games. Suddenly, at the end of 1912, he was assailed by his Oedipus complex, whose import and implications he did not know. In *Amerika*, this complex assumed on three occasions the forms of temptation, sin and Adam's condemnation in the earthly paradise. But *Amerika* is still not a book inhabited by God. During the months from September 1912 to August 1914 the Oedipus complex settled in the depths of Kafka's mind and conscience; it expanded, became more complicated, accepted succor from all parts of the soul and culture, until it was transformed into the most grandiose and complex theological system in the modern world. He did not know that he carried it within himself, just as the bachelor did not know that someone was hiding in his room. Thus God descended into his life, suddenly, without warning, like the angel with the large white wings and the brandished sword. But was it truly God? Or only his counterfeit, his shadow, a wooden figurehead? Whatever he might think, Kafka lived for the rest of his life beneath the light of this fearful visitor.

With *The Trial*, Kafka turned his back on the grand novel, which he had superbly attempted in *Amerika*. A novel is a concentration of time, which unfolds and moves before our eyes, with now a slow, now a swift rhythm; in *The Trial* this temporal continuity and fluidity is absent. Each chapter is a fragment of time—two hours or a day—wrenched from the course of time, rigidified and paralyzed; and between these fragments there is no connection or relationship or mediation, but a crevasse that is often difficult to cross. The second hand of despair—as Günther Anders said—runs without pause and at a mad speed; but the clock is broken, and the hour hand does not move. The structure could not be more elementary. Whereas a novel is a symphonic intertwining of motifs, the plot of *The Trial* is a series of polar encounters between Joseph K. and the minor characters (the wife of the doorman, Miss Bürstner, the uncle, the lawyer Huld, Leni, the industrialist, Titorelli, Block), who usually appear only once and never meet each other. All narrative play is lacking, all modulation of plot, all *fondu*. In the central part, there is a total novelistic void, filled by Huld and Titorelli's great Platonic discussions, to which K. listens almost in silence.

What a distance from *Amerika*! Then Kafka had tried to take hold of the world and redeem it by imagination, and a thousand direct and delicate links tied him to Karl's destiny. Now, as he wrote alone in his deserted house, he had withdrawn at the same time from the world and from his own book; he had turned to stone, like Karl Rossmann in the course of his peregrinations. He wanted to have nothing to do with his own hero and caused an inhuman wall of ice to descend between himself and Joseph K. All the world's colors and lights have disappeared; everything is black or a gloomy gray; there no longer is any open air, and we stifle, like Joseph K. in the Court's attics.

CHAPTER SIX

The Trial

K afka's writing is a roll of the dice flung into the void, which simultaneously hazards opposing hypotheses, to exhaust the mind's possibilities. Written at the same time as *The Trial* and "The Nature Theater of Oklahoma," "In the Penal Colony" informs us that God is dead; that the machine for punishment and ecstasy, which formed the old religion, has gone to pieces; that God's last worshipper has died on his cross; and awaiting us are times of tepid illuminism. In *The Trial* the immense unknown God, whose name we never hear pronounced, has a life so intense and a power so boundless as perhaps he has never had throughout time. He invades all reality, also the reality that should be most alien to him; from the very first pages his messengers slink into the room where Joseph K. is sleeping and arrest him, as no human power would be able to do.

What is the name of this God? Or what are his names? Or perhaps it is not a matter of God but of a multiplicity of gods, each of whom possesses infinite names and endlessly generates other gods? At the beginning of Kafka's theology stands a great omission: no one says that the Law is the house of God, or that the Court is an emanation of God, even though the superscription IN FRONT OF THE DOOR persuades us that we are dealing only with him. This omission does not surprise us, because any consequential mysticism, Jewish or Christian, in the end leaps beyond the name of God. So then, can we attribute the Law and the Court to God? That is what will be done in the course of this book; even though, in so doing, we are committing a betrayal, because the lack of the name creates a void, an absence, a kind of death in God's body, which we replace with the fullness of a name.

The second sentence of *The Trial*'s theology informs us that God is transcendent: no one in ancient or modern times, not even the great Dionysian theologians, or the Islamic mystics, perhaps ever affirmed God's absolute transcendence with a faith so desperate and cutting as Kafka did during the last ten years of his life. There is nothing else we can say, because nothing can be said about this God without a name. On the basis of some sentences in *The Trial*, we confine ourselves to imagining that He forms a pyramid with infinite steps, of which not even "the initiates can have a complete vision." On the highest steps dwell the supreme judges: exceedingly distant, mysterious, invisible, similar to the lost center of the world, to the emperor of China dead in his palace, to the forgotten idea that inspired the Great Wall. We do not know what they are doing, and whether in other times, wise or mad demiurges, they created the world. Today their task is only that of guarding the Law: now majestic, now arbitrary, now cruel as the assassin's knife, now supremely meek and delicate as the rays sent us by the moon. Higher up, above all this, does there stand a hidden and absent God, a One, as *The Castle* and "The Great Wall of China" seem to suggest? Or does the pyramid move away endlessly into the sky? We can say only that, in some part of the universe, there is a *total gaze*, which takes in all of the Trial's complexity, and the multiplicity of that which has become incarnate. As for us, who live in *The Trial*, we cannot discern either God or the gods; we cannot take in their

mysterious totality; any relationship with them, even the
most remote and indirect, is impossible; and none of our
prayers or implorations reaches the summits of the heavens.
This transcendent God is light and can be nothing but
light. Even though we are at the end of the great Platonic-
Christian tradition, Kafka reaffirms twice, and with particular solemnity, that from the door of God's house erupts an
"inextinguishable radiance," a "blinding light." What does it
matter that we see it so rarely, and perhaps only when we are
obscured by the blindness and nearness of death, like the
countryman? Despite everything, the fact that the God
without name is light consoles us like an irrefutable truth.
But this light has a singular property. When it descends upon
our world, and especially upon the sacred places of this
world, it generates blankets of darkness, as though a cosmic
law compelled the luminous gods to let us know only the
night. So here are the cemeterial shadow that reigns in the
Court's attics, the candles in Huld's house, the feeble
glimmer on Titorelli's stairway, the most complete darkness
that will encompass the cathedral. This light has another
property. Striking the Court's roof, God's fiery sun makes
the air in the attics inhabited by the Law sultry, oppressive,
unbreathable. The divine places are places of cloistering, like
the "little room similar to bathrooms in the countryside,
darkened by smoke and with cobwebs in all the corners"
where Svidrigailov in *Crime and Punishment* imagined that
eternity dwelled. The Law contaminates life's air, destroys
the freedom and freshness of the universe, suffocates us and
prevents us from breathing freely. Someone might add
that only Joseph K. finds the atmosphere in the attic unbreathable; the clerks (and those tried a long time before)
lived in these tenebrous and mephitic places, these under-
grounds below the roof, as though it were their natural
atmosphere. For the elect, the vitiated air of the attics is the
pure celestial air.

For dozens of centuries we have been accustomed to

believing that God, or the gods, are the supreme Truth and
the supreme Justice. The God of *The Trial* will not let himself
be imprisoned in these too-human categories. He does not
love the word *truth:* or, more accurately, he stands above any
single truth, any affirmation tied to yes and no; truth, for
him, resides in the acceptance of opposites. God is at once
truthful and deceitful, close and distant, accessible and
inaccessible, open and closed, luminous and tenebrous; two
thoughts that exclude each other can be, for him, equally
necessary, because "necessity" is the category closest to the
sacred. So we are not surprised if, like Greek gods, or those
of Goethe's *Lehrjahre*, the gods of *The Trial* have a very strong
predilection for everything that is mendacity, falsehood,
deceit, theater. The guards of the court lie when they assure
Joseph K. that "he will know everything in due time"; the
Court lies when with some excuse it lures K. into the
cathedral; the priest deceives when he interprets the inscrip-
tion; the portraits of the functionaries are false; and from
what vulgar variety show have the Court's executioners
come, these theatrical automatons in their top hats? As for
justice, the Court is supremely just: its judgments are
infallible and no one can influence them, although a cruel
irony decrees that it is a corrupt informer who affirms this
truth. Like Titorelli or Huld, Kafka is convinced that it does
not and cannot make mistakes. If we are not told of any
acquittals, it is only because, unlike human courts, the
heavenly Court with miraculous intuition accuses only the
guilty. But it is a strange justice. Infallible, evenhanded,
haughtily detached from men, at times it appears to us like
the goddess of the Hunt or the goddess of Vengeance, so
much pure hatred is enclosed in its inflexible heart.

Like the Hebrew, Christian and Islamic Law, that of the
Court is a written Law, a Law of the book: some angel has
dictated it to a human hand, or made a seer or prophet
swallow it with its flavor of honey and gall, or has inscribed
it in a heart. We hear from the priest that somewhere there

exists a Law, always identical with itself, accompanied by Scriptures that introduce it and by the insatiable observations of commentators who always try to reinterpret it. This Law is secret: only a few initiates turn the pages of the great Book; and as for the Trial, everything the judges compile—charges, documents, final sentences—is inaccessible to the accused as well as the lawyers, and sometimes even to the judges. The wisdom of the heavens must remain hidden. If we wish to know more, we must turn to "In the Penal Colony." Here the simple words of the sentence, carved on our bodies, are surrounded by a decorative labyrinth of closely hatched lines, which cross each other continually and make them incomprehensible to unaccustomed eyes. The written Law is therefore a dreadful game that the divine powers are engaged in with us; this game has the purpose of hiding the truth from us and at the same time revealing it to us, because only the slow impression of the labyrinth on our bodies allows us to know the divine voice, attain the dolorous ecstasies of the sentence and perform the sacred rite. Joseph K. does not understand the enigma by which the heavens protect us: he demands arrest warrants, charges, documents, sentences, something written on paper. He does not understand that, beyond the divine enigma, there exist only useless and desacralized scrcedar the vacuous memories of lawyers and their senseless autobiographical attempts, which the encoded calligraphy of the heavens derides with its tenebrous and blinding light.

To reach the heart of the God of *The Trial*, we must repeat the paradox that has tormented almost every religious conscience. That God so transcendent, so remote and distant, similar to the coldest and most invisible star, to the emperor of China lost in his great palace, is at the same time immanent in the world, present in infinite reality, even in what should be most repugnant to him. This is revealed to us by that most assured of guides, the equivocal painter Titorelli, with his habitual irony. When Joseph K. is molested by some little girls, the painter bends over him and murmurs into his ear:

"Also these little girls are part of the Court." "What?" K. asks, pulling back his head and staring at the painter. The painter sits down again on his chair and says half in jest and half in explanation: "Everything is part of the Court." There can be no doubts: not only the invisible summit of *The Trial*, with its high secret judges, but everything that appears in these pages, even the most repugnant guards, even these corrupt and depraved thirteen-year-old girls, *is* the Court. All reality has become the Law: all of everyday life has become sacred; God has incarnated himself in all things and firmly dwells in them. This is how we can resolve the apparent contradiction that runs through the book. On the one hand, hidden in the high attics, the Court is secret, or, as one of the functionaries says, "is not very well known to the population." On the other hand, it has no need for privileged edifices, because it establishes itself in all houses, commands all persons and all men, even the bank, where another power should triumph; its emissaries are everywhere; and we soon become aware that all of the book's characters—the old people who look out the window, the landlady, the bank clerks, the small manufacturer, the passersby, the sacristan— know about the mysterious Court and are informed, we do not know how, of the strange trial brought against Joseph K. The Court is secret and manifest, concealed and apparent, invisible and most visible—as is God.

In *Amerika*, the space of Robinson, Delamarche and Brunelda, the equivocal and parasitic world of the "louche," stood outside the Law's walls, like a colorful meadow to which it paid no attention. Now, in *The Trial*, the "louche" has been accepted into the Law and has assumed a metaphysical value; these guards, these functionaries, these prostitutes, these painters, lawyers and executioners are signs of *something else*. While God's sphere is enlarged and dilated beyond measure, the sacred is degraded: it has pitched its tent in the infamous and base, as had already happened in Dostoevsky. For a baroque writer, this process of dilation would have been a triumph; what could arouse more enthusiasm than God's omnipresence, than a universe totally dominated by his Law? But for Kafka this process was a tragedy without equal. All reality had been assumed into the Law, while remaining exactly as it was, or even more debased than at the time of *Amerika;* and now it moved against him, dominated by its new, atrocious divine power.

The degraded sacred does have its privileged edifices, in whose attics it dwells. They are the same edifices where, half a century before, Dostoevsky's most famous hero had appeared. When Raskolnikov is summoned to the police station, on the fourth floor of a new building, he descends into the world's "underground." The stairs are narrow, steep and filthy, awash with dirty water and filled with empty shells; all the kitchens of all the apartments on all four floors give on the stairs, remaining open almost all day long and spreading their suffocating stench; and also in the tiny rooms of the police station there is a dreadful fug—the air is saturated with the smell of cheap varnish made from rancid linseed oil. It is here that Raskolnikov faints.

In writing *The Trial,* Kafka has paid passing homage to his great master: by identifying the police station offices of *Crime and Punishment* where Porfiry Petrovich rules, the clownish judge of the "underground," with the first location of the Court, as though to signify that he too had descended into God's "underground." The first Court building is tall, gray, inhabited by poor people; the entrance courtyard is full of locked vans. Three entrances lead to as many stairways; along the stairs that Joseph K. climbs, the doors to the apartments are open, and in the small kitchen–living rooms women hold nursing babies and work over the stoves, while half-naked girls run about busily. On the fifth floor, the Court's location, a young woman is washing children's clothes in a tub. In the squalid adjacent room the air is filled with vapors; dirty daylight turns the atmosphere whitish and dazzling. On the upper floor, where the attics are, there is a long hallway, divided by broken doors, almost without light, with long wooden benches on which the defendants sit, their backs curved, their knees bent, like beggars. Behind plain wooden gates are the offices, where the functionaries spend the night. The tenants' clothes are hung to dry; the air is damp and heavy and Joseph K. is on the point of fainting like Raskolnikov in the Petersburg office. The Court's second building, with which we become acquainted a few months later, is even more repulsive. The neighborhood is even poorer, the houses are even darker, the streets full of filth on the melting snow. Through a crack in the main door pours a disgusting liquid, yellow and steaming, which puts to flight a pack of rats; and from the workshop's door in the courtyard a large sheet of leaded tin casts a livid light on the faces of three shop boys. The stairs are narrow, without railings, enclosed between walls pierced by small windows; the doors to the apartments are of rough wood sloppily painted red; and the sultry, oppressive air once again torments the wayfarer in the celestial underground.

In these degraded places live the basest representatives of the Court. Corrupt and crude guards, parasitic and scurrilous, lying and depraved, festive like dogs; errand boys with an equivocal air, miserable ushers, badly dressed clerks, vain, louche and familiar judges, infamous painters, repugnant henchmen; and a procession of prostitute-custodians and prostitute-maids who offer to one and all their infantile and indecent charms, comfort and molest, both spies and accomplices of the accused. There is no world more depraved than the world that vegetates on the lowest steps of the Law. And yet, in a mysterious and paradoxical manner, these figures below the level of daily existence reveal to us something about the Law. The very same guards, whom Joseph K. despises, have a subtle theological knowledge of the mysteries of the divine world; and regarding guilt and the Law they say the same thing that the priest will reveal many months later. There is only one Court. The Law is identical up high and down below, in the supreme judges, in the angels with their colored wings, who perhaps perceive the ultimate mysteries of the God without name, and in these guards who steal their lunch, these judges who read pornographic books. "No man hath seen God" (John 1:18), and we cannot reach him directly, as *The Castle* will repeat, but through a boundless multitude of mediators and procuresses. Perhaps his intense, intolerable light has to be veiled by something dark; perhaps his majesty must be brought into relief by contrast with something repugnant; or what is sublime can express itself, on earth, through the basest. These are God's mysteries, before which Kafka bowed his head; but only a great mystic, such as Rūmī or 'Aṭṭār or St. Teresa, certainly not poor, modern Joseph K. with his puny bank-clerk's thoughts, can grasp them.

We do not know all the activities of the Court, of this kind of secret freemasonry, interwoven with the entire life of the universe, like the Society of the Tower in the *Lehrjahre*. If we must believe Kafka's book, today the Court has only one activity: that of staging trials. But they are peculiar trials. The Court does not accuse the defendant of having committed this or that misdeed, having broken this or that commandment of the Law, as do all human tribunals, or as happens also in "The Penal Colony," where the broken commandment is inscribed on the bodies of the sentenced persons. When K. is arrested, the guards do not bring any specific accusation against him; and not even later, when the trial is already well under way, nor even under the executioner's knife, will he know what his crime is. What are we supposed to assume? That the Court conceals his crime from him to the very end? Or that Joseph K.'s crime is original sin, which forever taints human souls? This does not seem possible, because only some men, in *The Trial*, are accused by the Court. Everything leads us to believe that K.'s sin (and that of the defendants in *The Trial*) is another. His is the crime without name and without motive, the ineluctable crime, neither distant nor close, that no one committed even at the earth's dawn, and which can weigh on many men, like a halo of darkness, like a stain they will never be able to wash from heart and hands. In a word, his is the atrocious feeling of guilt that tormented Franz Kafka throughout his life.

The Court therefore has no need whatever for inquisitors and policemen, as human courts do, which try to find out whether a certain forbidden act was or was not committed, whether Raskolnikov really robbed and killed the two old women. "Our authorities," as one of the guards puts it with great precision, ". . . do not look, so to speak, for people's crimes, but are attracted, as it is stated in the Law, by the guilt." The Court possesses a kind of superior sense which reveals to it the presence of sin: a magical olfactory sense which helps it discover who, among all men, is tainted by the crime without name, just as the Furies smelled from afar the scent of spilled maternal blood and pursued the murderers. Thus the woman guard, who never saw Joseph K. before, recognizes him immediately when he knocks at the Court's door, asking: "Does a certain carpenter Lanz live here?" and in the same way the sacristan and priest recognize him in the cathedral's dense darkness.

Between Law and guilt, between God and sin, judges and sinners, there is a close affinity, as Kafka already told us in "The Penal Colony." If the Court is attracted by guilt, the man who bears the gift of guilt in him is attracted by the Court: accusers and sinners cannot live without one another and magically communicate thoughts to one another. On the morning of the first hearing, no one informs K. of the hour of the session or the correct staircase in the large tenement, and yet K. arrives at the appointed hour and without uncertainty goes up the staircase to where the Court's attics are hidden. On the evening of his last day of life, nobody announces the visit of the two executioners, and yet he awaits the assassins' arrival and puts on his dark ceremonial suit. The other defendants are endowed with the same keen sense of smell as

K. He meets some of them in the Court's attics; never before
has he seen persons so tortured by the feeling of guilt:
neglected in their attire, their faces humiliated, their backs
bowed and knees bent, looking like beggars or dogs who lick
the hands of their torturers, seated on the benches placed
in the hallways, they futilely wait for acquittal or sentencing, the end that will never come, the conclusion of the
inexhaustible trial. When K. lays a hand on the arm of one of
them, he gives a heartrending cry as though he had gripped
him with a red-hot pincers: we will later find out that he read
or thought he read his sentence on K.'s lips. Among them we
meet neither women nor the poor, for neither of these know,
according to Kafka, an indeterminate sin but commit only
precise sins. The lawyer Huld informs us that all of them,
even the most repulsive, become beautiful with the passing of
time. As in "The Penal Colony," any procedure of the
court is an election; neither crime nor punishment, but only
the Trial, which degrades and demeans them, imparts a
strange beauty to their features.

The trial-process is unknowable, as are the Court's
highest hierarchies and the unknown God that presides over
them. The judges, hereditary and childish, capricious and
vindictive, without any sense of reality and human relationships, do not know it as a whole: each one of them knows the
smallest fragment of it, and for the rest does not know
"where it comes from" and "where it continues." As for the
lawyers, they are barely tolerated: the Court derides them
most cruelly; they cannot consult any of the documents or
testimonies or charges. So then what good are those memo-
randa, full of Latin, of unspecified appeals, self-praise, hu-
miliations, analyses? Only the total gaze, which descends
from the highest darkness of the superior gods, can grasp the
totality of the trial-process; and can let fly and strike the
precise judgment. In the expectation of that supreme moment, the trial proceeds down its slow, long road: especially
in modern times, when its step has become exceedingly slow

and enervating, perhaps because our guilt feeling is much
more tortuous and unseizable than that of our ancestors.
Everything breathes procrastination: an always unchanged
movement, neither ascending nor descending; whereas the
accused yearns for the debate, the Court, to make us suffer
more and at the same time obey its enervating and labyrinthine nature, aims at the indefinite prolongation of the pretrial investigation. Sometimes the trial-process comes to a halt.
The defendant receives a certificate of "apparent acquittal,"
but the accusation continues to hang over him intact, and a
judge can again issue an order for his arrest. So the pretrial
investigation resumes, with new canceled acquittals, new arrests, and new remands: it stagnates, slows down and is lost
like a trickle among the court's dusty papers. Until one day,
without advance notice or warning, the trial—the defendant,
the meticulously drawn-up briefs, the lower-court judges—
is taken away from the attorney and vanishes. Everything is
gone. Everything has been transferred to the competence of
inaccessible courts, of invisible gods, from whom comes
down—just as suddenly—the definitive sentence.

What this sentence proves to be is the only certain thing
about the interminable trial-process. Attorney Huld alludes
several times to trials with "a happy ending," but he does not
offer us any details; and for the rest his task is that of keeping
his clients in the abject condition of hope. Titorelli says he
does not know "any real acquittal"; the usher and uncle think
the same. Joseph K. is not mistaken in adding: "A single
executioner could replace the entire Court." As Kafka says in
"The Penal Colony," "guilt is always certain." The Court
does not have theological pretensions: it does not insist that
all men are guilty; it does not exclude, purely as a matter of
principle, that some may escape the enervating process; but
it possesses precise vision, an unerring flair for uncovering
sin, and all the persons that it accuses are proven to be guilty
of the crime without a name. The exceedingly slow trial
apparatus serves only to confirm the Court's first, lightning-

like intuition. Nobody is innocent, nobody is absolved—this is the dreadful postulate on which Kafka has constructed his book. Only a few legends, similar to the Catholic legends about the cult of saints, of which Titorelli speaks with veneration and scorn, continue to assure us that, yes, in the past, the distant past, perhaps the same past in which Anthony and Francis preached to the animals, someone had returned home enveloped in the radiant light of absolution.

When Kafka conceived Joseph K., to whom he gave his own age, part of his name and something of his room, he canceled every trace of himself; he ventured into a place much further from him than his master Flaubert was distant from Frédéric Moreau. He was bound by tender affection to Karl Rossmann; in *The Castle*, he admired K.'s very bold theological attempt; but what could he possibly care for in this average "modern man," this excellent bank clerk, who does not believe in heaven and has no trust in the invisible? As Kafka depicts him for us, Joseph K. is a lonely man, arid, sure, arrogant, presumptuous, certain of his own good faith and his innocence, orderly, aggressive, authoritarian, egotistical, incapable of understanding others, greedy for earthly success, at times a megalomaniac. He has all the faults of "modern man." Unlike Karl Rossmann, he has killed in himself every trace of childhood and does not allow the unconscious to nourish him; he refuses to look into his heart, learns nothing from his own experience, does not love and does not want to be loved, detests the irruption of chance; and he expects to impose the iron play of his will on reality. If Kafka selects him from among all the characters that perhaps crowded his mind, it was only because of a quality K. would prefer to ignore. Although he does not believe in sin, like all laymen he is ridden by a very strong feeling of guilt. This is the only stigma of his mediocre life. As though it wanted to redeem him, the trial-process makes this feeling of guilt grow, mature, become more complicated; it renders his intelligence more restless and subtle, to the point that it leads him to pronounce words that previously he would not have even dared to think.

One morning Joseph K. is arrested. The landlady's cook, who brings him breakfast around eight o'clock every day, does not come to his room. This had never happened before. When K. rings the bell, there appears an unknown man, thin and robust, in a strange black suit, while the other rooms of the boardinghouse are occupied by equally unknown guards. Like "The Metamorphosis," the novel begins with a break: the irruption of the unusual and unexpected violently shatters a life petrified by habit. This irruption occurs in the morning, during the most risky moment of the day, because the danger exists that, overnight, the world might change completely and we might wake up in a different bed surrounded by different furniture and walls, in a country or planet or galactic system that knows nothing about us and our habits. Till that day, K. had always been unaware that the trial-process is the essence of human life; and all of a sudden the reality of the trial-process is revealed to his eyes and spirit. But a second, no less peculiar thing takes place. Joseph K., the arrested man, is released, just as Raskolnikov is given his freedom by Porfiry Petrovich: the Court, which has its seats everywhere, has no need to lock Joseph up in prison. He remains free and a prisoner, without chains and a confined man—like all of us, who in the same way live in a prison without bars.

When the guards arrest him, Joseph K. questions the existence of the Court, the Law and God. "I do not know the Law," he says. In the anonymous modern city he is the only one (perhaps together with Miss Bürstner) who does not know that the Law inhabits all the attics and from there, unobserved, governs the world's destinies. He does not accept the arrest; he wants the guards to show him the documents; he despises the guards, who in their depravity still possess an august and luminous remnant of God's Law; and he is sure of his innocence, as no one should ever be. He would like to erase the irruption: by putting the furniture and night tables in their customary places, removing the cups, dishes and cutlery of his breakfast, abolishing every trace of the guards, he hopes to kill divine intervention in his life. When he goes to the first hearing, he is surprised to find himself in a place that rejects all forms, ritual and even decorum, not understanding that the Law of God derides all of earth's formal crystallizations. Confronted by those black ceremonial jackets, those long, rigid, sparse beards, those tiny, flitting black eyes, he parades his superiority and his spiritual nobility; he is aggressive, ironic, cutting, sarcastic, sure of himself, exhibitionistic, and he impersonates the role of the knight fighting against terrestrial injustices. As Kafka lets us understand, K. has not understood anything of what has happened to him. His gravest sin is lack of attention: he does not possess the delicate, molecular patience, the meek passivity that alone assists us in matters of the spirit. Within a few hours the obsessive circle of trial and sentence closes around him. Nobody, not even the old Mrs. Grubach, shakes his hand, as though he were infected by the plague. His fate seems to be sealed.

After his arrest, Joseph K. leads the same existence as before. He works at the bank, continues in his mediocre habits, mingles as before with the gray sounds and colors of the world. But it is impossible to be more clearly marked by prison bars than this man who continues to roam the streets freely. Like the lowest of convicts, he lives only within the trial's dimensions, incapable of erasing from his mind the thought of that morning, the unknown men in his room, the aggression in his house—whereas, if he knew how to forget, the guards, the judges and the Court's hierarchies would most likely go back into the void from which they came. Subjugated by his own repetitive obsession, he goes so far as to perform the scene in Miss Bürstner's room in his boardinghouse. The great shadow of guilt envelops him completely. When he walks along the street, he feels spied upon by real or imaginary eyes; when he is at home, he feels soiled by suspicion; and he goes to the Court without anyone's having summoned him. As the months pass over him, he loses all strength. Early in the morning he is already crushed. He sits in his office, his arms stretched out on the desk and his head bowed, like a defeated, bloodless man, like a somnambulist. He does not receive clients, does not answer when spoken to, is unable to think and remember—and all along, for hours on end he watches the snow which continues to fall silently outside the window. In his dreams or when awake, he stares fascinated and obsessed at the most insignificant details; he abandons himself to fantasizing and playing with the images of his mind; his person, his body, his name, everything that really concerns him is a burden; and he feels that he is the only man under accusation in the entire universe, while all the other men are his accusers. To stand at the window and contemplate things morbidly, to dream of escaping from life—repeating, at least in this, Kafka's destiny—seems to have become his only salvation.

Restless, doubtful, without faith in his attorney, Joseph K. decides to defend himself. Since the Court does not reveal the charge, he will simply have to interrogate himself, becoming his own cross-examiner, and write his own biography. Thus, desperately, he begins this interminable task, this infinite labor. Stealing time from office hours and sleep, asking for a period of leave from the bank, Joseph K. retells his own life, summons up its events with meticulous care, examines his behavior in each case, probes on all sides and in every place and every corner, trying to discover the fissure through which the sentence's sting might penetrate. If he wants to defend himself, he must give up living, leaving his job, forgetting habits and thoughts, the fugitive consolations of mornings, evenings and nights. The defense against his guilt thus becomes, as in Kafka's own case, a substitute for existence: an exhausting labor, performed by writing on behalf of the accusation and against the accusation. But will this autobiographical memoir not be a new mistake on K.'s part? Who can assure him that his questions are the same as the Court would have addressed to him? Who can believe that he is able to track down all the tiniest events of his life? Who can imagine that he is capable of penetrating the deepest depths of his unconscious, where the guilt nests? As Kafka thought, autobiography, this weapon of the rational I, does not in the least assure us of reaching the truth about ourselves. This truth is gained only by the self-destruction of the I, or through the impersonal metamorphosis of story or novel, in which the self is dissolved in a fabric of objective relationships.

Meanwhile, the trial, as interminable as the autobiography, continues. We know that the other defendants are interrogated several times a week. As for Joseph K., we know only of the first hearing, when he accuses the Court, and of another interrogation, about which we are told by his cousin in a letter to the father. Nothing else: either Kafka thought of describing some sessions in chapters he planned but didn't write; or he did not intend to describe the trial. The latter is the more likely hypothesis. After the omission of the name of God, this is the second great omission in the book. No direct account describes for us the interplay of questions and answers, the Court's accusations and K.'s defense, the slow ascent of the litigation toward ever more sublime courts and hierarchies, toward the absent space where the ultimate Judge lives. Kafka sets another void at the center of his book. Nothing can fill it: because Huld's and Titorelli's stories, these indirect Platonic discourses around the Law, which we must interpret as the philologist interprets a torn and fragmentary papyrus, do not offer us any certainty.

Within the immense and desolate space of the trial, Joseph K. encounters two figures, the lawyer Huld and the painter Titorelli, who offer him two contrasting possibilities of salvation, similar to the great allegorical figures of confession and renunciation. The attorney Huld lives in the darkness that God has cast over the world; the house in which he lives is dark, his nurse-waitress, Leni, illuminates with a candle the lightless entrance hall and the dark room where the lawyer lies, unshaven, in bed. But there, enclosed and buried in darkness, Huld tells Joseph K. that he will be able to save himself from the Court's sentence only if he will follow the path of faith, devotion, unlimited religious obedience and trust in "grace" (*Huld* means "grace" in German), which descends from above to save doubting and guilty men. His juridical talent, his Talmudic exquisiteness must not deceive us. For the accused who live together with him, he is much more than an attorney: for them he enacts the role of God the Father who gave his people the tablets from the Sinai. "Who is your lawyer?" he asks the merchant Block. "You are," says Block. "And besides me?" the lawyer insists. "No one but you," Block says, repeating the words of the Jewish people and of millions of men who from then on believed in God.

At Huld's feet sits the servant-nurse, Leni, who enacts the role of the sacred prostitute. Leni does not prostitute herself to all men in the slums of the great city: only those accused by the Court, with the strange beauty set afire in them by the criminal proceedings, only men marked by the sign of guilt awaken her erotic desire. Before letting herself be possessed by K., she shows him a membrane of flesh that joins the middle and ring fingers of her right hand. Leni therefore is the siren, the great temptress, and her dark, slightly protruding eyes, her pale cheeks, her temples and rounded forehead, her long white apron, her obscene and childish charms must forever bind the accused to the Law. She devotes to them that mixture of disgusting eroticism and sentimental affectation which distinguishes Kafka's women. She kisses them, soothes them, looks after them, consoles them, comforts them, humiliates them and renders them debased; and, if we are to believe her, she is even capable of sacrificing herself for them, just as the lawyer Huld immolates himself in the name of their redemption.

In the figures of Robinson and Delamarche, Kafka had depicted the colorful and picaresque debasement that occupies the heart of reality. In the character of the tradesman Block, accused by the Court, debasement becomes one of the paths that allow us to approach the sacred. With maniacal and inflexible dedication, Block consecrates time and spirit to the trial that has been hanging over him for five years. He leaves his home, lives locked up in the dark lumber room in Huld's house, physically and spiritually close to the Law. All day long he reads the sacred book the lawyer has ordered him to read: all day long the same page, while his finger glides along the lines—and his reading is prayer, dazed worship, supplication. He is always there, waiting to be called by his lawyer-god.

When Huld does call him—one never knows when, the lawyer is capricious, the bell might ring even at night—Block advances on tiptoe, his hands contracted at his back, leaving the door open behind him. As soon as he hears the lawyer's voice, he totters as though someone had struck him in the chest, halts, bends in two and raises his hands to protect himself, ready to flee. The lawyer speaks, and Block does not have the strength to look at him; he keeps his eyes fixed somewhere in a corner, so as not to look at Huld's hidden resplendence. He trembles, falls to his knees, invokes him as though he were God, crawls on all fours, stretches toward the bed where the lawyer lies, cautiously caresses the feather quilt and finally kisses his old hand three times. Then he subsides, waiting to hear his voice, with head bowed. He has reached the ultimate degree of servitude, humiliation and degradation: intelligence and sensitivity have grown dim in his mind. Like Robinson on Brunelda's balcony, like the man in the legend who prays to the fleas in the doorkeeper's fur—he has become a dog; and we would not be surprised if

he crawled under the bed and barked. The sacred demands
this mystical abjection from its devout. But degradation is
not enough: Huld and Leni demand still more. Like Circe,
Leni the siren offers her bed to Block, to Joseph K., to all the
accused, so that they will confess, repent, or at least pretend
to confess and repent. Only when the process of degradation
and confession is accomplished does the lawyer Huld
promise—but in vague, uncertain words, without a shadow
of the certainty craved by K.—that one day the Court will
put an end to the infinite proceedings and they will be able
to issue, tamed and bowed but absolved, into the light of
the sun.

If Huld lives in the heart of the night, Titorelli inhabits
hell. We have already become acquainted with the wretched
district of the city, the street door from which pours liquid,
steaming manure, the rats in flight, the workshop's livid
light, the narrow, almost lightless stairs, the wooden door
badly painted red, the corrupt little girls; and now we enter
the miserable little wooden room, covered with portraits and
landscapes, where the air is polluted and oppressive, close to
the Court's attics. In his nightshirt, barefoot, wearing a pair
of wide canvas trousers, Titorelli talks, chats at length with
K., voluble, futile, brazen, cynical and impudent. On the
one hand, he belongs to the Court's hierarchical nobility,
since he inherited from his father the position of painter and
the traditional standards for painting the judges, like a
painter of icons. But his portraits, his allegorical figures, his
monotonous landscapes of heaths are so crude that they show
us to what depth of degradation the sacred tradition has
fallen in the modern world. He has nothing of Huld's
lawyer-like and Talmudic majesty—he hasn't even read the
Law—and he has obscene relations with the corrupt girls on
the stairs, who at every instant pop into his room. Those who
know him treat him as a beggar, liar and adventurer. We,
who have taken from him the most precious information
about the Court, realize that he is one of the thousand

Ulysses-like tricksters* in the modern world. His closest kin is Goethe's Mephistopheles, from whom he derives his lucid, corrosive intelligence; like Mephistopheles, he never deceives us (even though he is a liar), dominated by that desperate spirit of truth that only tricksters know. In Kafka's world, heaven delights in choosing these ironic and depraved mediators between itself and earth.

The universe of the Court is very strange. Titorelli is employed by the Court as a religious painter and confidant; therefore he belongs to the sacred. And yet he resolutely turns his back on the divine world; he lives in the sacred as if it were no longer sacred. With ironic sobriety, he declares that he is not interested to know how it is formed and where the supreme Tribunal is located. For him, all of Huld's categories have no value: in his sphere, real absolution is impossible; one renounces salvation and the hope of salvation; repentance, confession, abjection or sacred prostitution are all unnecessary. Chatting with K. in the stifling little room, Titorelli informs him that he can hope for "apparent absolution" and "procrastination." In the case of the first, the accused receives a certificate that releases him from the charge; but the charge continues to hang over him, and then it moves, rises to the superior courts, returns to the lower courts, oscillates, halts, begins to move once more, until a judge again orders an immediate arrest; and, lo and behold, at that the possibility of apparent absolution reappears, and of a new arrest, and so on ad infinitum. On the contrary, procrastination consists in the fact that the trial continues to remain at a lower stage, revolving in the small circle to which it has been reduced. What the two proceedings have in common is to prevent both the defendant's sentencing and his real absolution. Thus all of existence becomes nothing but the trial and pretrial investigation, a succession of canceled acquittals, of postponed sentences. We live in

* English in original.—Trans.

eternal culpability as though it did not exist, resigned to the endless proceedings, renouncing salvation, without truth, without the absolute, without innocence, freedom or hope. The proposal advanced by Titorelli is modern life, as Kafka imagined it: this mediocre life, this monotony, this repetition, this remand, this desperate absence of light and levity; the life that Joseph K. always knew and loved before the fatal morning on which, "without his having done anything wrong," the guard penetrated into his room.

Joseph K. is changed. The sin without name, which has been awakened in him, and the tormenting abrasion the trial has imposed on his soul have lifted him above himself, opening his mind to spiritual intelligence and occasionally pervading his behavior with a tragic nobility. He understands that neither Huld nor Titorelli promises him acquittal; not even Huld can help him glimpse the light after he has crawled through the mud of debasement. So with desperate courage he rejects both roads. On the one hand, he defends the human dignity vilified by Block (although Kafka probably considered mystical abjection a goal of the spirit). On the other hand, K. wants to be freed forever from the taint of guilt: he cannot tolerate that more shadows should surround his soul; he cannot endure postponements, compromises, delays, half measures, procrastinations, appearances; and he would like to face the High Court. With all his desire, rediscovering in himself forgotten or never existent yearnings, he dreams of the light.

At a moment in the writing of *The Trial* that we cannot determine, Kafka thought of saving his transformed hero. We have a trace of this in two dream fragments, which have been analyzed with great subtlety by Walter Sokel. In the first, Joseph K.—heavy, dark—undergoes a total transformation. Titorelli embraces him and pulls him along with him. When they arrive at the building of the Law, they run up the stairs: at first up, then up and down, without any effort, light as a light boat on the water. And precisely at that point, as K.

looks at his feet, over his bent head the metamorphosis takes place. The light, which until that moment had entered from behind, changes direction and erupts, blindingly, from in front. K. raises his gaze and contemplates it. What a tremendous change! Until then K. believed that the Law was weight, opacity, darkness and persecution; now he understands that God is only an irradiation of light, an ecstasy of lightness, which has the gift of making also us supernaturally light.

In the second dream, Joseph K. is walking in a cemetery. It is a very beautiful day; all around him there is a strangely cheerful atmosphere, flags slap against each other with joyous violence, and he glides along a small path as though over a swift stream, with the floating typical of dreams. An open grave, in which a tombstone is wedged, attracts his attention. An artist begins to write with his pencil on the upper part of the stone; he writes sharply etched, beautiful letters, deeply engraved in perfect gold. "HERE LIES . . ." When he has written the two words, he looks back toward K.; he is unable to continue, as though there were some obstacle, and full of embarrassment he again turns toward him. All the earlier joy and vivacity have vanished. Joseph K. is desolate because of the sculptor's embarrassment: he begins to weep and sob for a long time, his hands covering his face. As soon as he calms down, the artist decides to continue writing, though with reluctance: the script is less beautiful, the gold is poor, the stroke pale and uncertain. A J is almost completed. Joseph K. finally understands the reason for his reluctance: that grave is being prepared for him. Then, using all his fingers, he digs up the earth, which offers almost no resistance; and, turned on his back by a slight current, he sinks into a big hole with craggy sides. While below he is received by the impenetrable profundity, up above his name darts over the stone, in powerful arabesques. At that moment he awakens, ecstatic. These marvelous pages remind us of the conclusion of "The Judgment" and "The Metamorphosis," but with more joyous and luminous accents. In his dream, Joseph K. understands that by now his life and his body are an obstacle; and without rancor and sorrow, without regret and emotion, he sacrifices himself, sinking into the prepared grave, so that his death will cause the triumphant harmony of the universe to burst forth. He dies happy, while the miracle of art darts in golden letters over his tombstone.

Just as he had thought of saving the "innocent" Karl Rossmann, so Kafka thought of also saving the "guilty" Joseph K. In the airy suspension of the dream, he granted his hero two supreme gifts: divine illumination, and the ecstatic reconciliation with his destiny and his death. *The Trial* too would be concluded with the miraculous gift of divine grace. Thus his great novels once more reveal that they are living fields of force, disposed to welcome every intellectual solution. We do not know for how long Joseph K. remained saved: a few hours, a few days, a few weeks. Then Kafka was again seized by his own destiny. He understood that in his world Joseph K. could not be saved. He must believe that God is darkness, violence, weight, oppression. He must succumb with reluctance, indignation, shame, in the night, without any artist assisting him with his darting gold letters: like a dog, while two sinister assassins twist the long butcher's knife in his heart.

Toward the end of the book, on a rainy day of late autumn, the Law—or at least a superior instance of the Law—reveals itself directly to Joseph K., without being concealed by the mediations of Huld and Titorelli. The prison chaplain encounters K. in the city's cathedral. But it would seem that the Law ignores all simplicity and clarity in its proceedings, that it cannot dispense with deluding and deceiving, moving in the most tortuous manner. Instead of being given an appointment by the priest, K. learns that an Italian client of his bank wishes to visit the cathedral and will wait for him at ten o'clock in the morning: he has the task of showing him the monuments, paintings and sculptures. At ten the Italian fails to show up; in the cathedral the sacristan and priest are waiting for him, two messengers of the Law. Already at this point the Law lets us know by which ambiguous means the definitive revelation, which should illuminate, will take place, and forever cast Joseph K. into the darkness.

When K. arrives, the narrow square of the cathedral is deserted. All the window curtains are drawn: no human spectator can witness the encounter between the Law and this innocent-guilty human creature. In the cathedral, also deserted, darkness gradually falls, and the anguishing event of the light which slowly grows weak, is extinguished, disappears from the earth, will form the background to the anguishing dialogue between Joseph K. and the priest. At first, on the main altar, a large triangle of candles glitters: a taper, large and thick, affixed to a pillar, instead of lighting up the paintings on the side altars, increases the darkness that envelops them. A lamp is set over a small pulpit. When the priest climbs onto the pulpit, the weather outside worsens— it is no longer a dark day, it is deep night; no stained-glass window can break through the darkness with its gleam—and the sacristan begins to douse one by one the candles on the main altar. The priest comes down from the pulpit, detaches the small lamp, and hands it to K. so that he will carry it for him. And so they walk side by side in the dark side nave, while the priest recounts the parable "Before the Law" and comments on it. Meanwhile the small lamp goes out; for an instant the silver statue of a saint gleams with its own silver reflection; and then on the church, on the soul of K., on the universe definitive darkness descends. In this gloom there takes place the sole revelation that light will encounter in *The Trial:* instead of illuminating, light becomes darkness, augments darkness, covers K. with darkness, prevents him from seeing the light, lets his soul be enveloped by the shadow of ignorance, guilt and anguish.

About halfway through this story of light and darkness I have just recounted, the priest climbs onto the pulpit. He checks the light of the lamp, turns up the wick a bit, then slowly faces the balustrade, looking around. What utter silence reigns in the cathedral! On tiptoe Joseph K. is about to move away, the stone floor resounds under his light steps, and the vaults send back a weak, uninterrupted echo. When he has almost left the space of the pews, he hears for the first time the priest's powerful, trained voice, which resounds through the cathedral ready to welcome it. The voice calls: "Joseph K.!" K. stops, staring at the ground. Then he turns; with a sign of his finger the priest calls him closer, and he runs with long, quick steps toward the pulpit. He halts at the first pews: but the priest, with his index finger almost at a right angle, points to a seat just below the pulpit. K. obeys him, even though he must bend his head backward to see him. He knows by now that he has exhausted all avenues: he has refused Huld's assistance, has rejected Titorelli's sly tricks; and the long labor of his autobiographical memoir wears him out and irremediably debilitates him. He no longer has any hope. He does not know that the priest represents, for him, the Law without mediations: the Law that approaches him; the only road to salvation and redemption for a man visited by sin. In the dark, empty and silent church, there takes place, infinitely tender, the encounter between the Law and a human creature. Even though he speaks to him from on high and does not wish to forget the distance of his office, the priest participates in K.'s anguish. Needy and desirous of help as he is, Joseph K. invites him to come down to his side: "Won't you come down? You don't have to preach to me. *Komm zu mir herunter.* Come down beside me." The priest descends, he holds his hand out to him and offers him the small, still luminous lamp. Later on he will repeat almost the same words. Just as K. has waited for the priest at the bottom of the steps, so the Law waits for K. if he will ascend to it: "The Court receives you when you come. *Es nimmt dich auf, wenn du kommst.*" The reciprocity seems perfect.

While they walk side by side, back and forth in the dark lateral nave, the priest tells Joseph K. the parable "Before the Law." The person commenting on the parable is a Catholic priest, the person listening to it is a man without faith; the matter of the parable is Hebrew, the "scriptures which introduce the Law" are like a Talmud preceding the Bible, the tone of their elaboration resembles that of the Hasidic legends; the custodian and doorkeeper of the Law, with his "fur coat, his big pointed nose, the long, sparse, black Tartar beard," seems an Oriental Jew—unless that "sparse . . . Tartar beard" alludes to an even more distant Orient, to the China conquered by the Mongols, where Catholics and Jews could merge before Kublai Khan's extremely white mantle. We are not surprised to see that the Law is spatialized: that the one Book becomes an edifice with a hundred halls, one inside the other, with hundreds of doors and hundreds of doorkeepers. The Torah as edifice is an image of the Hebrew Gnosis, which arose again in Kafka's mind with prodigious fidelity without his knowing anything about it.

Before the Law a doorkeeper stands on guard. One day a man from the country comes to this doorkeeper and begs him to let him enter into the Law. But the doorkeeper says that for the moment he cannot permit him to do this. The countryman looks at the open door of the Law, the door-keeper's face, and decides to wait until the moment when it will be granted to him to enter. For years he sits on a stool to one side of the door; he vexes the doorkeeper with his prayers, makes small talk, vainly tries to corrupt him, grows old and little by little becomes acquainted even with the fleas on the doorkeeper's fur collar. At last his eyesight fails, and he no longer knows whether it is really getting dark around him or his eyes are deceiving him. But at that moment, in the darkness he perceives a splendor, which streams inextinguishably from the door of the Law. He is about to die. He beckons to the doorkeeper because he cannot lift his stiffening body. The doorkeeper bends over him: "What do you want to know now?" he asks. "You are insatiable." "Everyone strives toward the Law," the man says. "How is it that in all these years no one but me has asked to enter?" The doorkeeper realizes that the man is nearing the end, and in order to penetrate his growing deafness, he shouts at him: "No one else could enter here, because this door was meant for you alone. Now I'm going to shut it."

How should we interpret this parable? What was the countryman's fate? What is this dazzling light? Was he deceived by the doorkeeper? Or is he guilty of not having entered the edifice? These questions, which we also address to the text, are the same that, on that morning, in the dark cathedral, preoccupied Joseph K. and the priest, and since then have disturbed all of Kafka's readers. The answer is paradoxical, like all of Kafka's answers to questions about God. On the one hand, Joseph K. is right. God "wants nothing" from man: he does not desire our love, or our good deeds, or our desperate search for identity with him. Distant, cold, unattainable like the most separate star, he waits for us: waits for us to come to him; and if we find the way and avoid all the deceits and perils along the road, he welcomes us into the edifice of a thousand halls that he inhabits. The door of the Law is open; the Law is accessible to all, as the countryman thinks; the countryman had reached the door that was meant for him, he was expected; and therefore the doorkeeper deceived him by forbidding him to enter. But on the other hand, the countryman did not have enough faith: he should have entered without asking, passed through the door, open before him, without any uncertainty; if he did not enter, it is only because his question did not have enough strength to call up the answer. Therefore he is guilty; the doorkeeper did not deceive him. But there is more. If he did not enter, it is because he respected the word of God's messengers and guards, the innumerable hierarchy of God's mediators, whom he must venerate. Therefore he is innocent. And so we could continue on, like the old Talmudists, interrogating and perforating the text from all sides, and we would always be led to face the same paradoxical reply. God waits for us, in his high Castle, but he does everything possible, through his very messengers, to make sure that we shall not reach him. God is near but far, accessible but inaccessible. The door to the kingdom is open to all men, and therefore, in Kafka's world, the most ecstatic hope of entering the kingdom is born. But no one goes through that door because of God's deceptions, and so hope is never fulfilled. God is the one who answers our words, but his answer is always mute.

Even though by a negative path, the parable describes what was for Kafka the supreme mystical way: the man who enters the Law, steps over a thousand thresholds, passes through a thousand halls, and when he reaches the heart of the Law he is dazzled by the splendor of the divine light. Kafka knows that this is the culmination of every universe, of his universe, but he also knows that it does not behoove him to represent the light's full irradiation and beatitude. The only mystical path that he can lay claim to is that of the countryman. He sits on his stool before the door, outside the door: he spends all of his life in expectation and exclusion, as Kafka thought of spending his life, waiting for an unattainable Felice. Little by little he becomes a dog: he uninterruptedly watches the doorkeeper, who is only the lowest of doorkeepers, comes to know the fleas on his fur coat, rots before the threshold, grows old and becomes so humiliated and abject as to beg the fleas to help him persuade the doorkeeper. Who would ever be able to distinguish him from the beggars, who in Kafka's books live in the mire and gutter? He resembles Block, although, unlike him, who will never come before the Law, he remains seated there, in front of the door. In this place, he has the sole vision that is granted him: he sees the splendor stream inextinguishably from the door of the Law, even though veiled by the shadow of his blindness, by the shadow of the darkness which has descended on the world, by the shadow of approaching death, by the shadow of the distance from the place where the light is born. I believe that Plato would have mocked the countryman and his miserable gift of light. But for Kafka he is the symbol of the highest metaphysical state that can be achieved: a state neither Joseph K. nor K. managed to approach.

The apologue that the priest tells Joseph K. overturns the meaning we had until now attributed to the difficulties of the defendant and all the world's defendants. The trial-process rotates upon itself, turns head over heels and appears in an unexpected light. We had believed that the Court accused Joseph K. of a sin without a name, against which he had tried in vain to defend himself. Instead, in the apologue, the Law hidden behind the door, the Law that the countryman seeks and that Kafka does not know he is seeking, reveals that it waits for all men, and above all for Joseph K. So in the trial-process, where until now we had seen only persecution and the arbitrary, we must discern a sort of invitation that Someone had addressed to him. The sin without name, the feeling of guilt of which Joseph K. and the other defendants are guilty, is in reality a divine election; this sin renders them "beautiful," while all other men, who do not live under this shadow, do not exist in God's eyes. God accused them and had them arrested by his disreputable emissaries, but this accusation was the sign of his search. All the investigations and the trial, the great machine on which the novel is constructed, were a sinister invention of the Court; the Law was playing a game with itself, for how is it possible to determine the meaning of guilt? The only relationship between the Court and the accused is their magical affinity, their hidden attraction. Joseph K. had not understood the

Law's invitation. In the base and trivial adventures of his Trial, he had not been able to recognize the beckoning of grace. If he had understood, if he had divined the path of his destiny, if he had opened the door prepared for him alone, it would have been flung wide to his entrance. But Joseph K. could not understand. No man can by himself travel the road that leads all the way to the Law, unless some sign comes to his aid; and K. had encountered only signs turned upside down, obscure messages, indecipherable invitations.

To us, who after so many years read these pages over which the world's mind has been racked, the priest's invitation seems clear. By relating the apologue, he is not proposing to Joseph K. that he confess and repent, as the lawyer Huld had asked; the path of confession, the key to *Crime and Punishment*, in which Raskolnikov climbs the narrow, malodorous stairs to confess to the murder, does not lead anywhere in Kafka's books. The priest proposes to K. that he enter the edifice of the Law, or that he wait near the door of the Law as does the stupefied, almost blind countryman, and as does the Law—distant, separate, hidden behind the door. The category of waiting is at the heart of Kafka's world: God's waiting, mankind's waiting. But the priest disguises his invitation. As he talks to a limited man, like K., he does not explain to him that the Law is paradoxical. He tells him the story of a deception: the doorkeeper's deception at the expense of the countryman. And in talking he deceives Joseph K. a second time, because his interpretation dwells exclusively on the doorkeeper's figure and does not touch on the essential points, those which closely concern K.—the countryman's search, his waiting, God's waiting. If K. had understood the parable, he would have been saved, redeemed by the light, or at least he would have waited for long years, sunk deep in sacred debasement, beside the door. But not even this time does K. understand, nor can he understand. Perhaps, being so active and aggressive, he is incapable of waiting. But even had he been capable of waiting, how could

he have understood that, up there, on the unattainable
summits of the Court, a door was open for him and that
someone awaited him? He understands only the most obvious
thing: the doorkeeper's deception. All the rest remains
obscure for him. Thus the new exclusion and the new
sentence take place.

Between the scene in the cathedral and the last chapter of
The Trial there falls an immense blank space, more vertiginous than the one that precedes the last chapter of *The
Sentimental Education*. We do not know what Joseph K. does
during the months that separate late fall and late spring: what
attempts he makes, what hopes still accompany him, and
whether some echo of the parable in the cathedral penetrates
his limited mind. We meet him again in late spring, on the
evening before his thirty-first birthday. As the Court demands, he has put on a black ceremonial suit, and seated on
a chair near the door he slowly pulls on new gloves that are
tight around his fingers. He is waiting for his executioners;
no one has announced their visit, but he has sensed it because
of the magical affinity that links guilt and accusation, victims
and judges. Around nine o'clock, two men in frock coats
come to his house, wearing apparently irremovable top hats,
with smooth, pale, fat faces and heavy double chins, from
which they seem to have just removed the greasepaint. They
do not say a word. They are like automatons with plastic,
lifeless limbs: perhaps two old, tenth-rate vaudeville actors,
or two old tenors. Like the Society of the Tower in the
Lehrjahre, the Court expresses itself through the appearances
of the theater; it seems to parody itself: the execution has
nothing sacred about it, such as those of many centuries
ago—but rather it is impious, empty, sinister, devoid of all
majesty and decorum. At that moment, Joseph K. admits
to himself that he expected a different visit. Whom did
he expect? A less undignified and theatrical death? Perhaps
the priest, who had taught him how to move through the
darkness?

He goes to the window—and looks once more into the dark street. Also the windows across the street—from which on the first day had appeared the avid spectators of his torture—are almost all dark; many have their curtains drawn. But from one window, still lit up, appears for the last time the moving spectacle of life, which will continue to renew itself after Joseph K.'s death: some babies, still unable to move about, play behind a grate and stretch out their little hands to each other. K. and the two executioners go down the stairs, reach the street, cross a deserted square and arrive at the bridge. K. stops for an instant, turning toward the parapet: the river's water, refulgent and tremulous under the moonlight, divides around a small island, on which cluster, almost crushed together, masses of trees and bushes. Then they continue walking, pass through small climbing alleyways, leave the town, until they reach a small stone quarry, abandoned and overgrown, near a house that still has a townlike aspect. "Everywhere there was the brightness of the moon, with its naturalness and quiet, with which no other light is endowed." How heartrending these words are! For the first time in the entire book, nature awakens from its absence and bestows on Joseph K. the quiet and tenderness he will never be able to possess. The mild splendor of the moon, which illuminates the murder, is a grace, like the splendor that illuminates the end of the countryman's life: the exceedingly sweet, dreadful grace that the Law grants only to the condemned.

After an exchange of courtesies, one of the men approaches K. and removes his jacket, vest and shirt. K. shivers. Near the quarry's wall rises a boulder. The men make K. stand upright, prop him against the boulder and place his head on the rock. Then one of the men opens his frock coat and from a sheath attached to the belt over his vest draws out a long, thin, double-edged butcher's knife, holds it up and examines its edge in the light. Once more the grotesque, disgusting courtesies, one man passes the knife to

the other man over the stretched-out body, and the other
man returns it to him across K.'s body. Joseph K. looks
around. His glance falls on the top story of the house beside
the quarry. The shutters of a window are flung open with a
flaring light, and a figure, faint and frail because of the
height, impetuously leans far out, holds its arms out even
farther. "Who was it? A friend? A good soul? Someone who
sympathized? Someone who wanted to help? Was it one
person only? Were there all of them? Was there still some
help? Were there objections that had been forgotten? . . .
Where was the judge he had never seen? Where was the High
Court, which he had never reached?"

These last questions are K.'s last hopes before death:
hopes that death renders vain. And yet this cry goes beyond
death, and not even the slaughter extinguishes it. Once more,
the Court reminds us that the Law waits for men and, up
there, in the shape of a question and a figure faint and frail
because of the distance, holds out its arms to us. Kafka's
world is open to hope as no other, and the hope is realizable,
because if it were not, it would no longer be hope. We can
only establish a simple fact: for all we know, the hope is
never fulfilled, the priest deceives K., and the executioners
kill him. "Outside of this world that we know is there still
hope?" Max Brod asked his friend. Kafka smiled: "Oh,
certainly, much hope, infinite hope, but not for us." Kafka's
smiling answer confirms the conclusion of *The Trial*. If
Kafka's world were without hope, it would be easier and
more bearable to live in it. But the fact that hope, despite
everything, is not dead, that it always blossoms anew, that it
flies high in the mild lunar sky, always to be again disappointed by pitiless hands—this is what makes Kafka's world
so desperate, tragic and unbearable.

Kafka knew the happiness of punishment. In a dream,
which he recorded in his *Diaries*, he was punished and
derived from this a "boundless happiness." "The happiness
consisted in the fact that punishment came and I welcomed it

so freely, convinced and happy—a sight that must have moved the gods: I also felt this deep emotion of the gods almost to the point of tears." In "The Penal Colony" he had described the ecstasy of punishment. The great machine incised the violated commandment on breast and back; during the first six hours the condemned man was nothing but pain; but starting with the sixth hour, he became quiet, deciphered the Law's writing through his wounds, his intelligence opened up, he compressed his lips as though listening; and the Law's light, incised on his body, was diffused like light from his transfigured countenance. In that sentence there took place the *unio mystica* between man and his God. Here, in the last pages of *The Trial*, the sentence does not generate any light or transfiguration: Joseph K. does not know the happiness of punishment, does not welcome it "freely, convinced and happy"; nor do we sense, above him, the deep emotion of the gods at his punishment and his joy.

Around K.'s throat are placed the hands of one of the assassins, while the other plunges the knife into his heart and twists it twice. Through eyes that are losing their light, Joseph K. sees the men close to his face, cheek against cheek, observing his death. No death can be more scandalous and undignified; nothing can redeem it: it is death to its darkest depth, with all the shamefulness of the word—shame for the crime committed by the Court, shame for the turpitude of the act, shame for K.'s guilt that survives the sentence. Never did the horror of the sacred strike with greater fearsomeness than in these lines.

CHAPTER SEVEN

A Sino-Greek Intermezzo

Like the Court's topmost hierarchies, the directorate of the Great Wall of China is located in an unattainable place. Despite all the anonymous Narrator's questions, nobody has ever found out where the directorate's office was, and who occupied it. Here, too, the center of the world is unknown. But in this unknown place, the world's supreme wisdom is gathered. Although the Great Wall's directorate is not, probably, divine, through the open window "the reflection of divine worlds" enters and illuminates the hands of the directors who are drawing up the plans. What is striking in the directorate's activity is its total scope. Up there is the harmonious seat of the All. Under the light from the broad windows illuminated by God arrive all of man's desires, fantasies and thoughts, all his accomplishments and goals, and the architectonic experiences of all known times and peoples.

The extraordinary thing is that this divine directorate, inspired by the breath of totality, has built only fragmentary walls. The Great Wall is not a single construction that begins in the northern steppes where the Mongols threaten, and, after crossing plains, mountains and deserts, ends at the foot of the Tibetan mountains. It is a series of partial constructions: walls five hundred meters long, each built by a group of twenty workers, and not connected to each other. Between one wall and the next, according to history or legend, great gaps intervene. But of what use can so fragmented a wall be? How can a wall so broken up protect? The barbarians can slip through between one section and the next, advance into the plain and demolish the walls built in the desert regions. In any event, no one has ever seen the barbarians. The Chinese read about them in old books, and the cruelties the barbarians committed make them sigh as they sit on their peaceful verandas. In the artists' realistic paintings they see those faces of the damned, those gaping mouths, those jaws armed with huge pointed teeth, those slitted eyes that already seem to be spying out the prey that their jaws will tear up and devour. Seeing these paintings, the children weep with fright. But that is all the Chinese know about the barbarians. "We have never seen them, and if we remain in our village we shall never see them, even if on their wild horses they hurled themselves directly at us, as they hunt— the country is too vast and would not let them get close to us, they would lose their way in the empty air." In fact, nobody ever thought to build the Great Wall against the barbarians. The directorate has always existed, as ancient as China's gods; and the architectonic project too goes back to the most remote past. The Great Wall is a philosophical idea, an ideal form, an architecture of the mind, which the celestial hierarchy invented to hold together the immense and multiform Chinese people.

China's paradox resides precisely in this. The total directorate wants to construct a partial wall, limited and full of gaps, because the totality of the celestial mind is best mirrored on earth in fragmentary constructions. The All is rigid, whereas the fragmentary is flexible, slow, disposed to adapt to reality's suggestions, to the solicitations of chance, to the differences offered by China's territory and population.

The fragmentary is like water, the emblem of the Tao. The directorate does not want to employ workers in a titanic undertaking, in which they would be overwhelmed by despair. It knows very well that the human creature (who has a basis in levity and resembles the dust that rises in the air) does not tolerate chains. When he is tied to an absorbing task, a superhuman undertaking, a single chain, after a short while he begins to rebel, feverishly rattle his shackles, tear apart and throw to the winds the wall, the chains and himself. Many, at that period, spoke of the Tower of Babel: some thought that for the first time in the history of humanity the Great Wall would provide secure foundations for a new Tower of Babel. At this point, our anonymous Narrator seems unable to understand. But the directorate's thought (Kafka's thought) seems clear to me. The Great Wall is the anti–Tower of Babel. The first is the daughter of patience, prudence and acceptance of human limitations; the second is the daughter of hubris, which intends to defy human limits and the God in heaven. The first is a horizontal construction; the second a vertical construction. The first is a fragmentary construction; the second, like the Court in *The Trial*, aims at reproducing the circularity and frightful tension of the All.

So, protected by the Wall, which does not defend it from barbarians but from itself, China lives its harmonious existence in the thousands of small communities that populate it: a China that, with a ductile hand, Kafka brings to life in the delicacy and tenuousness of its colors. We are in a village of the South. On a summer's evening (China's time is sunset), a father holds his son by the hand on the river's bank, while his other hand runs along his long, very thin pipe as though it were a flute. He thrusts out his broad, sparse, rigid beard, enjoys the smoke from his pipe while gazing on high beyond the river; his pigtail drops down, rustling faintly against the gold-embroidered silk of his festive gown. A boat stops near the bank; the boatman whispers something into the father's ear. The old man falls silent, looks at his son thoughtfully, empties his pipe, slips it into his belt, caresses his son's cheek and presses his head against his chest. When they return home, the rice is steaming on the table, some guests have arrived, the mother pours wine into the glasses; the father repeats the news just learned from the boatman: in the North the emperor has begun the construction of the Great Wall.

A section of the Great Wall is completed. During the enthusiasm of festivities, the chiefs are sent far away; and during their journey they see rising here and there sections of the completed walls, they pass before the quarters of the high chiefs and are presented with badges of honor, they hear the exultance of the masses of workers who come in streams from the villages, they see the felling of whole forests, which are destined to become scaffolds for the Wall, they see mountains being shattered, in sacred places they listen to the songs of the devout who pray for the completion of the construction. All this appeases their impatience. They return to their villages. Their tranquil lives at home give them new vigor, while the authority they enjoy, the humility with which they listen to the reports, the trust that the simple citizen places in the future completion of the Wall help to keep the soul's strings taut. Then the frenzy to resume work becomes invincible, and they bid farewell to their native places, like children animated by perpetual hope. They leave home early; half the village accompanies them for long stretches. Along all the streets, clusters of people, banners, flags: never before had they seen how great and rich and lovable China was. Every peasant is a brother for whom a protective wall is being built, and he is grateful throughout his life. Collective labor had until then been for Kafka a mechanical, anguished and lifeless operation, as in *Amerika*. Now, for the first time in his books, it becomes a sublime people's utopia: from the veins of the individual the circle of blood flows softly, with a perpetually repeated cycle, into the veins of illimitable

China; and this collective harmony of individuals takes place only because the Wall is not a total and rigid construction, but a patient, prudent, flexible inlay of fragments.

At the center of China stand the emperor-God and Peking: its living body. How immense the emperor is! He is a space, a city: dwellings without end; the inner rooms of the imperial palace, swarming with the realm's great personages; palaces upon palaces, stairways, courtyards, gate after gate, and at last "the imperial city, the center of the world, filled to overflowing with its dregs." Wherever a Chinese lives, even if he is a few miles from Peking, an incommensurable distance separates him from the center. Wherever he may live, he lives at the farthest periphery and from there he avidly listens to the reports and legends that come from the very distant capital. But he knows almost nothing. He does not know which emperor reigns, and he is even doubtful about the dynasty's name. As for the past, in his village emperors long since dead are worshipped: battles of ancient history are only now being fought, and the neighbor, his face glowing, brings the news: ancient imperial concubines, swollen with a frenzy for power, excited by lust, swamped in luxury, continue to commit their misdeeds; an empress of thousands of years before is just now drinking her husband's blood in long gulps. The people live outside Peking's and the emperor's time: they live past events as though they were present and the present as though it were the past.

The Chinese behave as though the emperor-God does not exist. They have no craving for the absolute. They never feel for their emperor-God that desire for identity, for mystical union, which torments the breasts of so many believers—and forces them to burn, fail, faint, in the terrible amorous encounter. If the emperor does not exist, neither does the idea and institution of the empire exist. The wise hierarchy knows that men must not be bound with chains that are too tight: the reins are slack, as the Tao teaches, so that the Chinese are not aware of being held back and will not begin shaking them wildly. The center is distant; the links between the diverse parts of the empire are labile and loose, the laws vague and never enforced. Some theologians of unity and totality, some heirs of *The Trial*, could maintain that this leads to chaos and so call for a compact Wall, unitarian, rigid, like the most rigid religion. But even though he is so uncertain, the anonymous Narrator of this story knows quite well that the Chinese people are held together precisely because the wall has gaps, the empire's construction is slack and free, Peking is distant, as though the emperor does not exist.

The emperor is dead: God is dead; perhaps forever. From his deathbed the emperor sends a message to his "most wretched subject, a minuscule shadow who has sought refuge from the imperial sun in the remotest reaches" of China. He bids the messenger kneel at his bedside and whispers the message to him; and so much does he care for the precision of his words that he has the messenger repeat them in his ear. With a nod of his head, he confirms. Never as here, in Kafka's work, does God, the God who is dying, show such delicate care for his subject: he sends a message not to the universality of his subjects, but just to him, a person, a particular individual among the hundreds of millions of individuals who populate China. The mysterious message never reaches the last periphery. "The multitude is so vast! Its houses are endless. If the fields were open and free, the messenger would fly, and instantly you would hear the splendid beat of his fists on your door. Instead he is not at all in a hurry; he is still trying to cross the chambers of the innermost palace; never will he be able to get beyond them; and were he to succeed, he would obtain nothing; he would have to struggle along the stairs; and even were he able to do this, he would obtain nothing; he would still have to traverse the courtyards; and after the courtyards, the second palace which encloses them; and again stairs and again courtyards; and another palace; and so on through the millennia; and if in the end he were to dash precipitously from the last gate—but never, never will this occur—before him will stand the imperial city, the center of the world, filled to overflowing with its dregs. Here no one can pass, much less with the message of a dead man. —You, however, seated at your window, dream about it when evening falls."

This last, very brief sentence contains an entire theology —the theology by which live all those who, after God's death, believe in God. The humble Chinese does not wait for the message surrounded by the complete darkness in which the priest in *The Trial* speaks to Joseph K., or the darkness in which the countryman perceives the inextinguishable stream- ing forth of the light. Sitting at his window, he waits for the messenger when the day comes to an end, interweaving light and darkness, glimmer and dusk. Like each of us, he is "without hope" (because God is irreparably dead) and "full of hope" (because God will never die). He knows the divine through the death of the divine; he lives as though the gods were not there, and yet he dreams about them; and he is forever immersed in their crepuscular light and their fra- grance. Thus, lost in his dream, he has an airy existence, free, natural, serene, mild, without the temptation of trag- edy. He no longer has the obsession of the sacred, as does the city dweller of *The Trial*; but he is surrounded by the aura and protection of the living and dead image of the sacred. Now that God is dead, he has resumed a tender and confidential relationship with the father, as is shown to us by the image of the two on the river's bank, the son's head tenderly resting against the father's breast—an image that in Kafka's work we encounter only here.

In "The Great Wall of China" God is an empty place, an absent and dying figure, an oasis of gentleness; and even though we do not know the message he sent to each of us, we cannot believe that he meant to seduce us with his fascinating words. Not all gods are like the remote emperor of China.

There are the potent and very beautiful figures of the unconscious: the Sirens, whom Kafka evoked some time later; the Sirens, who, after so many centuries, stretch out on the rocky meadow, turn, fling to the wind their frightful loose hair and spread their claws over the rocks. They sing as they did in Ulysses' time: no longer, as then, tales of the Trojan War, but mysterious and terrible words that the gods reveal to men. Their song penetrates everywhere, seduces minds and hearts; the chains with which the sailors tie themselves to the masts no longer serve, nor does the wax in their ears to which Ulysses has recourse. All those who listen to the sacred voice are lost: they cannot bear the revelation; and on the rocks lies a heap of bones and shriveled skin. But from Ulysses' time to ours, the Sirens have become even more powerful. Now their supreme temptation is silence. Whereas in "News of the Building of the Wall: A Fragment," a preliminary version of "The Great Wall of China," the gods disappeared and died, here they pretend they are dead. The death of the gods—the theme that fascinated Kafka during these years—is therefore only the most insidious of their ruses. In this silence there is an intolerable seduction. As soon as they fall silent, we commit the sin of hubris: we think we have reduced them to silence with our strength; overwhelming pride swells our heart; and what we thought was our victory is transformed into our definitive defeat—our blinding.

When Kafka's Ulysses reaches the sea of the Sirens, they are not singing; they think they can overcome him with silence, or they forget to sing at the sight of the beatitude that pours from his countenance. They no longer have the desire to seduce: they want only to clutch for as long as possible the splendor that shines from his great eyes. To protect himself from them, Kafka's Ulysses is even more cautious than Homer's: he has himself chained to the mast, fills his ears with wax, whereas in The Odyssey, as a great expert of temptations and mysteries, he had left his ears open to the Sirens' song. He delights and trusts in his inadequate and puerile means, while all other voyagers had discovered that they were useless. He does not hear the Sirens' silence. He thinks that they are singing and imagines that he alone, with his ears stopped with wax, is kept from hearing them. Fleetingly, he sees them stretch their necks, breathe deeply, notes their eyes filled with tears, their barely opened lips, and believes that all this accompanied the melodies which, unheard, are lost around him. The spectacle barely grazes his eyes, turned toward the distances of his return. If he saves himself and defeats the Sirens, it is because of his limited, resolute, decisive character. He is a simple man, a positivist, a man of action—the opposite of the polymorphous, intricate figure, most attentive to divine voices and spells, that he was in *The Odyssey*. He does not even imagine for a moment that the Sirens' songs could defeat his ridiculous defenses; and he is so insensitive to the gods' lethal silence as to mistake it for a song he does not hear. But he is not an impious man: he does not let himself be overwhelmed by the pride of having killed the gods. Thus, because of a curious combination of circumstances, Ulysses is the one man who survives the disappearance of the divine.

Though with many cautious qualifications, Kafka offers another version of the legend of the Sirens: the only one in which, evidently, he believes. Ulysses is not at all the limited, puerile hero whom, playfully, Kafka had supposed: he remained the man of *The Odyssey*, endowed at once with the most subtle religious wisdom and those human ruses which allow us to deceive the gods and coexist with them. When he sees the Sirens stretch their necks, breathe deeply with tear-filled eyes and just barely open their lips, he does not believe that they are singing or that the artifice of the wax prevents him from hearing. He understands that the Sirens are silent, that he is witnessing the silence and death of the gods. But contrary to the other men, he does not let himself be defeated by the seductiveness of this silence, believing he had defeated them with his own powers. Cunning as a fox, he pretends he believes they are still singing. This modern

Ulysses is Kafka, the man who has taught us to coexist with the death of the gods. When the last Chinese in the provinces does not receive the emperor's message, he understands that the ancient god is dead, and yet he goes on living, "without hope and full of hope," in the dream and memory of him. Ulysses understands that the death of the gods is the supreme test the gods impose on us in our epoch, the ultimate divine stratagem in the course of the long battle with men. If he wants to survive he can only meet trickery with trickery; and he pretends he is a limited, puerile man, who believes in the protection of the mast and the wax. Who could be more of a fox than he? But at the same time more devout and religious than he? Because in the desolate world that the death of the gods opens in the hearts of men, he continues to listen to their immortal voices—so terrible, so implacable and rich with seduction, as they had never been until now.

I confess to having a predilection for this Sino-Greek experience, this untragic space, nourished with the colors of the Tao and *The Odyssey*, that Kafka attempted in 1917, on the margins of the tragedy that the revelation of his tuberculosis was for him. It occupies a unique place in his work. Little more than two years before, he had completed *The Trial* and "In the Penal Colony." This had been the absolute experience of the center: like the countryman, he had tried to enter into God's luminous-tenebrous edifice, and had desperately sought for union with him. But this experience had ended in death and defeat: the ecstatic death of the condemned man in the old colony, the shameful death of the officer and of Joseph K. Now, during those years of quiet living and the loosening of his ties with Felice, during this time of small stories and small tests, Kafka had moved away from the center. Three years later, in a letter to Max Brod, he would express with marvelous precision the meaning of "The Great Wall of China" and "The Silence of the Sirens": "The Greeks . . . were particularly humble people. . . . They imagined the divine as far away from them as possible, that whole world of gods was simply a means of keeping the decisive element from the terrestrial body, to grant air to human breath. . . . In theory there exists an earthly possibility of perfect happiness, that of believing in what is decisively divine and of not aspiring to attain it. This possibility of being happy is as blasphemous as it is unattainable, but the Greeks were perhaps closer to it than many others."* In these two prose pieces Kafka had experienced at least as an intellectual hypothesis the "perfect happiness," which he later considered blasphemous. This was the one experience of distance from the center that he ever attempted. Faith in God in death and in the silence of God: the fragmentary, gap-filled wall, which envelops the earth; flexible, slow, mild, airy, patient, prudent life; the cautious bond with others; the tender love between father and son in the summer evening; the cunning of Ulysses with the Sirens . . . Kafka had never known so luminous an image of celestial and earthly life.

---

* The central or third sentence was already written in the third octavo notebook, on December 19, 1917.

CHAPTER EIGHT

The Zürau Aphorisms

During the night between August 12 and 13, 1917, Kafka had his first serious hemorrhage from the mouth. It was four o'clock in the morning: he woke up, wondering about the strange amount of saliva in his mouth; he spat it out; and when he decided to turn on the light, he saw the large stain of blood on his handkerchief. He thought this would continue all night long until he slowly lost all of his blood. How could he close up the source, since he hadn't opened it! Agitated, he rose from his bed, went to the window, looked out, paced the room, went over to the washstand, sat down on the bed—blood, more blood. At last it stopped, almost suddenly; and immediately, seeing that the definitive sentence had been pronounced and it was useless to discuss it, he fell asleep as he had never slept during the last three years. Sometime later, in writing to friends, he said the illness did not surprise him. He had foretold it in "A Country Doctor," when the doctor discovers in the boy's right side a wound as big as the palm of a hand: "pink in color, with diverse shades, dark at the bottom, lighter toward the edges, slightly granulated, with irregular clots of blood, open like the entrance to a mine."

He had no need to remind himself of the outward symptoms of his tuberculosis: the incessant insomnia, headaches, fevers, the fearful nervous tensions, which had distressed him during the five years of his engagement to Felice. By now he was accustomed to read all the events of his life as a symbolic tapestry, of which he was the involuntary center. On the stage of his existence there had been a struggle between the world—Felice was its representative—and his ego, or two parts of his ego—the good one, which wanted to marry Felice, and the wicked one, which did not want to marry her. The good ego, which belonged to Felice, had suffered defeat. And now, weak, tired, almost drained of blood, it leaned invisibly on her shoulder and, disheartened, watched the big wicked man who began to commit his vulgarities. Kafka insisted: "I shall never get well. Precisely because this is not tuberculosis, which laid in a deck chair can be cured, but a weapon, whose extreme necessity remains as long as I live. And it is impossible for both to remain alive." Or perhaps another struggle had taken place, which also had a symbolic relationship to Felice. After years of anxieties, his brain could no longer endure the preoccupations and pains imposed on it. He said: "I cannot go on, but if there is still someone who cares to preserve my life let him take some of my burden and it will be possible to stay alive for a little longer." At that his lungs, which hadn't much to lose, came forward, and after frightful negotiations they assumed the burden. If he had had a tolerable loss of blood, he would have been able to get married, and in his private universal history this victory would have had "something of the Napoleonic." But the stain was immense, like the frightful red flower that had opened in the boy's side in "A Country Doctor."

The play of symbols led ever higher, toward that Other, that tenebrous-luminous principle from which his life was suspended. As with many interventions of the Other, he sensed in this intervention something gentle (especially "in comparison to the average of recent years"), but also extremely simple and crude. Was that all? he thought. Was the celestial intervention nothing but a gush of blood, a pink stain on his handkerchief? The illness, which he had not sought out, took on in his eyes a strange protective and maternal quality. "Today I have for tuberculosis the feeling a child has for the folds of his mother's skirt to which he clings." He did not experience the illness as a test or a battle, which he had to endure like a stoic combatant. He was not made for tests: they did not fortify him, and his first instinct was to go to meet the blows and disappear under them. He wanted to get well; but he also wanted the contrary—to disappear once and for all, under the batterings sent him by God.

The symptoms of the illness did not preoccupy him much. He wrote to Brod that he "almost did not feel it." He had no fever, he did not cough much and was not in pain. He was short of breath—true enough—but if he lay down or sat he didn't notice it; and when he walked or did some sort of work, he easily put up with it: "I breathe twice as quickly, that's all, it's no great nuisance. I've come to the conclusion that tuberculosis, as I have it, is not a particular disease, an illness worthy of a special name, but only a greater intensity of the general germ of death, whose importance right now cannot be evaluated." He put on weight: a kilo in a week, two and a half kilos in three weeks. He made merciless jokes about the physicians' diagnoses. After the first examination, they had said that he was almost completely healthy; after the second, that he was even better; then there was a bit of bronchial catarrh on the left; later on, signs of tubercle bacilli on the right and left which, however, would disappear in Prague quickly and completely; and finally he could even expect, but only for a day, an undoubted improvement. He had the impression that the others had become exceedingly good to him: they all were immediately ready to make sacrifices, from the humblest to the highest. "But probably I am mistaken, they are like this only with someone for whom no human help can be of use. A special sense of smell reveals such a case to them."

It seemed to him that doctors and friends wanted to screen off with their backs the angel of death, who stood behind them, and then gradually they moved aside. But he was not afraid of the angel of death; and this was the sign that he was rapidly abandoning life and its allurements. With bitter irony he accepted death, which every day in his apparent health took a step forward. While the others saw a past, present and future, he no longer saw anything: it seemed to him he was something dark that ran precipitously in darkness, and at times he felt he had not even been born. "If I could save myself like a bat digging holes, I would dig a hole." Max Brod reproached him for being "happy in unhappiness." The reproach hit home. Almost with the same words he replied to Max and to Felice that to be "happy in unhappiness" (which also meant being "unhappy in happiness") was probably the condemnation marked on Cain's forehead. He who bears that mark on his forehead leaves life, shatters the world, no longer walks in step with the world; unable to reconstitute it alive, he is pursued and persecuted through its rubble. Did he too bear the mark of Cain on his forehead? To both Max and Felice he protested he did not. Despite his protestations he accused himself of not having recognized the happiness that had been entrusted to him, and of desperately enjoying his own misfortune.

All that was left to do was to leave Felice. On September 21, when she came to visit him in the country, Kafka had the impression that the tuberculosis was the final weapon he had invented to torture her. "I have committed the wrong for which she is being tortured, and besides I serve as the instrument of her torture." He pushed her away, with a gesture, and, as he said a few days later, played out his part: "The scene I saw . . . was too infernal for one not to have the wish to come to the aid of those present with a bit of music capable of distracting them." He saw Felice again at the end of December, in Prague. He accompanied her in tears to the railroad station; then he went to see Max Brod, at the office. His face was pale, hard and severe, but suddenly he began to weep, as he hadn't done since he was a child. He was sitting on a small chair next to Brod's desk, where debtors, pensioners and petitioners usually sat. With tears streaming down his face, he murmured: "Isn't it terrible that this must happen?" Brod had never seen him so bereft of support. During the following days he wrote in the *Diaries:* "F.'s departure. —Weeping. Everything difficult, wrong and yet right." Then: "Not fundamentally disappointed." Finally: "Of his own will he turned like a fist and eluded the world."

On September 12 he left for Zürau, in the Bohemian countryside, where his sister Ottla lived; and two years later he wrote that those eight months spent in a village where, under the tutelage of illness, he thought he had become detached from everything had been the best time of his life. He had a warm and airy room, before which spread the open countryside. "There cannot be, in any sense, anything better for breathing." The house was quiet—although sometimes noises tortured him even there: the sound of a piano, a worker beating wood and another beating metal. He felt free as he had never felt before: free from family, work, Felice, reality, literature and, in a certain sense, even from worries about his future, since his illness delineated the horizon line with precision. There were no tests he had to confront: he did not have to suffer comparisons; Ottla carried him "on her wings through the difficult world." He lived with her in a small, pleasant, everyday ménage; he surrendered to its rhythm gently, quietly, patiently, and with great goodwill. With her there never was the violent tension of a short circuit as with Felice and later Milena, but rather a tranquil, placid, sinuous current.

He kept away his friends, who would have asked questions he did not want to answer; and he did not want to break the evenness of his time with a trip into the inferno of

Prague. He did not enjoy seeing his father and mother. Confined in the countryside, far from the railroad, close to the indissoluble evening which descended without anyone or anything opposing it, it seemed to him that he was repeating the destiny of a member of his family: his uncle, the country doctor, with his subtle bachelor's or birdlike irony. He had changed his life's regime on an essential point: he no longer wrote at night, as when he had struggled with the nightmares of Gregor Samsa and the degraded gods. His time was wrapped in silence: he lived almost without talking, almost without listening to words. He lay down close to the window, reading or not reading. He lived very well among the animals; he fed the goats, which with their muzzles reminded him of the face of his attending physician, or Jewish physicians and lawyers, or some girl, she too Jewish. A homemade lounging chair had been put together for him out of an old wide upholstered armchair, with two stools in front of it; and it was carried to a large, semicircular hollow surrounded by a chain of hills. He lay there "like a king," without a shirt, where no one could see him. He listened to the voices of the world thin out and fall silent; he caught sight of a beam, a streak of sunlight, and he thought he could see happiness descend among the earth's hills; and he experienced a total sense of fullness. "Not a drop runs over, but there is no room for another."

However, this was not only a sojourn filled with light. One night, about the middle of November, he was again assailed by horror of the mute, insidious animal strength that he sensed in himself and in the world. Every so often, during that fall, he had heard a subdued gnawing, and once he had risen trembling from bed to see what it was. But on that night he witnessed the soundless and noisy rebellion of the frightening mouse population. At two o'clock he was awakened by a rustle near his bed, and from that moment on it did not stop until morning. "Up on the coal bin, down from the coal bin, a race from corner to corner of the room, circles traced, wood nibbled, faint whistles even during their rests, and all along the sense of stillness, of the secret working away of an oppressed, proletarian people, to whom the night belongs." He had tried to save himself through thought by placing the chief commotion near the stove, at the other end of the room—but the noise came from all corners, all sides, and from time to time the entire tribe leaped down in a compact mass from some piece of furniture. He was utterly distraught: he did not dare get up; he did not dare turn on the light; he simply tried to frighten them away with a few shouts. He was afraid of that relentless, crafty presence: he had the impression that they had pierced the walls in a hundred places and lay there in ambush, lords of the darkness. In the morning he could not get up because of nausea and depression; he stayed in bed until one o'clock, straining his ears to hear what those tireless beasts were preparing for the coming night. Then he took a cat into his room. But he was afraid of her too. He did not have the courage to get undressed in her presence, do his exercises and go to bed when she was there; he hated her to jump on his knees or dirty the floor.

In Zürau, in the thoughts that he disseminated in "octavo notebooks" and in letters, he boldly confronted his past. He had failed in everything. In the city as well as in the family, in his profession, society, friendship, his engagement and literature—he had not "acquitted himself well," as had not happened to anyone else around him. He had done nothing but ask questions: questions of all kinds; questions that were always more vexed, lofty and arduous, and he had never received an answer. Now he did not understand how he could have deluded himself that he had really asked questions. He did not have the air in which he could breathe; he had no ground—laws, habits, thought, religion, literature— on which to set his feet. All his books—and the fragments which could only make him blush—he had written in the language "of possessiveness and its relationships," not that of the spirit; and now all this seemed to him a pile of useless paper, thousands of ink-stained pages, to be thrown away with a single gesture, or to be entrusted to a merciful bonfire. All that was left of his life was an atrocious feeling of shame, almost as though he had died wretchedly, or had been killed like his Joseph K., with a shame that survived his death.

Now, there, almost alone, protected by his sister's wings, with a few books, he wanted to find an answer to all the questions that had tortured him, and had tortured men, ever since Adam had been driven from the earthly paradise. He had little time. He wanted to start from scratch, as though nothing had ever been written, as though time had never existed, and with one bound, like his daring acrobats, leap with joined feet straight into the eternal. No one protected his back, but he always forgot this and again sought protection, at no matter what cost. As he told Brod, he was trying to achieve clarity on the ultimate things, whereas the ideas of West European Jews were not clear about anything. He wanted to "lift the world into the pure, the true, the immutable." Separate truths no longer interested him—only metaphysics, theology: God, nothing but God. But what else had he done, during recent years? From the first glimmers of *Amerika*, to *The Trial*, to "The Great Wall of China," what had his work been if not an incessant search in which only the name of God was omitted? In reality, he had tried to reach God through the world: degraded reality, the lowest emissaries, the Wall's gap-filled construction. Now, for the first time, he would confront God face to face, with a pure effort of his thought.

The first lines he wrote in the third notebook allow us to believe that he, like Pascal, wanted to conduct an intellectual battle against his time and all times. "I cannot fight my personal battle." In this battle he was not alone: he did not make war on his own, as he had thought; he had allies, couriers, rear guards, snipers on his flanks, even though it is difficult to imagine who these allies were, seeing that Kierkegaard had also abandoned him. But on the other hand, he claimed the right to use the weapons of his adversaries. Wasn't his condition perhaps essentially ambiguous? Didn't he stand at all the crossroads, all the meeting places of thought? A child of the night, he found himself fighting for light; nourished only by gaps and empty spaces, he intended to build an edifice of solid brickwork; child of the negation of his time, he sought to construct a metaphysic of the One.

What a paradoxical task! On the one hand, his supreme obligation was that of constructing an All. He wanted to learn the letters that composed its invocation, invoke its dream, dream its existence, intuit its closeness, brush close to its design. And then, as he held the All in his hands, attack something or someone with a raised fist, "as one clutches a stone to throw, a knife to butcher": to immolate and be immolated, because that knife was also the sacrificial knife— and he must die at the foot of the All. But on the other hand, where was this All? He held only fragments: a myriad of thoughts, a quantity of aphorisms, disjointed, unharmonious sentences, splintered stones that would not have been able to form even the gap-filled barrier of his Chinese wall. He did not want to construct an All. He did not want to elaborate a theory—because he detested theories that do violence to the world, oppress it, deform it and end by destroying it. Even though his work was totally molded by thought, it escaped all existing forms of thought. "Only from within" can one preserve "oneself and the world in silence and truth." And where were those allies he had dreamt of, and together with whom he hoped to conduct a philosophical or metaphysical battle? He was truly alone. "You are the task. Nowhere is a disciple to be found." It was fortunate that the ground on which he stood could not be greater than the space covered by his feet. Digging right there, in that inexhaustible soil, utilizing its faults, its gaps, the absence of foundation, its chasms, he would construct the most fantastic of Chinese Walls.

The premise of the Zürau research is an undemonstrated and undemonstrable hypothesis: there exists a point of arrival, whatever its name might be, God or the One or Being, or "the indestructible," as Kafka calls it, in the manifest desire not to name it. Which is the road that leads to it? Which is the way to the point of arrival? The first answer distresses us deeply: There is no road, not even a high mountain path. The "true way goes over a rope," and to traverse it one must be an acrobat, a tightrope walker, one of those performers whom the young Kafka loved, and who reappear here as the only mediators on the road toward Being. But here a new difficulty arises: the rope is not stretched up high between two houses, over a square or lake. The rope is stretched at ground level; and probably one must walk on it without touching the ground with one's foot. Thus the old balancing aerialist who walked along the wire or across the void with his extended arms taking the place of a pole becomes a grotesque figure going into contortions on the ground, with none of his old prestige and nihilist glory. The rope no longer communicates between two points over the void. "It seems to be there more to trip you up than to be walked on."

This is the most favorable hypothesis. At times not even the ground-level rope exists, and there is "no way." What we call the way is nothing but our hesitation, or our uncertainty, our restlessness, as Joseph K. knew quite well. Or there is a road, but it goes down a craggy slope, just as steep ahead of us as it is behind us; and instead of going up we go down. Or the unmarked road goes through the desert, like the one that led to the Promised Land; it is not a long straight route through the desert but a labyrinthine road which goes back and forth, sideways and crisscross, and allows us to touch every single grain of sand with our foot. Confronted by the second case, Kafka gives us a bitterly ironic piece of advice:

You must not despair, precisely because the road climbs up and "its regressions can also be caused by the conformation of the terrain." But is it not precisely this that could lead us to despair? That the terrain that takes us toward the Single One should be so steep that we shall never be able to surmount it? That we shall never, at any price, reach the top?

Kafka asked himself whether he might be able to reach the point of arrival with the help of the art of questions and answers, and he tried to interrogate the mechanism of this art. And with what renewed anguish! In his hands the mechanism turned upside down, breaking down irreparably. While we imagine that the question has an open face, as have all those who ask, it has, for him, "an inaccessible face": the stone face of the sphinx, the enigma. While we believe that this question travels along attainable paths, it plunges, for him, down the most remote and absurd tracks. While we suppose the question (with its flowing question mark) is "in ambush, timorous, hopeful," for him it is the answer that interrogates, indeed slithers like a snake around the question: while we imagine a question to be in motion and the answer immobile and firm, for him the question is motionless and the answer is in eternal motion; while we can believe that the question may be "desperate," for him the answer is inexorably desperate. If the question moves and slithers, shy, hopeful, desperate, it is possible that the answer may satisfy it. But if it is the answer itself that slithers and despairs, who will ever be able to answer? Between question and answer there opened an impassable abyss, which no voice bridged.

The final paradox is that, despite these uncertainties, these obstacles, these arrests, these labyrinths and abysses, the true way truly exists, perfect and intangible, and we cannot "subtract from nor add anything to it." It is up there, and it awaits us, and we can follow it. Or perhaps "follow it" is not the right description. We are carried to it, moved to it, swept to it in flight. As the maxim says, "he who seeks does not find, but he who does not seek will be found." Someone finds us. So we must overturn everything we have said until now: the way that passes along the rope stretched at ground level, the road without a road, the steep upward road, the labyrinthine road through the desert indubitably lead us to our point of arrival.

Up there, at the point of arrival, in the Place toward which all our life and our way tend, what do we find? This is one of the questions most discussed by Kafka's interpreters and at first sight it seems insoluble. But Kafka is not Kant, nor is he Nietzsche. His intellectual battle, his edification of an All composed only of fragments, his task which concerns everyone but in fact him alone, does not conclude with the construction of a systematic theory. With despair and hope, with violence and gentleness, Kafka hazards, speculates, attempts intellectual hypotheses in all directions, continually thinks one thing and its opposite. Like an old rabbi, he incessantly glosses the first chapters of Genesis, and probes and turns their meaning this way and that. From the mass of thoughts gathered in the octavo notebooks, a small part of which ended up flowing into his aphorisms, we may derive at least two great images of the life of the spirit. In the first (if such cultural labels have any sense) Kafka is a monist with a resolution and completeness rare in the history of thought; in the second he is a Manichean.

The first world culminates in the symbol of the tree of life. Whereas the tree of knowledge distinguishes between good and evil, the tree of life describes a good that exists before (or after) the distinction between good and evil: harmonious unity between the opposites of existence, the abolition of contraries, light without the taint of shadow. Whereas the tree of knowledge invites its devotees to adhere to the virtues of active life, the tree of life recommends mystical quiet: the gift that none of Kafka's characters ever knew or ever will know. Whereas we have already eaten the fruit of the tree of knowledge, we can have only a presentimcnt of the fruit of the tree of life; perhaps we will know it on the day that the separation between God and ourselves will fall away, and yet we already know it, because when we live in the light of the eternal, we encounter the tree of life, the flower of all eternities. Up to here Kafka adheres to the Biblical text. But on one point he modifies it radically. If in Genesis the cherubs protect the garden of Eden against the return of men with "the flame of the flashing sword," Kafka assures us that the garden still exists, even without us, and still today is destined to serve us and is made for us. Despite the expulsion, the indestructible that was in us was not destroyed: original sin did not completely transform our nature; we have acquired divine knowledge. But there is an even more consoling piece of news. Not only is paradise still open, but we inhabit it, we live up there while we dwell in our time, even though few or perhaps none of us realizes it. We live already here, now, in the eternal. Eternity is not something that will come later, as the Christian and Persian religions affirm; it is unthinkable that something so corrupt as temporality should be overturned in the eternal, and thus be justified. There are two lives, as there are two trees in the Terrestrial Paradise. On one side, temporal life runs restlessly; on the other, like a quiet lake of light there extends and rests eternal life, which, in a fashion incomprehensible to us, perhaps comprehensible to Kafka, "corresponds" to the temporal life.

If from Edenic knowledge we pass to man's knowledge, if we join psychology to theology, we obtain the same truths. Everyday reality does not exist: in the universe there is nothing but the soul, nothing but the spirit, only *Seele*, only *Geist;* and this "deprives us of hope and gives us certainty." But Kafka prefers to avoid this language charged with secular resonances and steeped in dualism; he purifies it, and he speaks of the "indestructible," which inhabits us and dominates us and unites all men, as the origin "of the incomparable, indivisible union" that forms mankind. That this "indestructible" remains hidden from us, that we lose faith in it, that we hide it behind all sorts of constructions and illusions, and perhaps even behind a faith in a personal God, has not the least importance; the indestructible exists and is the sole foundation of our life. Evil on the contrary is nothing but appearance: it is totally *other* in respect to man; it can tempt man, seduce him, deceive him, subjugate him, but it cannot become man; and in fact Satan was compelled to agree to be incarnated in the serpent.

Although Kafka avoids the name of God, his psychology is enclosed in a monist metaphysic. The fire that is within us, that is to say, the "indestructible" in us, is sucked up by God: "to believe means to liberate the indestructible in oneself, or, more accurately, to free oneself, or, more accurately yet, to be indestructible, or, better still, to be"; and *Being* is simply a word to indicate God. A last sentence says: "The sky is mute, and acts as an echo only to him who is mute." It is unimportant that God does not speak to us, or even that he is dead, as "The Great Wall of China" had told us. Kafka reverses every sentence about God's death. This sky, which is mute, is in accord with us, acts as our echo, answers us, if we too are silent, in accordance with that quietude of the soul, that mild inner silence which is counseled us by the tree of life.

Where God and absolute truth exist, there no longer is speech or any form of expression whatsoever. "Mutism is an attribute of perfection."* This ineffability of God, or of truth, or of good, or of the soul, or of the spirit, is determined by a more profound cause. The immense soul, which constitutes the sole reality of the universe, does not know itself: quiet, mute, enclosed in the infinite silence of its darkness. Truth cannot be known: "it is indivisible, therefore

---

* The German edition of *The Notebooks* does not include this aphorism, which is found only in the Italian translation (p. 718). But the aphorism is without a doubt Kafka's. Ervino Pocar collated the text published by Brod with the manuscripts.

it cannot recognize itself; he who wishes to recognize it must be mendacious." In the Zürau aphorisms, analytical spirit, self-consciousness, consciousness of the other are always possessed by evil: evil knows itself and knows good, whereas good rests in its own mild and obscure indistinctness, as the tree of life teaches. We do not need experience; as always, it is enough to read the first chapters of Genesis. Sin has been generated in man by his desire for knowledge—"what provokes sin and what knows it is one and the same"—and should we wish to climb from the tree of knowledge, this first indispensable step, all the way to the tree of life and thus reach eternal life, we must cancel in us everything that acts as an obstacle—knowledge, your own self which speaks and knows.

Kafka does not have enough words to condemn Joseph K.'s vain desires: confession, self-observation, self-analysis, psychology are all disguised forms of evil. "Confession and the lie are the same thing. In order to be able to confess, one lies. What one is one cannot express, precisely because one is that; one can communicate only what one is not, that is, the lie. 'Observe yourself' is the advice of the serpent." Analytical psychology only mirrors the terrestrial world on the soul's celestial surface. If we want to attain the indivisible truth in ourselves, we must forget ourselves, destroy ourselves, as the mystics teach: to find what we are beneath appearances, not to act or construct ourselves or impose on ourselves a self-discipline—but passively to contemplate the immense circle of our quiet soul.

To live in accordance with the tree of life generates a particular art of seeing. In the first place, the gaze of our eyes must overlook ourselves and fall upon our ego as though it were an extraneous object—one of those thousands of objects that do not belong to us. Kafka also advises the same renunciation as regards the world. Any person who observes in a certain sense participates in life, becomes attached to life, tries to keep in step with the wind; and then we must not observe, or if we have observed sinfully, we must forget and cancel all that we have seen, transforming our memory into an empty reservoir. If the stimulus is still to be too strong, our eyes must cast upon the world a light so dazzling as to dissolve it and make it vanish into nothingness, as though it had never existed. Thus the art of seeing becomes an art of not seeing. Only by being blind, as if we were without speech and without knowledge, can we preserve the supreme gift: the uncontaminated purity of the gaze.

He who lives in the eternal knows only the soul, has no knowledge and has no knowledge of himself, does not see and does not see himself—he accomplishes a radical renunciation of the world, much more radical than Kafka had ever imagined. Now he is alone: never had the Stranger and the Bachelor been so alone as this quiet mystic who for eight months stayed in the Zürau countryside. But this total renunciation overturns itself and becomes its opposite. While the Bachelor feared that solitude might prevent him from loving man, by flinging him into the desert that spreads around the land of Canaan, now, precisely at the heart of this solitary renunciation of the world, Kafka discovers love for the others. He understands that he cannot love men "within the world" as he had done in his youth, because he who, "within the world," loves his neighbor commits the same injustice as he who, "within the world," loves himself. He cannot love this person or that; he must shun single passions; and from his ascetic renunciation blossoms the love of all men, of all mankind, "of true human nature, which one cannot but love, provided one has nature's dignity." So, thinking desperately alone, with his back unguarded, mad as an acrobat, Kafka in a few months acquired a theology, a science of the soul, a mysticism, an art of seeing and a morality. He no longer lacked anything. That edifice of the All, which he had dreamt of, stood clear, evident, before his eyes. How could he avoid discerning at last the *place*, the utopian place, the place of light to which all his life had aspired? "I've never been in this place: breathing is different here: beside it shines a star more dazzling than the sun."

Here and there we encounter blazing maxims that we do not know how to interpret. What does this mean: "Good, in a certain sense, is *trostlos*"? We could interpret it in the most obvious manner: good is "disconsolate," "comfortless," "sad," "aggrieved," "inconsolable" (because a goal is lacking, it cannot attain what it dreams of). Or instead, is it "without hope for improvement" (good is the supreme achievement, it cannot become better)? Or, finally, is good "discomforting," "mortifying," "discouraging," "desolate"? Everything leads us to assume that this, the current interpretation, is the correct interpretation; and therefore we ought to believe that good emanates little attraction, arouses scant desire, is enshrouded by a kind of grayness, mediocrity and desolation. Another aphorism seems to exalt the metaphysics of Being, but with what a reversal! "To have does not exist, only to be exists: only a being which yearns for its last breath, for suffocation." The paradox of this Being is that it does not aim at eternity, immutability, the light without shadow, but at the shame of death, a death that we do not know is natural or provoked, but which might perhaps be unworthy, like that of Joseph K. Whenever did Being, which is God, dream of dying of suffocation?

These distressing maxims can probably be explained by the supreme nobility and supreme weakness of good as expressed in the aphorisms: its ignorance, its inability to know, its desire not to know. But it would be mistaken of us to believe that the Zürau theology of good occupied an absolute place in Kafka's world. Never, not even during these months of meditation, did he share the pure innocence of good; his art never renounced the gift of knowledge; his theology, even if it was overturned as here in the expectation of Quiet, sprang from a dramatic, almost desperate intellectual tension; and while reality was annulled in the unknowing soul, he continued to be the sole paradoxical observer who scrutinized it. There is one thing that Kafka will never be able to accept: to attribute exclusively to evil the dreadful strength of understanding the universe. Good, such as he pursued it all his life, was not only a mild, quiet and obscure force: it was a tortured good, divided, wounded, shattered— but fortified by all the light of knowledge, animated by an immense will to understand.

The second intellectual edifice that Kafka constructed at Zürau is Manichean. It rests on the fact that in the Terrestrial Paradise we have sinned: be it by having eaten the fruit of the arid tree of knowledge, be it—and above all—for not yet having tasted the blessed fruit of the tree of life, which constitutes the symbol of perfect existence. "The condition in which we find ourselves is sinful, independently of any guilt." Under this double, intolerable burden, Kafka's man is a sinner as no man had ever been: Augustine's man, the child who, "pale, with a bitter gaze," envied the brother who sucked milk from the breast of the same mother, the child who stole a few pears from a tree for the simple pleasure of doing evil, is an innocent compared to him. So he has forever been driven from Paradise: the flashing flames of the cherubs' swords have been raised to defend the gate; and now he lives in the world's desert, without hope of ever again seeing the garden, immersed in evil's everyday mud.

Never, in modern literature, had evil perhaps ruled over so gigantic a space and cast so sinister a shadow on the universe. The wicked figure we meet in the aphorisms is not, as some believe, an optical illusion or a projection of ours; this is not the small, everyday perversion; and neither is this something purely objective—that which is "here," as the maxim wishes to assure us. In these lines we encounter the atrocious majesty of Absolute Evil: the transcendence of Evil; a sort of upside-down Being, which some could venerate and worship. If we were to accept a brief story without reservation, we could affirm that Evil is the only Being in the universe.

Evil knows itself: none of its chasms, its twists, its ruses, its enigmas is unknown to it; all those who practice analysis, confession, reflection and psychology are its pupils. Evil knows the entire vastness of the universe: the innocent and obscure extension of good, the great soul that ignores itself, the secrets of the individual spirit. "Do not let evil persuade you that you can keep any secrets from it." This theology culminates in a great enigmatic aphorism: "Evil is the starry sky of good." Confronted by such a sentence, analysis must come to a halt; and, after gathering together all the analogies, relationships and absent and present thoughts, it should admit that the intellectual content burns in the blinding light of the enigma, of the absolute sentence, which renders its own content vain.

The point of departure is the celebrated sentence of modern philosophy: "Two things fill the soul with ever renewed and growing wonder and awe . . . : the starry sky above me and the moral law within me." The first interpretation is clear: evil (which knows itself and knows) is light, while good (which is unaware of itself and is unaware) is darkness. But perhaps Kafka tacitly invited us to read Kant's entire page, in which the starry sky helps us know, on the one hand, the place we occupy in the palpable external world, and extends our connection to "an interminable grandeur, with worlds upon worlds and systems of systems, and then also to the unlimited times of their periodic motion, their beginning and their duration"; and on the other hand, "annuls our importance as an animal creature, who must restore again to the planet (a simple point in the universe)" our body's matter. Does evil therefore impart to good the consciousness of its infinite relationships with the universe which it—by itself—would not possess? Does it impart to good the sense of its finiteness? All this will remain forever-mysterious. In our mind persists the image of this prone, quiet, innocent, tenebrous, silent good, which looks to evil as its light—and perhaps as the aim to which it aspires.

Like Baudelaire's evil, Kafka's evil is the greatest actor, quick-change artist and illusionist that ever existed, whereas good, in its undivided simplicity, is incapable of play-acting. Evil knows how to impersonate all the roles offered it by the repertory of the universal theater; nobody surpasses it in the part of the Evil One; it is always play-acting because it is always split, and yet a kind of weakness, or a hidden inferiority complex, leads it to don the role of the good above all. So we can witness terrifying spectacles. Before us, who must choose, stand good and evil; they are not opposed figures; it is always evil, now in its authentic nature, now in its role of the good. If we do not realize this, we can only succumb, because spurious good is much more alluring than true good. But if we do realize it, a pack of devils drives us toward spurious good: like repulsive objects, we are rolled, jabbed, swept toward it by a barrier of pinpoints, while the claws of spurious good reach out to seize us. We then pull back a step and with yielding sadness are swallowed by true evil which, at our backs, has waited all this time for our decision. Out of delicacy toward us, or so as not to frighten our souls, or because of an artist's scruple, or because, for once, he has been enslaved by evil, Kafka has glossed over the most significant fact. Our choice is between two forms of evil. It is not that good is less alluring than evil. Good has vanished from the visible universe. The world, where until now we have seen only the divine Being, is completely occupied by this enormous, very intelligent, very agile, very luminous, very mobile negative Being.

We have not yet encountered the masterpiece of evil's scenic art. Until now, it remained outside us and had confined itself to performing perfectly the role of good. But evil can do better. If it wishes, it marvelously transforms itself into you yourself: it becomes, indeed, your very own lips, lets you nibble with your teeth, and as you are nibbling you realize that your old lips—those you thought were *yours*—were never so docilely well suited to your bite. Then it makes you speak. It doesn't make you speak, as some naive person might think, blasphemous words which offend the good, or God, or the tree of life; but to your surprise, you pronounce the "good word." After having demonstrated this illusionistic power, it has no trouble seducing you. The first artifice is the simplest. As Baudelaire revealed, as soon as it slips into us it tries to make us believe that it does not exist: we are safe, with our secrets, protected by its omniscience. It can also choose a different path. What is more noble than fighting openly, frankly, without half measures, without pause, against evil? Or what is sweeter than to converse with friends, breaking the quiet of silence? These are some of evil's ruses: among the many that Kafka knew.

Some stupendous aphorisms which already have a story-like mode recount man's intermediary condition. We know that, as in Platonic mythology, on the one hand he lives in the Terrestrial Paradise or in heaven and, on the other hand, in the world of the Fall. We are double, woven of heaven and earth. In appearance, one of the texts repeats this condition: every man is at one and the same time "a free and secure citizen of earth" and "a free and secure citizen of heaven," and he therefore has at his disposal all the moral and imaginative possibilities. But Kafka's images completely transform Platonic mythology. The single man of the myth splits into two men who, in dramatic scission, in total schizophrenia, never meet. The "free and secure citizen of the earth" becomes an earthly prisoner: his neck is fettered by a chain long enough to allow him to reach any earthly place, but it prevents him from going beyond the limits of the earth; if he tries to ascend to heaven, earth's collar chokes him. The "free and secure citizen of heaven" becomes a celestial prisoner: his neck is bound by an analogous chain; if he tries to descend to earth, he is choked by the collar. The completeness of the double experience is lost. The inhabitant of the Terrestrial Paradise, the man inhabited by the eternal, the "indestructible," has become a prisoner: what seemed to be his salvation is now his condemnation, because nothing allows us to believe that heaven's prisons are more agreeable than those of earth.

Confined in the earthly prison, we experience the desire to die: as in Plato, this is the first sign that we are beginning to comprehend. "This life seems unendurable to us, another seems unattainable." We are no longer ashamed of dying. Christian faith assures us that at the moment of our death we will ascend to heaven, free from all constriction and all weight; the Greek faith speaks to us of successive metamorphoses, which will bring us to a higher form of life. In Kafka there is no liberation, no leap, no ascent, no sudden opening of the sky. We continue to live in an unstoppable cycle of iron destinies. As in the Gnosis, we are "transferred from the old cell we hate into a new one, which we must still learn to hate." The universe is a prison from which one never issues. Hope, which seemed to have been revived on the deathbed, is immediately negated. And yet despite the inexorability of repetition, a thread of hope remains: an ironical, paradoxical hope, founded on nothing, documented by nothing—the only one that Kafka knows and which every time is disappointed. "Perhaps, during the transfer from the old cell to the new, the Lord will by chance be passing down the corridor, He will look into the prisoner's face and will say, 'That one should not be locked up again. He comes with me.' "

In the parable in Plato's *Republic*, men see the shadows of the ideal world reflected on the walls of the cave. In Kafka Plato's cave has become a modern railroad tunnel. A group of travelers has suffered an accident: they are in a place from which the light at the entrance is no longer visible, and the light at the exit is so small that their eyes must continually search for it, and continually lose it. One isn't even certain whether that light of a struck match comes from the beginning or the end of the tunnel. The travelers stay there, unable to reach the exit, which, perhaps, does not exist. They do not know what they ought to do or why they ought to do it: every moral question, every ethic of action, every explanation of causes seems absent from their lives. And yet life continues. With their senses in disarray, confused or hypersensitive, they create monsters for themselves; they abandon themselves to a game which is "kaleidoscopically fascinating or fatiguing, depending on the individual's mood and wound": the loves, passions, desires and illusions that make our existence so colorful and painful. Despite the similarity of the theme, the distance separating Kafka and Plato is unbridgeable. While the shadows in *The Republic* are reflected by the sun and the real world of Ideas, in Kafka's cave the light of the sun is not reflected. The monsters and the travelers' kaleidoscopic games are merely a simple fantasy of our excited senses, our whims and our sorrows, to which nothing objective corresponds. In contrast to what happens in Plato, no educator will ever be able to free us from the tunnel and lead us, little by little, out of the shadows and into the light of the sun.

The fourth small story is the most upsetting. A long time ago, men were asked to choose between becoming the king and becoming the king's couriers: gods or couriers of the gods. An enigmatic sentence: Who posed the choice? God? But at that moment there was no God, as we will learn soon after. A God without name? An absent God? Or was this an anonymous choice, undifferentiated, posed by life itself? In any case, as Genesis affirms and "Investigations of a Dog" suspects, men, at the beginning of their history, could have become gods and "lived eternally": promulgated the law, contemplated the stars, lived clustered around the tree of life. But because of their incurable childish frivolity, attracted by horses, multicolored garments, bells, stagecoach stops, active life, they chose to become the "king's couriers." So now we live in a world without gods, because at that original time the gods were not created. No one hands down the law, gives orders, promulgates the various messages. There are only men, couriers, who gallop throughout the world, and since there are no gods, they shout their senseless messages to one another. What does it mean to continue a life so empty and absurd? To continue carrying incomprehensible messages? The couriers know this and would gladly be done with their miserable existence and the entire universe. If they continue to run about with their peaked caps, their bells and their meaningless messages, it is because of the courier's oath that they took at the world's beginning: an oath to a nonexistent god, a pact woven of the void, a commitment to nothingness.

A few years later, Kafka would describe this part of his search with another stupendous aphorism: "*We* are digging *the pit* of Babel." In the land of Sennar, Noah's descendants had built a city and a tower using brick instead of stone, bitumen instead of cement; they wanted to remain united, so as not to be scattered upon the face of the earth, and to raise the top of the tower all the way to the sky, so as to gain knowledge of God's secrets. Kafka had not built a tower, not even a Great Chinese wall, so that it might protect his immense territory. His description of the luminous place of Being had perhaps been only an illusion. But he had dug the Pit of Babel: like Dostoevsky he had delved ever more profoundly in the night and the abysses; he had descended into the animal's burrow, into God's underground; he had described the dreadful Being of Evil, the existence of man in sin, the double prison, the dissipation of the king's couriers. What a superb pit of Babel! As he wrote down his aphorism in Berlin, he must have been assailed by disquiet. Perhaps he too was guilty of hubris, like the men of Sennar, even though it was a reverse hubris. Perhaps he too, desperately wanting to remain united, had been scattered on the face of the earth, inducing men to imitate him. Perhaps the result of his excavation had been only a confusion of tongues—a message without meaning and incomprehensible, like the message of the king's last couriers.

CHAPTER NINE

Milena

In the first days of April 1920, Kafka arrived at Merano, in order to treat his tuberculosis in a milder climate. When he saw it for the first time, the Ottoburg pension did not appeal to him: it was small and resembled somewhat a "family tomb," indeed a "common grave." A few days later, on April 10, he returned there; and the pension, despite its funereal air, or precisely because of it, pleased him. The guests were all Christian Germans. Kafka had asked to be seated at an isolated table, because of his vegetarian habits and his adherence to the Fletcher method, which obliged him to chew every mouthful a hundred times. But as soon as he sat down, a colonel, who acted as head of the table, immediately invited him to the table d'hôte so cordially that Kafka could not refuse. Above all he liked the balcony of his room: it was on the first floor, exposed to the sun and sunk in the garden, surrounded, almost covered by bushes. Lizards and birds came to visit him; and in the background, the hedges in full flower, tall as trees, formed a kind of theatrical backdrop, while farther on, other large gardens—the trains from the railroad—seemed to rustle. He spent the greater part of the day lying almost naked on the balcony. One day, beside him, a beetle fell on its back and was desperate at being unable to right itself; Kafka did not help it because he was reading a letter from Milena; a lizard slithered over the beetle and righted it, for one instant the beetle remained immobile, as though it were dead, and then in great haste it climbed up the wall of the house.

During those April days he wrote two letters to Milena Jesenská, a young Czech woman who led a sad life in Vienna, at the side of a husband who tortured her. He had met her in Prague in October 1919, when Milena had told him she wanted to translate his stories into Czech. While he had remembered, even to the point of obsession, every detail of Felice's face, he remembered nothing about Milena's: in his memory had remained a figure, a dress, an aura. He turned that frail memory over and over; it seemed to him that under that delicate appearance he recognized an almost peasantlike freshness; and as ever more glowing letters arrived from Vienna, he transformed the impression of the letters into a remote vision, as precise as in a mediumistic communication. The epistolary style became the light of her eyes, the breath of her lips, the movements of body and hands, so rapid and so resolute—but when he approached the face he saw nothing but fire. Milena had told him that she no longer "could breathe" in Vienna. The sense of her unhappiness attracted him, and with the audacity of the shy he immediately invited her to Merano. "I do not give advice—how could I advise?—but simply ask: Why don't you leave Vienna for a while? You are not without a country like other people. Wouldn't a stay in Bohemia give you new energy? And if for some reason that I do not know, you perhaps do not wish to go to Bohemia, you could go somewhere else, perhaps even Merano would be fine."

With speed and naturalness, as though he had known her forever, Kafka immediately confided to her the great secrets of his life: his tuberculosis, the psychological explanation of the tuberculosis, the Trial to which he was being subjected, his engagements, his feeling of guilt. Did he do this only with Felice and Milena? Or was there in him—the solitary, separate person—the gift of opening his heart to others, so as to bind them forever to himself, like Christ who says: "*Vide, cor meum*"? Not only did he open his heart, but he tried to make her open hers, insinuating that her lungs too were sick for psychic reasons, and presenting himself as confidant and doctor. He was immediately curious about everything that concerned her, as he had been with Felice, though not in such a detailed way: "Do you have a beautiful house?" He asked her to surrender herself to her illness: "Every now and then there ought to be ready for you, in the shadow of your garden, a deck chair with a dozen glasses of milk within reach of your hands. Above all, in any case . . . draw from the illness . . . the greatest possible sweetness. It contains a lot of it." For her, he extracted from his wounded heart the delicacy and almost exhausted gentleness that was hidden in it; and with an insinuating charm, with subtle verbal caresses and kisses, he began luring her into his world: "It's not that you are not in full command of German. Generally, you have an astonishing command of it, and if at times you don't, it spontaneously bows to you, and this is more beautiful than anything; something that a German doesn't dare expect from his language, because he doesn't dare write it so personally. But I would like to read some of what you write in Czech, because Czech belongs to you, because only there are you completely Milena . . . while here you are still just the one from Vienna or the one preparing herself for Vienna." This light stirring of his heart's placated waters provoked a crisis of insomnia. But she slept tranquilly. With his gallantry at once of a boy and an old gentleman, he remarked: "So if at night sleep passes me by, I know the road it takes and I accept." He knew that sleep was the supreme mercy and that he, the insomniac, was the man of darkness, the supreme culprit. But for once he mitigated his guilt. If he didn't sleep—he explained—it was because his body had no weight, and instead of entering into the heaviness that was sleep, it fluttered about capriciously even as high as the ceiling.

A great part of this love was created by Kafka: most of it he drew from his incendiary imagination. Whereas Felice had remained passive under those epistolary flares, the imaginative Milena collaborated with continual inventiveness in the creation of this long-distance relationship. Immediately Kafka sensed in her the "fire" of passion: she was fire and her letters generated fire, and he was like the gnat or butterfly of the Iranian fable, which was burnt by the flame. Without really meeting, the two souls were inflamed by each other; separation kept them more united than proximity; the bodily act, the kiss, the embrace, was not necessary; the uncontaminated impulse of desire was enough, as though only distance could cancel the limits of persons confined in themselves. So Kafka saw Milena's image all day long in his room, on the balcony, in the clouds: the beloved had traversed space and breathed next to him, upon him. "It is true that my room is small, but the true Milena who evidently escaped from you on Sunday is here and, believe me, it is marvelous to be at her side. . . . And what's more, it would be lying if I told you that I miss you, this is the most perfect, most painful magic, you are here exactly as I am and even more; wherever I am you're there with me and indeed even more so."

Faced by Milena's amorous assault, Kafka surrendered immediately: passive, enervated, in a condition of total dependency, lost, reduced to a shadow, as had never happened in his relationship with Felice. He was Samson, who had revealed to Delilah-Milena the secret of his strength and his life. With her he lost everything, even his name. At times, especially later on, it seemed to him "a sacrilege" to be so dependent on another human creature, and this dependency gave birth to anguish—not the anguish innate in love, but the anguish of amorous subjugation. He repeated that she belonged to him, even if he were never to see her again, and so it would have been necessary for her to have the same dependency on him—but he knew very well that this was not true; he did not want from her the marriage he had asked of Felice, but only happiness—full, burning, unendurable happiness. His letters were already an earnest of this future happiness: from them he drew joy, gaiety, salvation; it seemed to him that Milena was immolating herself for him; and with a great rush of gratitude he thanked her for the simple fact of existing. During the very long epistolary relationship with Felice, something in him had always remained rigid; now he abandoned himself, relaxed and gave himself with an immediacy he had never known before. For the first time in his life he sensed what it meant to be free.

He immediately had the presentiment that love, between them, could be only anguish and tremor. He feared that Milena, after attracting him, would push him back into misery: but precisely this eventual rejection fascinated him. More profoundly yet, he was afraid of the upheaval that love would be, that it already was for him. "You are thirty-eight years old and you are weary in a way that one cannot be because of age alone. Or, better put: you are not at all weary, but restless, and you are afraid of taking a single step on this earth bristling with traps, therefore you always, so to speak, keep both feet simultaneously suspended in midair; you are not weary but you are only afraid of the enormous weariness which will follow this enormous restlessness (you are not Jewish for nothing and you know what anguish is)—weariness which can be thought of as a stunned staring into the distance. . . . You've already become an invalid, one of those people who begin to tremble as soon as they see a toy pistol, and now, now all of a sudden, it is as though you'd been summoned to the great struggle to redeem the world." At the slightest untoward incident, he became hysterical: a wave of anxiety and frenzy poured over him; he was stripped of control and defense. "This crossing and clashing of letters must cease, Milena, they drive us crazy, one doesn't know what one has written, and what one receives in reply and, in

any case, one is always trembling. . . . My nature is: anguish." The voice of Milena, who wanted him with her in
Vienna, was for him the terrifying voice of God himself who
called to the prophets: like the prophets, he was only a small
frightened child—or a sparrow pecking crumbs in his room,
trembling, listening with its head cocked, its feathers ruffled.
The whole world collapsed around him. "I'm really beginning to tremble as under the hammering of an alarm bell, I
can't read it, and of course I read it anyway, just as the
animal who is dying of thirst drinks, and I have anguish upon
anguish, I search for a piece of furniture under which I can
burrow, I pray trembling and completely beside myself in a
corner so that you, just as you have entered roaring with this
letter, can fly away again through the window, I can't keep a
hurricane in my room: in such letters you must have
Medusa's grandiose head, for that is how the snakes of terror
writhe around your head and, around mine, even more
savage, writhe the snakes of anguish." His answers to Milena
were not the fluid, interminable letters he had written to
Felice, but shards, splinters, sometimes elliptical, obscure,
nebulous, darkened, often falling back, as though to protect
himself, on the literary figures of his adolescence.

At the end of May, Milena invited him to stop off in
Vienna, during his return trip to Prague. But Kafka de-
murred and refused, fearing that love might again take on the
dreadful face it had assumed during his first engagement. "I
do not want (Milena, help me! understand more than what I
say), I do not want (this is not stammering) to come to
Vienna because I would not be spiritually able to support the
effort. I am spiritually ill, this pulmonary disease is only an
overflowing of the spiritual illness. I'm so very ill because of
the four, five years of my two first engagements." He had
received a telegram from Julie, his present fiancée: "Appointment Karlsbad the eighth please write confirming." He told
Milena about her, "the most disinterested, most tranquil,
most modest" being; he said that perhaps he had sent Julie a

letter on the back of a letter he had begun for her; and he confessed that, when he received the telegram, he kept looking at it unable to read it. It was as though on it there were a secret sentence that wiped out what was written and said: "Go through Vienna on your journey!"

He made childish tests: he threw some bread for a sparrow in the middle of his room; if the sparrow entered, he would go to Vienna. From the balcony the sparrow glimpsed his life's nourishment in the shadows, it was afraid but enormously attracted, by now it was more in the shadow than in the light—but when the moment of the test came, he spoiled it, making the sparrow fly away "by a very slight movement." He insisted that he would never go to Vienna— or to Karlsbad; he certainly wouldn't come, but if to his most frightful surprise he were to arrive in Vienna, he would need neither lunch nor supper, but rather a stretcher on which to rest for a moment. He imagined his arrival: "A tall, gaunt man will appear, he will smile gently (he will always do so, he takes after an old aunt who also always smiled, but nei= ther of them does it intentionally, only out of timidity) and he will sit down where he is told. With this, the party will be over, because he will say almost nothing at all, he lacks the vital energy to do so. . . . He will not even be happy, for this too he lacks the vital energy." Finally he bowed his head before Milena's will and amorous violence: yes, he would come, at the end of June. He dreamt of his journey. He had forgotten her address, the street, city, everything; only the name Schreiber somehow surfaced in his mind, but he didn't know who that was. Milena was lost. In his despair, he made several cunning efforts, which, however, were not carried out, and only one of which remained in his memory. On an envelope he wrote: "Milena," and below: "Please deliver this letter, because otherwise the administration of the Treasury will suffer an enormous loss." With this threat he hoped to set in motion all of the state's resources to track down Milena. Or he dreamt that Vienna was simply a small tranquil square, one of its sides formed by the house where Milena lived, across from the hotel where he would stop: on the left the West Station, where he would arrive, and on the right the Franz Joseph Station, from which he would depart. Then he refused again: he would not go to Vienna. Such a journey exceeded the spiritual energy at his disposal.

Before meeting Milena he had already formed an image of that girl in Prague, who would dominate his existence for years. Felice had been for him the devout wife, without a trace of eros, the woman who would lead him to the land of Canaan. Instead, Milena was a powerful, radiant erotic figure; but her fascination was not rooted in sexuality and had nothing of that nocturnal atmosphere, that desire for dirt and filth which he connected with sexuality, and which he depicted in the relationship between K. and Frieda. Milena's eros breathed the air of the earthly paradise before the sin of Adam and Eve. As Kafka explicitly said, Milena was "the Mother": the immense, vital, nurturing, erotic maternal figure, born from his incestuous dreams, which he had repressed throughout his life. When it came to Milena, he imitated the figure of the son, the child and pupil: "I would like to be your pupil and continually make mistakes so as to be reproached by you: I sit at my desk in school, I scarcely dare raise my eyes, you bend over me and from on high continually flashes your index figure with which you accompany your remarks"; "and here I stand before you really like a child who has done something very bad, and now finds himself before his mama and cries and cries and makes a vow: 'I'll never do it again.' " Since she was the mother, Milena was also the sea, with its infinite masses of water, its inundations, the force of its tide which attracts and is attracted; her letters were water to drink; and, reciprocally, his love must be the wave that engulfed her, with no longer any of the rigidity he devoted to Felice. So Milena, in reality or dream, had all the material qualities: equilibrium, calm, trust, clarity, the strength of truth, the inability to lie, clairvoyant intelligence, courage, greatness of soul, sweetness which keeps away suffering.

But Milena was also the opposite symbolic figure: the chaste moon, unattainable in its remoteness, which attracts the waters of the sea; the maiden, the virgin, the Beauty—the opposite to him, dark animal of the woods. If Milena-mother with a gentle hand pushed away all suffering, Milena-moon brought all suffering; her eyes shone with the world's suffering, she suffered and caused suffering—and she was the queen of suffering. In her Eros had the face of Thanatos. Already at the beginning of their correspondence, Kafka saw her as the angel of death, the most beatific among angels, who robs men of the strength and courage to die. But Milena was also something more terrible. From her letters, Kafka conjured up a dark story of horrors, which had accompanied her youth; and he perceived in her Medusa, with the serpents of terror around her head, looking at him with so penetrating an eye as to petrify him. He was terrified by her intelligence, her strength, courage, vital energy, despair, her hidden debasement, the grandeur of her soul. Only one thing in him did not fear her: literature. While Felice, marriage, the land of Canaan put literature to flight, Milena's sweet and free erotic embrace protected literature—and, perhaps, enclosed it in itself.

On June 24, Kafka wrote to Milena that he had decided to arrive in Vienna on the twenty-ninth, a Tuesday—"unless something unforeseen happens inside or outside." But he did not have the strength to make an appointment with her right away: "I would be suffocated until then, if today, now, I were to tell you of a place and for three days and for three nights I saw how empty it is and how it waits for me to stop there at a particular hour on Tuesday." He arrived in the morning at ten, almost fainting from anguish and fatigue. He hadn't slept for two nights. He wrote to her immediately, from a café at the South Station: he would wait for her the next morning, Wednesday, at ten, at the Hotel Riva. "I beg you, Milena, do not surprise me by arriving from the side and from behind." Meanwhile he would spend the time of waiting "looking at the monuments," visiting the places that Milena frequented: the Lerchenfelderstrasse, where she lived, the post office where she received Kafka's letters *poste restante*, the southern traffic circle, the charcoal vendor's—all of it, if possible, without being seen. But Milena did not have the patience to wait so long for her extremely complicated lover: she checked all the hotels near the station, and finally found him, at an hour we do not know, on June 29.

So, at that unspecified hour—he almost in a faint, she affectionate and self-assured—there began Franz Kafka's four and a half days in Vienna: the only days of intimacy with Milena. We do not know much about them; they spent many hours in the woods near Vienna; they lingered below Grillparzer's statue in a park, went to a stationery store; he saw the house she lived in and her room, dominated by a most imposing wardrobe closet; and on Sunday morning, the day of his departure, she wore a "madly beautiful" dress. Here we have two versions: Milena's—positive and vitalistic—and Kafka's—more perplexed. Some months later Milena wrote to Max Brod: "When he felt that anguish, he looked into my eyes, we would wait a moment as though we were unable to breathe or our feet hurt us, and in a little while it all went away. There was no longer any need for effort, everything was simple and clear, I dragged him all over the hills around Vienna, I stayed in front of him running while he walked slowly, stomping his feet behind me, and if I close my eyes I can still see his white shirt and his neck scorched by the sun and I see him struggling along. He walked all day, up hill and down hill, exposed to the sun, he did not cough even once, he ate a frightful amount of food and he slept like a rock, he was simply healthy and during those days his illness seemed to us something like a bit of a cold. " Kafka made a distinction between the days: "The first was uncertain, the second too certain, the third contrite, the fourth good"; and the year after, writing to Brod, he said that "happiness was only the fragments of four days wrested from the night." Sunday morning at seven, Kafka left for Prague; Milena accompanied him to the station. "How beautiful you were at that moment! Or perhaps it wasn't even you? It would have been very strange for you to have gotten up so early. But if it wasn't you, how could you know with so much precision how it was?"

As soon as he got back to Prague, filled with happiness and a mad exhilaration, that Sunday evening Kafka wrote Milena three letters. "I need all of time and a thousand times more than time and indeed all existing time to think about you, to breathe in you." By now there existed nothing in the world but her and him: that "we" that he now declined ad infinitum; neither past nor future existed any longer, but only the present that she irradiated with the light of her great blue eyes. He annulled himself in her, lost himself in her without leaving anything behind; there was no longer husband or friend, and that "we" was so gigantic as to fill the world. He was no longer afraid to die: indeed, he wanted to die of amorous happiness, and then be born again thanks to the gift of that happiness. In the sky there was an immense bell which tolled: "She will not abandon you"—though, actually, mingled with that bell a tiny little bell insistently rang in his ear: "She's no longer with you. . . ." Lost in this ecstasy, Kafka profoundly wounded another human being, in a way he had never done before. He was ruthless with Julie, his fiancée. He met her in Charles Square, talked to her about Milena, and for many minutes the girl stood at his side, her entire body trembling. He could not keep from saying that next to Milena the entire world disappeared and was reduced to nothing. She formulated her last question: "I cannot leave, but if you send me away I will go. Are you sending me away?" Kafka answered: "Yes." And she: "But I cannot go." She insisted on writing to Milena, and Kafka agreed, though knowing he wouldn't sleep for two nights. The story of this letter ended tragicomically. Kafka had promised Julie to go on an outing on a steamboat on Tuesday, at half past three in the afternoon. But he spent an almost sleepless night; and early in the morning he sent her a letter by pneumatic mail, postponing the appointment until six. He added: "Don't send your letter to Vienna until we talk about it." But the fact is that early that morning Julie, almost beside herself, not knowing what to say to Milena, had already written her letter and, in her anxiety, had mailed it. Now, on receiving that pneumatic message, completely under Kafka's domination, she ran in great distress to the central post office, managed to retrieve the letter to Milena, grabbed it and—she was so happy—gave the postal employee all the money she had on her: an enormous sum.

Thursday morning Milena's first letter arrived. And immediately the Eden of the present, of pure memory, of ecstatic happiness, in which he had lived for four days, was shattered. Milena talked about her husband; Kafka would have liked to leave for Vienna and tear Milena away from her husband and take her with him to Prague, or at least, he proposed that she should return to Prague together with a friend, Staša. This would confirm him in his existence: precisely he, the pariah, the pawn of a pawn, would for the first time occupy the place of a king in a game of chess. Then he understood that Milena was not going to come. He began coughing again day and night. Everything turned dark—also Vienna, the distant city, although it had been so bright for four days. "What is being cooked up for me over there, as I sit here and stop writing and clutch my face between my hands?" The "marvelously tranquilizing-disquieting" effect of Milena's physical proximity vanished as the days passed. He had nothing, except for anguish; and clinging to it and convulsed, he rolled with it through the nights. At moments he had an absurd hope: he looked at the rain from his open window, and then—a most natural and obvious possibility— he thought the door would open and Milena would appear. No letters arrived on Friday—and not even on Saturday, the tenth of July, Sunday, the eleventh. He was desperate. *Never* would anything arrive again. On Saturday he went to his office every two hours to see if there was any mail: in the evening he went to the *Tribuna,* a newspaper, to see Laurin, a journalist he knew, who told him about a letter from Milena, and just the thought of a letter from her made him happy; he spent the evening with Laurin, heard Milena's name several times and was grateful to him for it. He got bored, but he kept telling himself: "One more time, only one more time I want to hear *her* name." Sunday was even worse. He spent the entire morning in bed, returned to the office to ask if there was a telegram, then knocked at the door of a friend of hers, simply for the pleasure of uttering the name of this friend, and finally he went to the Café Arco, where Milena used to go, looking for somebody who knew her. There wasn't anyone. But Monday, all at once four letters arrived—"this mountain of despair, sorrow, love, requited love."

In one of these letters, Milena wrote something that wounded him deeply: "Yes, you are right, I am fond of him, but, Franz, I am also fond of you." He read this sentence very carefully, word by word: "and yet, due to some weakness, I cannot succeed in grasping the sentence, I read it over and over and finally I once more transcribe it here so that you too can see it and we can both read it together, temple against temple (your hair against my temple)." He was wounded by that "also" with which Milena put him after her husband. He had understood that Milena loved her husband deeply—with a love composed of passivity, erotic subjection, complicity and debasement. And yet he accepted this: dark though it might be, that love did not make him envious; he did not demand exclusive affection, as he had demanded it from Felice. "And if we should unite . . . that would be on another plane, not within his domain." And what was this plane? Kafka asked for the exclusiveness of conjugal attentions: of these he was extremely jealous; he wanted all cares, kindnesses, the money needed to support her to come only from him. "Write to me immediately if the money has arrived. If it got lost, I'll send you more, if that gets lost, still more, and so on, until there's nothing left and only then everything will be in order." As for Milena, he couldn't bear to hear her telling him that her husband needed her, had an intimate need for her and could not live without her; Kafka could not bear this relationship of dependency; above all, he could not bear the external attentions she bestowed on him, such as the habit of shining his shoes with scrupulous, devoted care. "You continually pour all the mystery of your unbreakable union, this rich and inexhaustible mystery, into your preoccupation with his boots. There is something that torments me! But it's very simple: if you should leave, he will either live with another woman or else go to a boardinghouse and his boots will be shined even better than now." Kafka's immense jealousy focused on things, on fetishes—instead of on emotions.

During those days, Kafka wrote Milena a strange and ardent defense of himself—perhaps the only one he ever offered. He was not—he said—even a street musician: he was one of those peddlers who, before the war, roamed through the outskirts of Vienna, or rather, in the economy of Milena's big house, he was a mouse who could be permitted to freely cross the rug at most once a year. "And yet, if you decided to come to me, if therefore—judging by musical standards— you decided to abandon the whole world to come down to me, to so low a place that from your position you could see not only little but nothing at all, that for this purpose you—strangely, strangely!—would not have to climb down but rather in a superhuman way reach above yourself, on high, to such a point that perhaps you would have to tear yourself to shreds, plunge, disappear." He lived in the lower depths—but to reach that peddler's or mouselike grayness, wings were needed. Then he realized that if she was tied to her husband by an indissoluble, indeed sacred matrimony, he too was tied—he did not know to whom, but the gaze of this terrible wife often came to rest on him; and these two bonds reinforced each other. Who was this unknown? Tuberculosis, literature, death—or something even more remote and mysterious, a bond of which one was not even aware? He understood that not only was Milena not going to leave her husband, but if she were to leave him she would not be doing it for him. He understood this with infinite bitterness and desolation; and with his usual guilt complex he attributed the cause to his nature as the last pawn in the chess game.

He continued for some months to imagine and to receive letters: he did nothing but write letters, read letters, hold letters in his hands, put them down, pick them up again, put them down and pick them up once more; and he stared out the window, like an adolescent. Despite everything, these letters—the dear, faithful, gay letters, bearers of happiness and salvation—brought him joy. Had there ever been in universal history an emperor better off than he? He entered the room, and there they were, three letters he had only to open them—how slow his fingers were—and rest on them, without daring to believe his own happiness. Then Milena's portrait arrived: something inexhaustible—"a letter for a year, a letter for eternity"—that he could look at only with a throbbing, apprehensive heart. When there were no letters, he lived with Milena's phantom; he sat her down on a deck chair and did not know how to embrace with words, eyes, hands the joy that was there and belonged to him. Or he dreamt of her. They were sometimes sad dreams. She would be talking; but her words contained something unfathomable, almost a rejection. Nothing betrayed her rejecting ways, but the rejection was there. Milena's face was powdered, even too noticeably, perhaps she was flushed, and on her cheeks the powder had formed patterns. He was always on the point of asking why she was powdered; as soon as she realized he was about to open his mouth, she affably asked: "What is it?" He did not dare ask the question; he sensed somehow that that powder must be a test, a decisive test, he understood that he ought to ask, and he wanted to do so—but he did not dare. During the day, despite Milena's prohibition, on the sly he read her articles in the *Tribuna*. He found one that distinguished between the styles of swimmers: there are some who swim elegantly, the body level with the water, and others who do so heavily, the body deep in the water. Naturally, he swam with the weight at his feet. Then he found an article about fashion—and sought all around him on the streets of Prague for the Bohemian girls who obeyed Milena's precious suggestions.

He still dreamt of living with Milena. How lovely it would be—question and answer, glance for glance. No matter what other people might say about her and no matter what she might do, whether she remained in Vienna with her husband, or came to Prague, or remained suspended between Vienna and Prague—she was right. For love of her, albeit with clenched teeth, he was ready to put up with everything: distance, anxiety, preoccupation, lack of letters; and the days without letters were not horrible, they were only heavy, the boat was overloaded, shipped too much water, and yet it floated on her waves. Often, as in Merano, he wanted to melt in her: rest his face on her lap, feel her hand on his head and remain like that forever. He would have liked to lose his name and form, and be only one of her objects, like the happy wardrobe closet in her room, which could look into her face when she sat on the deck chair or was at her desk or went to bed to sleep. At the start, when writing to her, he had signed his letters "Franz Kafka," then only "Franz," and then only "yours": he wanted to lose his name, flinging it into her shadow, forget his own identity. Finally he wrote: "Franz

wrong; F wrong, yøurs wrong, no more, silence, deep woods."
He himself, possession and love were lost in the darkness of
Vienna's woods, in the darkness of all the silences and can-
cellations and dissolutions and woods and deaths of the universe.

How far away they were a month later—those four and a
half days spent together in Vienna—the walks through the
woods, their purchase at the stationery store, the stop in the
park, the wardrobe closet—even though they had been only
the tatters of happiness. Now there was only darkness: on all
things. And torture. The swords slowly approached the
body; when they began to nick him, it was so frightening that
immediately, at the first cry, he betrayed her, himself,
everything. Milena tried to comfort him, proposing a future
life together. It was impossible: in no case was there the
possibility they had thought they had in Vienna; they did not
have it even then, he had looked "beyond his hedge," he had
clung to its top—then he had fallen back, with torn hands.
"The world is full of possibilities, but I do not yet know what
they are." They were never going to live together: in the
same house, body against body; and before that "never" there
was another "never." If she had come to Prague, he would
have passed a test, perhaps the only one: he would have
demonstrated to himself that he deserved the love of a
woman—but he had failed it. So now he did not want to see
her for a few days in Prague. "This morning, for example, I
suddenly began to <u>fear</u>, to <u>fear</u> lovingly, to <u>fear</u> with an
aching heart that, deflected by some fortuitous trifle, you
might unexpectedly arrive in Prague." Nor would he go to
Vienna; he did not want to separate her from her husband,
and every reference to this trip was a fire that she brought
close to his bare skin.

At the end of July, Milena heard from Max Brod that
Kafka was gravely ill and decided to see him immediately.
She did not love him: he was too angelic and unreal, while
she planted her firm, brave and imaginative feet on the

colorful ground of reality. But she understood him—with intelligence, precision and feminine force. At first Kafka refused; like a scrupulous pupil, he did not want to tell lies at his office: the office—and before that grammar school, high school, the university, the family—was for him something alien to the point of absurdity, but to which he was joined in a way that demanded respect. He sensed a secret anguish in her, he did not know whether for him or against him, a restlessness, a sudden haste. The appointment was set: they were to meet at Gmünd, on the border between Austria and Czechoslovakia. Then the plan fell through: Milena could not come. Like a mole, Kafka had dug a passage from his dark apartment all the way to Gmünd and had thrown away everything he had found in this passage which led to her. Now he suddenly ran into the impenetrable rock of a "Please—do not depart," and he was forced to go back again through the tunnel he had dug with such haste, and fill it with what was there.

On August 14 and 15 they met in Gmünd. The mole had once again joyfully gone down into the dark tunnel, digging through the earth to reach the light. He arrived there with a strange feeling of assurance, like the "owner of houses." But there he found no joy: they spoke to each other like two strangers, separated by too many thoughts. He had the impression of sinking: lead weights dragged him into the deep sea; or he had been *torn* away, on the smooth wall there were no handholds to which he could cling.

Back in Prague, all he did was sit, reading desultorily: he did not want to see anyone; and he spent his time listening to a very slight pain gnawing at his temple. He began coughing again: every evening he coughed uninterruptedly from quarter past nine until eleven, then he fell asleep, but at midnight as he turned from left to right he began coughing again until one. He no longer cared for Milena's letters. In the past he had read them to the end and would become ten times hungrier and thirstier; now he bit his lips and nothing was more certain than that slight pain in his temple. He began to be afraid of the letters. When none came he was more tranquil; if he saw one on his desk he had to summon up all his strength. He could not endure the sense of sorrow: it came from the torment, incurable, and gave him only torment, incurable; and if he wrote to her, sleep was out of the question. Disquietude and anguish tore him apart. "Love is for me the fact that you are for me the knife with which I probe inside myself." Bitterly he repeated: "Yes, torture is very important to me, it is my chief occupation to be tortured and to torture." He dreamt of her one more time. Milena was on fire, and he tried to smother the flames, beating her with an old garment. Then the metamorphoses began. She vanished, he began to burn and beat himself with the garment, without its having any effect. Now he was Milena, now Milena was he. Then the firemen arrived, and Milena was saved. But she was completely different: spectral, inanimate, drawn with chalk on the darkness—and she fell into his arms. Or perhaps it was he who fell into someone else's arms? And so he lived between darkness and fire, going from one transformation to the next, from sorrow to sorrow, without certainty. Only one thing was certain. Someone had sent him off from the Ark, like the dove of salvation; he had not found a trace of green; and now he had again—forever—slipped into the dark Ark.

To Milena he had written that anguish was the best part of him, perhaps the only lovable thing about him, and the only thing with which Milena had fallen in love. It wasn't only *his* anguish, but absolute anguish, the anguish of all faith since always, and it forced him to be silent forever. It compelled him to withdraw from the world; he thought that then the pressure of the world would diminish. Instead, as he withdrew and locked himself away in his castle, the world's pressure increased, and the anguish grew; and he gave heed to it, nourished it, poured himself into it, with a sort of sinister enthusiasm, a deadly ecstasy. He felt its hand at his

throat—"the most horrible thing I have ever experienced or
may ever experience." Then, calling him back into life with
her high spirits, Milena had helped him endure anguish;
there had been days when anguish had been only a light,
smiling pressure against his temple, a light caress against his
throat. But now, as everything collapsed about Kafka, his
amorous passion inflamed, dug up anguish, made it a hun-
dredfold. Precisely the asexual and incestuous eros, which
had attracted him to Milena, was a source that could never be
placated. Anguish, not desire, was his erotic stimulus. In
appearance, outside of this, there was only a "yearning for
something," for the "unknown nourishment" that had devoured Gregor Samsa's soul; this yearning seemed to leap
beyond all emotions—and yet no, it was precisely the
yearning that more than anything else aroused anguish.

He wrote to Milena: "I am dirty, Milena, infinitely dirty,
that is why I make all this noise about purity. No one sings
as purely as those who are in the deepest depths of hell: what
we think is the song of angels is their song." He was not
dirty: he was infinitely less so than we; but he lived in
darkness, in the underground, in the animal world, among
mice and moles, he wrote at night; and he dreamt of celestial
food. He had met Milena: the Beauty of the fairy tale,
Gregor Samsa's sister. "Things stand more or less like this: I,
a sylvan beast, was not, one might say, in the forest, I lay I
know not where, in a filthy ditch (filthy, naturally, only
because of my presence) and then I saw, out in the open, the
most marvelous thing I had ever seen, I forgot everything,
forgot myself entirely, rose, approached, fearful in that new
and yet innate freedom, so I approached, I came all the way
to you, you who were so good, I huddled next to you as
though it were my right, rested my face on your hands, I was
so happy, so proud, so free, so powerful, so at home, always
like that: so at home. . . ." He had lived for a while in light
and knowledge, as Gregor Samsa had lived playing in his
dark room, while his sister in silent communion brought him

food. Now he understood that "The Metamorphosis" had prefigured the fate of his love for Milena. Like Gregor, he had experienced the desire for "unknown nourishment" and the craving to return to his den in the forest, dragging Milena along with him. "If only I could take her with me!" he thought, and the counterthought was: "Does darkness exist where she is?" But he realized that it was not possible: darkness and light are incompatible; he must write in the forest's darkness and anguish, Milena must walk radiantly in the light. So, almost without wanting to, he decided to return to the darkness and silence whence he had come; he must obey, he could not do otherwise. He broke off the correspondence: the only way to live was to be silent; and for a last time, not in a dream, he had a vision. Milena's face was hidden by her hair, he managed to part it to right and left, her face appeared to him, he caressed her brow and temples, and held them between his hands.

The November letter was not the last: others, which were lost, followed until January, while Kafka was in a sanatorium in the mountains at Matliary. Milena did not want to break with him: for almost two years, she kept going to the Vienna post office to see whether there were any letters for her at the *poste restante*, whereas he tried to avoid suffering at all costs. "the desperation that scratches and lacerates the skull and brain." At the beginning of January 1921, gathering all his strength, he asked for a last favor: not to write to him any more, make it impossible for them ever to see each other again. Indomitable, insatiable, Milena wrote him another letter that was supposed to be "the last," and another in April. Kafka asked Brod to tell him if Milena was in Prague so he could avoid stopping there, and to let him know if Milena by any chance was coming to Matliary, so as to escape in time. But at the end of January, toward morning, he had a dream that filled him with happiness. On his left sat

a child in a camisole; he wasn't sure that it was his son, but
he didn't care; on his right, Milena. They both clung to him,
and he told them the story of his wallet, which he had lost
and found again. He cared for nothing but having those two
at his side, in the early radiant morning that changed into a
sad day.

At the end of September 1921, back in Prague, he heard
that Milena was also in town, and he was afraid the
sleepless nights would begin again. A few days later, at the
beginning of October, he gave her his *Diaries*, with the twofold desire of being fully understood by her and of freeing himself from his past. Between October and November
they saw each other again four times; perhaps they went back
to using the formal address, which they had used during
the Merano period. What did they say to each other?
Did they talk with the old passion, tension, sincerity? Was
one the other's knife? Did they suffer and love to suffer? Did
anguish reappear? Did the swords come close to their bodies
again? Or instead had the veil of mitigated and defeated
passion already descended on them? When Milena returned
to Vienna, Kafka wrote in his *Diaries* that he was "infinitely
sad" because of her departure; and that Milena was "a
beginning, a light in the darkness." The year after, they saw
each other again; in January, perhaps Kafka talked to her
about the idea for *The Castle*. In April, he dreamt about her
once more. They understood that a last possibility existed
between them: that something or even much was still alive;
but both of them carefully guarded a closed door, "so that it
shouldn't open or rather that we shouldn't open it, since it
did not open by itself."

Two months before, Kafka had written her an unusual
letter, using a formal address full of politeness, distance and
affection. People—he said—know of only two ways to
communicate: if they are distant they think of each other, if
they are close they clasp each other. "Everything else
surpasses human strength. . . . How in the world was the

idea ever born that people can communicate with each other by means of letters?" In the first place, writing multiplies misunderstanding. Besides, it is nothing but an intercourse with one's own ghost, which apparently sits at the desk; with the recipient's ghost, expecting from us who knows what words—and with all the other ghosts that populate the world, before whom we lay ourselves bare, and wait at the threshold for the letters carried by the mailman. "Written kisses do not reach their destination, but are drunk by phantoms during the journey." Taking nourishment from this abundant alimentation, the phantoms multiply and the world becomes nothing but gray, perfidious ghostliness. All of his life's misfortune came from the perverse habit of writing letters. With his exquisite grace—the grace of an acrobat and ghost—Kafka played and invited Milena to play by writing one of her articles on the subject of letters and phantoms, so as to show "them" that they have been recognized. But it was a serious joke. His entire amorous life had existed through letters: a few meetings in Berlin, Marienbad and Vienna, and then nothing but letter after letter: he had thought that thus he could avoid the terror of proximity—and instead he had lost himself forever in transparent, disquieting, all-enveloping ghostliness.

Despite the phantoms, the amorous, implacable Milena continued to write. Sometimes Kafka answered, and told her about his fantastic plans to emigrate to Palestine, his trips to the Baltic Sea, his transfer to Berlin, where he lived almost in the countryside. On December 23, 1923, he wrote her the last letter. He was ill. Also there in Berlin, his old troubles had discovered, assailed and defeated him: everything he did was an effort; every stroke of the pen seemed too great, beyond his strength. If he wrote "Kindest regards," would these regards really have the strength to reach Vienna, the noisy, busy, gray urban Lerchenfelderstrasse, where he and anything to do with him cannot even breathe? Well, he would send them anyway, his kind regards. What did it matter if they fell to the ground as soon as they reached the garden gate, without the strength to get to the Potsdamerplatz, much less Vienna, just as the emperor's last message will never reach the house of his last subject, who waits for it sitting by his windows, and dreams about it when evening falls?

CHAPTER TEN

The Year of *The Castle*

At the beginning of October 1921, Kafka started a new notebook, and he remarked that from now on his diary, which had kept him company for almost twelve years, would completely change in character. By now he was almost a dead man. Like the dead, he had received the gift of a terrifying memory: everything was memory, his life, his loves, his errors were all fixed in his mind; he was incapable of freeing himself from the slightest fragment of the past, and therefore he had lost the ability to sleep. So he no longer needed his diary to assist his memory, recording the events of this external life: just as he holed up in his predeath den, the diary would hole up in the darkness. From that day on, Kafka's diary became even more concentrated: sharply pointed, desperate, increasingly lucid, it gathered around the great themes of his life and expressed them with an intellectual tension that perhaps he had never attained before.

If Tolstoy tried throughout his life to discover what was enclosed in the invisible and secret treasure of happiness, Kafka could not endure happiness: he feared that the joy of living might make him inattentive to the voice of destiny. His obligation was to listen to anguish and despair and go wherever they advised. No one was as wretched as he: around no one's head did the black raven fly as continually as around his; no one had taken on so difficult a task—"it is not a task, not even an impossible task, not even impossibility itself, it is nothing, not even that son a sterile woman's hope might dream of." It was the air in which he breathed, as long as he must breathe. He knew that the man defeated by life, the man dead in life, the survivor—such as he was—has a clearer, more lucid and penetrating gaze, and discerns everything that is hidden under the rubble. Despair is the most potent weapon of the art of seeing. But on the other hand, he wasn't a theologian of anguish either. Despair too, if it was too great, could distract or dim or obfuscate the gaze: torment too could completely close him in himself, paralyze him and prevent him from writing. So if he wanted to keep an open gaze and transform it into words, he must find a kind of quiet inside anguish.

He read Exodus again. His life was in the desert: he incessantly traveled over every grain of sand, every track, every mirage, every rare oasis; he would pitch his tent here and there, wait, hope, but he would never reach Canaan, like Moses, "not because his life was too short but because it was a human life." And yet at other times he thought that some people had reached Canaan, indeed had always lived in Canaan: wasn't his father's world Canaan, the desired homeland, which had always excluded him? As for him, his journey had been the opposite of Moses'. Forty years before, by being born, he had left Canaan, and for forty years he had lived permanently in the desert. Everything in his life had been desert: literature; and his engagements, his loves, his "puerile hopes" as regards women (because women belonged to Canaan) had been only "visions of despair." If he thought about it, he carried within him the desert's stigmata. He was extraneous to men like an animal or a stone. He could not stand human bodies—so fixed and limited. "What in these limited, speaking bodies with flashing eyes ties you more tightly than to any other thing, let us say to the pen holder in your hand? Perhaps the fact that you belong to their species? But you do not belong to their species, that is precisely why you formulated this question." He did not know how to establish a relationship with someone, or endure an acquaintance, and he was filled with infinite amazement when looking at a merry company or even when faced by parents with their children. He had never loved a woman. "It is mistaken to say that I've known the words 'I love you,' I have known only the silent expectation that should have been broken by my 'I love you': that is all that I have known, nothing more."

The uniqueness of the pages he wrote in his diary at Spindlermühle in January–February 1922 consists in the fact that, for the first time, with a trust that surprises us, he accepted being a denizen of the desert. Indeed, he proclaimed himself fortunate at having reached the desert: the road to Canaan was most complicated, and yet he had found it; he might have been crushed by the exile decreed for him by the Father; he might have met with a decisive rejection at the border and been unable to pass it, remaining in the most horrible place—the soundless, empty place, neither Canaan nor desert. Instead he had arrived—and there at times he even found a strange, exhausted, cold and crystalline happiness; freedom of movement; and the gift of attracting others, who loved him precisely because he was made only of sand. Now he lived there: he was the desert's smallest, most fearful inhabitant—and in a flash he could be elevated but also crushed "beneath millennial marine pressures." The greatest faculty he possessed was his "instinctive perception of Canaan": the sense that life's splendor is ready all around each one of us and in all its plenitude—but "*veiled*," in the depths, invisible, very distant—and comes to us if we call it with the right words. Even though it was impossible and unattainable, Canaan remained the land of hope, because for men no third country exists.

During the first days of 1922, he suffered a frightful psychic collapse which he analyzed with his usual clairvoyance. He couldn't sleep, he couldn't stay awake, he couldn't bear life and the tempo of life. His clocks did not run in accord, the clock of ego had totally dissociated itself from the clock of reality: whereas the first ran at breakneck speed in a demonic or diabolical and in any event inhuman fashion, at a velocity that he never represented in his writings, the second laboriously followed a monotonous rhythm. But why—Kafka asked himself—had ego's clock accelerated its beat so much? He couldn't give a certain answer. Only one thing was evident. Kafka observed himself; analytic observation did not bring calm to his ideas but rather brought them to the surface of his mind, probed, scrutinized, studied them; and then this thoughtful gaze became the object of another observant gaze, and this in its turn of another, and so on, ad infinitum. The diabolical element lay in the intelligence's fury, which he had condemned in Zürau as the expression of Evil. Thus the two opposing worlds—that of reality and that of the ego—were severed: Kafka felt pierced and savaged by this tension; his introspective fury aimed at the extreme, tore him away from humanity, reduced him to frightful loneliness and risked plunging him into the dissociation of insanity.

There was, perhaps, one possibility of salvation. Instead of opposing the demons, Kafka could let himself be carried along by the fury: find a moment of quiet in the horror, hold himself upright and so dominate it. Then self-analytical fury would be transformed into literature. Now he had become the exclusive site of a great battle, a double assault would take place in him: assault from below, on the part of the human, "against the last earthly frontiers"; assault from above, on the part of God, down, toward him, against him, against the human that was in him and in all men. Thus mad self-analytical fury would find peace, destruction would end in creativity, being transformed into a "new esoteric doctrine, a cabala." Kafka spoke in the future tense, as if about a task that still remained to be done. Actually, he should have spoken in the past tense: that "new esoteric doctrine," that "cabala," born from the twofold assault by man against God and God against man, was already written in his Zürau notebooks.

On January 29 he left for Spindlermühle, a mountain locality in the Riesengebirge. It seemed to him a place at the end of the world, buried in snow; and the abandoned road that went past the village beyond the bridge seemed not to have an earthly goal, like the road that in *The Castle* leads to the village. During the first days the mountain air did him good. And he slept as he hadn't slept for three weeks. He rode on the sled, climbed up the mountain, even though physical exercise tired him. He even thought of putting on skis. At the hotel he had a curious adventure. He had written his name on the guest list, the clerks copied it correctly twice, and yet the hotel's blackboard still displayed the name of Joseph Kafka, the hero of *The Trial*. The incident amused him, and then it worried him: literature was ironically reminding him that it possessed him, that he thought he was Franz Kafka, whereas he was only a character, a man doomed to being sentenced to the most shameful death. His incognito had been revealed. "Should I clear up the misunderstanding or wait for them to make it clear to me?" A few days later, he was again seized by insomnia—to the point of despair. He had the impression that the place's phantoms had awakened and attacked him on the abandoned road, at the end of the world. He tried to escape, with a few jumps. He sought shelter in the house under the silent lamp. And yet that light seemed to beckon to them from the windows, as though he had lit it to help them find the way. Once, perhaps, he had the impression that his aggressor was God. What could he do faced by enemies who were so exceedingly powerful, who attacked him on the right and the left? He must avoid the battle, flee through the mountain pass, which only a man with clear vision can find, and search for breathable air, the free life—"behind life," in death.

On January 22 he had written an enigmatic phrase in the *Diaries:* "nocturnal decision"; and during the following days he told of having spoken about it with Milena, even though in an inadequate fashion, and he complained because the "nocturnal decision" remained just a decision. The excellent publisher of *The Castle*, Malcolm Pasley, conjectures that this "nocturnal decision" was the first flash, the first vague idea of *The Castle*—of the pilgrim in search of God. This is possible, even though it is not at all certain. As soon as he arrived at Spindlermühle, the inability to write was lifted: with a pencil, the same one with which during those same days he wrote the pages of the *Diaries*, he sketched the first pages of *The Castle*'s beginning, and after that the impetuous tide of inspiration was endless, until it came to halt, one doesn't know why, at Planá. If this reconstruction is correct, we would have here another example of the extraordinary speed with which inspiration crystallized in Kafka. He had arrived in the mountains with a confused idea of his book. At Spindlermühle he took walks through the snow down the road that led to the bridge: in the *Diaries* he recorded some thoughts about the desert and the land of Canaan—and all at once, all this was transformed into the opening scene of *The Castle*, with K. crossing the bridge and asking for lodging at the inn.

In less than a month, Kafka's condition had been completely reversed. He had suffered the "collapse," the assault of the inner clock, the fury of self-analytical passion, which goaded and drove him to madness; and now, as he was writing the first lines of *The Castle*, he experienced "the strange, mysterious, perhaps perilous, perhaps redemptive consolation" of literature, which independent of reality follows the pure laws of its own movement and finds its own "incalculable, joyous, ascending" path. With this consolation in his heart, he wrote to Max Brod, inviting him to join him in the mountains. "It seems to me that I am in high school, the teacher paces to and fro, all the pupils have finished their tests and have already gone home; only I strive to develop the fundamental error of my math test and keep the good teacher waiting." But what did it matter? If Max came for a few days, they would continually roam the mountains, take rides on the sleds, ski; and in the evening, having escaped the attacks of the spirits, they would write their books, to summon the end, to hasten the death that was waiting—"a peaceful end."

On February 17 he returned to Prague, clinging to the book as though it were his last resort. He protested that even though he sat at his desk from seven in the evening, he got nothing done: his book was "a trench dug by scratching with fingernails during the world war"; but in reality, he wrote at his prodigious pace, his pace of a "large, tall soldier of fortune" who leads "desperate men through the mountain passes," since in two months he had written one hundred seventy printed pages. He seemed dominated by fury, by a kind of neurasthenic rage, cleaving to his oyster-book; he kept all disturbances at bay, all friends, all preoccupations; he tried to shut out all noises; and just knowing that somebody wanted to see him—even beloved Klopstock or most beloved Milena—was enough to plunge him into insomnia. But his most serious enemies were internal. He feared a renewed assault by his self-analytical fury: "And what if one were stifled within oneself? If, by dint of insisting on self-examination, the opening through which one pours out into the world were to become too small or close up entirely?" He feared, above all, the attacks of "the enemy"— the terrible, devouring anguish, which took on an external form. "The attacks, anguish. Rats that tear at me and I multiply them with my gaze. . . . Felt it coming on already for two days, yesterday an explosion, then the pursuit, the enemy's great strength . . . the serious 'attack' on the evening walks . . . at moments ruination, desertion, inanity, incommensurable abyss."* At times, he hoped to use the strength of external and internal enemies, of terrestrial and celestial assailants, and transform it into defensive strength or a forward thrust. On July 1 he was retired on a pension. A few days before that he went to the insurance institute to collect his things: in the wardrobe closet there was only his second jacket, gray and worn, which he kept there for rainy days. He removed it and took some papers with him. For the moment the office, where he had worked for fourteen years, remained empty. Left behind on the table were a small glass vase with two pencils and a pen holder and a blue and gold teacup. One of the clerks told the cleaning woman, Frau Svétkova, to throw away Kafka's "rubbish."

At the end of June he left for Planá, in the country, where he was to live with Ottla and her family. As at Zürau, Ottla protected him with her maternal tenderness. When he sat at the table in the big warm living room, she did not disturb him, taking her little daughter into a smaller, cooler room. Then she let him have the master bedroom with the two windows, from which he could see the woods. But noises managed also to creep into this Eden: the children would come to play on the lawn in front of the house and Ottla was not always able to send them away; the small balls of Ohropax in his ears dazed him slightly. Once he was chased from his bed, from the house, with aching temples through fields and woods, without a shred of hope, like a nighttime owl.

At the beginning of July, his old friend Oskar Baum invited him to Georgental. At first he decided to go, then he gave it up. He didn't want to leave his desk, his sheet of paper, *The Castle* which was moving toward its end: "a writer's life truly does depend on his desk, and if he wants to avoid madness, he mustn't, strictly speaking, ever leave his

---

* The first and third fragments are not included in the German edition, but only in the English, French and Italian editions of the *Diaries*.—Trans.

desk, he must cling to it with his teeth. . . ." He did not
want to call the attention of the gods to himself. He had the
feeling that if he continued to live there in his den, like a poor
old pensioner, while the days passed regularly one after the
other, the gods would not notice him and would continue to
pull at the reins mechanically. But if he freely went to the
railroad station with his luggage under the high sky, putting
the world and above all his own heart in a turmoil, then the
gods would wake up and persecute him. It was too grand a
gesture for his condition; and immediately insomnia caught
up with him and he spent the entire night without sleeping.
He had no illusions. He understood very well that he was
behaving like a madman. If he went on like this he would
reach absolute immobility, living death, like certain schizo-
phrenics who spend their lives staring at a spot on their
blanket or a stain on the wall. "It is thus decided that I must
no longer leave Bohemia, hereafter I will be confined to
Prague, then to my room, then to my bed, then to a
particular position of my limbs, then to nothing at all."

While meditating during that sleepless night, Kafka once
again realized that if so little was enough to distress him so
deeply, he was not living like other men with his feet planted
firmly on stable ground. He lived in a den, which collapsed
and crumbled on all sides, subjected to the attack of an
unknown wild beast; or in an abyss without walls and
unfathomable, a vertiginous, defenseless tunnel in which all
the powers of night were free to rage, completely destroying
his life. All he could do was transcribe the interminable
babbling voice of the night, the insinuating perverse voice of
the demons. "This descent to the dark powers, this unleash-
ing of spirits bound by nature, the problematic embraces and
all that may happen down there, about which nothing is
known up here when stories are written in the light of the
sun. Perhaps there exists another way of writing, but I know
only this." He was therefore a sinner, one who renders
"service to the devil." But he was also "mankind's scapegoat":

he immolated himself for other men, not to defeat the demoniacal and expel it from the world, but to bring it to light while leaving it surrounded by its horror and tenebrous fascination, thus permitting men to know—"without guilt or almost without guilt"—that awesome sin which he himself had committed.

In the evenings he walked in the forest near the house. The racket of the birds quieted down and here and there one heard only a timid warble: the birds were afraid not of him but of the evening. He sat on a bench—always the same one—at the edge of the wood, before a broad panorama; but here, instead of birds, one heard the horrible voices of the children of Prague. Everything was beautiful, tranquil, transparent, full of quiet happiness—but if a night or a day were troubled, if the assaults of the "spirits" had tortured him, the birds' wood also became the center of restlessness. He was at ease only with Ottla, when his brother-in-law wasn't there and there were no guests. His neurasthenia, anguish, insomnia and terror of insomnia, his nameless fear and inability to decide grew day by day, right to the brink of madness. He suffered four psychic "collapses": the first on a day when the children made a terrible racket under his window; the second when Oskar Baum invited him to Georgental; the third at the beginning of September, when Ottla wanted to go back to Prague and leave him alone at Planá; the fourth some days later.

Speaking to the landlady, he told her that he would like to spend the winter at Planá, and that only the thought of having to eat at the restaurant made him hesitate. The landlady offered to take him in and feed him. He thanked her, glad of the offer. Everything was decided: he would spend the winter at Planá. When all was said and done he was content: he very much wanted to live through the winter alone, quiet, not spending much, in this region which pleased him immensely. But as he was going up to his room, the fourth "collapse" took place. Above all he realized that he would not be able to sleep: the heart of the future power of sleep was torn out with one bite; indeed, he was already sleepless, he anticipated his sleeplessness, suffered as though he'd been sleepless the night before. He left the house, full of anxiety. He could think of nothing else; he was seized by an enormous fear and, in the most lucid moments, by fear of this fear. At a crossroads he met Ottla by chance. If she had approved his plan, even with a single word, he would be lost for several days; he would have to struggle with himself, an annihilating struggle which certainly would not end by making him stay. Luckily, Ottla said that he couldn't stay: the air was too harsh, there was mist. But Kafka was still worried: he still had to turn down the offer he had just accepted. He had aroused too many things which already lived a life of their own and it was impossible to calm them with a single word. As on all other evenings, he went into the wood that was dear to him; it was already dark, and all he experienced there was terror. That night he could not sleep. In the morning, in the garden under the light of the sun, the tension dissolved: Ottla spoke to the landlady and, to Kafka's great astonishment, the small matter that was on the point of tearing the universe apart was cleared up with the exchange of a few words. "All day long I still sit with my eyes sunk deep in my head."

On September 18 he left Planá together with Ottla. *The Castle* too remained unfinished.

CHAPTER ELEVEN

The Castle

The book begins: "It was late in the evening when K. arrived. The village lay under deep snow. The hill could not be seen, mist and darkness enveloped it, and not even the feeblest ray of light indicated the large Castle. K. stopped for a long time on the wooden bridge, which from the main road led to the village, and looked up into the apparent void." The entire year that I have described—the search of despair, the psychic collapses, the mad pace of the inner clock, the anxiety, the terrors, the "assaults," neurasthenia, dissociation, almost madness—dissolved, as though Kafka had never experienced it. The great book seems born in the loving womb of Quiet. Kafka had experienced the discontinuity of time: the struggle between two hostile times—one diabolically fast, the other slower—which fought each other almost to the point of tearing him apart and killing him. Yet as soon as he sits down at his desk, he immediately achieves a marvelous evenness of tone, continuity of breath, fluidity of the speaking voice, which only the interminable night could bestow on him. Not a break, a change of pace, a lowering or raising of tone. The voice proceeds at the same level—forever, to the end of the world.

As in "The Metamorphosis" and *The Trial*, the beginning is an absolute beginning: we have the impression that, *before*, nothing ever happened, and that the universe, Kafka's life, the history of literature begin that evening when K. arrives at the foot of the hill enveloped in mist and stops on the wooden bridge. Everything is simple, linear, light: there is no dramatic-expressionistic intensification of the narration. Whereas *The Trial* was a series of symbolic fragments, *The Castle* is a novel in the great classical tradition, with a unity of space and time, an incessant temporal fluidity, a skillful symphonic interweaving of motifs, the return of characters, attention to minor figures and even some moments of relaxation and idleness, as though Kafka wanted to remind us that not everything in his book is equally significant. After the book's first half, something incalculable happens. The action slows down. The classical novel, with its balanced alternation of action and dialogue, comes to an end. Immense and immobile monologues, reported now directly, now indirectly, replace the narration, without any concession to the theatricality and vivacity of the spoken word. Perhaps this grave monological pedestal was to prepare an unexpected solution in the final part.

Eight years after *The Trial*, the fundamental situation appears changed. There, the gods occupied the entire universe and its center, of which the anonymous city was a metaphor. Here they have withdrawn to the outermost periphery: in a separate place, forgotten, outside the world. Elsewhere the gods are dead. The Castle, the village at its feet, the two hotels where functionaries and servants stay are the only places in the world where the gods are still alive. Did they seek refuge here, coming from their ancient domains? Or have they always lived in the old tower? Whereas in *The Trial* the gods were mixed together with the nondivine (the bank, the state), the Castle is the utopian place, the impossible place, where the divine is chemically pure. Here there are only gods, and the breath of creatures devoted to the gods. This is the last strip of the land of Canaan, where the people live with them. Nobody, in the entire book, reminds us of the face or figure or history of some predecessor of K.'s, who is therefore the only one, the last one to set out in search of God. The great religious or metaphysical or mystical adventure no longer interests the men of the modern world, save for a derelict with a dubious past who is dangerously prone to mendacity. Even though some people arrive, the teacher informs us that the Castle "is not liked by any stranger."

From two fleeting allusions we can assume that the rest of the world still exists: there are southern France and Spain, to which Frieda is drawn by longing; and some "neighboring towns," "a meadow outside the village, along the stream," where public festivities take place. About these places we know nothing: no traveler has told Frieda about the colors, villages, seas and beaches of southern France or Spain. The only space is this: the Castle, the village. The rest of the world seems swallowed up by one of Kafka's enormous blanks. Whenever anyone takes a step beyond the bridge, he takes a leap beyond the frontiers of reality, enters another space and another time, like Ulysses at Cape Malea, when the winds drove him beyond the route of the real, into a pure mystical element. The Castle is segregated from the rest of the world: just as Canaan is segregated from and protected by the desert of sand, the Castle is separated and protected by a desert of snow, which can be traversed only on foot.

The God of *The Trial* was light: "the inextinguishable splendor" which streams from the law's gates, the "blinding" dazzle which erupts from the palace of justice, even though afterward this light became shadow and darkness in the places of the book. Here, there is no longer any trace of light. There reign extremely long, dark and monotonous winters, very short days, nights that are interrupted for an hour or two, and immediately after it is night again; the roads are covered with snow which reaches up to the windows of the

huts and lies heavy on the low roofs; and the interiors of the
houses are dark or semidark. Spring and summer also exist,
but they are instants which, in memory, seem no longer than
two days, fablelike dreams; and it snows even then, though
with splendid weather. Is not perhaps the name of the
supreme god who rules over the Castle West-West, sunset-
sunset? Without saying a word, K. experiences a terrifying
surprise. Like the ancient pilgrims, he has crossed the snowy
desert to be welcomed by the amorous arms of Canaan; and
he discovers that the site of the gods is the country of
darkness, deadly cold, eternal sunset. The gods live here,
where the light is at an end, because they are dying.

The morning after his arrival in the village, K. for the
first time sees the Castle, which the darkness of evening had
concealed. From afar, it corresponds perfectly to the image of
the divine, which inhabits it. While below, in the village,
snow, the symbol of weight, lies heavily on the low roofs of
the huts, on the hill there is little snow; and everything seems
to rise freely into the sky, dominated by the leap of lightness.
The wintry air is limpid, and clearly and sharply defines the
outlines of the building. Lightness, freedom, limpidity—
what words could better define the divine? When K. approaches, everything changes. The Castle is no longer a great
edifice, orderly and compact, "but a miserable little town, a
hodgepodge of village houses": long ago, they had been built
of stone, and now the plaster has fallen off and the stone itself
seems to be disintegrating. The gods have shabby, peeling,
rickety houses, just as in *The Trial* they inhabited the
suffocating attics of infamous houses. That leap of lightness,
which had struck K. from afar, had been an illusion. As he
looks at the Castle, K. remembers the bell tower of his
childhood village. How decisively it rose, without hesitation,
becoming slimmer toward the top, all the way to the roof
covered by red tiles! It was, of course, a terrestrial building—
we can build only terrestrial things—but it aimed toward the
heights, how light and luminous it was, how saturated it was

with celestial desires! On the other hand, the "hodgepodge of village houses" that forms the Castle, and the very tower with which it culminates, have no upward thrust at all: it is the domain of the *here*, of weight, limitation, degraded gravity.

The Castle's tower is a round and uniform construction partly covered by ivy, with small windows that glitter in the sun; and it terminates in a kind of terrace whose uncertain, irregular and crumbling battlements cut jagged into the blue sky. K. has curious impressions. It seems to him that the tower is a sad inhabitant—perhaps a sick man, an unhappy person, more probably a person guilty of an obscure crime— who, in keeping with justice, should remain locked up in the most remote room of the house but has instead broken through the roof, rising up high to show himself to the eyes of the world. The divine is sad, gloomy, segregated, menacing: bereft of all grace. Two more details strike K. and above all us who contemplate the Castle for the first time through his eyes. The light of the wintry sun, which strikes the small windows, has something of the *Irrsinniges*, the senseless: the light does not shine, dazzle, blind, as in *The Trial*—but it seems to engender madness. As for the uncertain battlements, which fret the blue sky, they seem drawn by a timorous or negligent childish hand.

Only one thing in the Castle seems worthy of the divine: the quiet, the silence, the superhuman or inhuman calm. When K. looks at it after a few days, he cannot discover in it the slightest sign of life: "Sometimes it seemed to him he was contemplating a person quietly sitting down, staring ahead, not lost in thought and therefore, isolated from everything, but free and carefree, as if this person were alone and no one observed him; and yet he must be aware of being observed, but this did not in the least disturb his calm." Man cannot bear the quiet of the divine: his eyes would like something up there to move, to agitate, to give some sign of itself; precisely because of this, his eyes cannot dwell on the building and they slip away, as though it were invisible.

The vision disappoints us. This miserable, shapeless edifice, peeling and crumbling, squat and sad, gloomy and menacing, chthonic, infantile, inhumanly quiet, with a light that seems mad: where is the divine in all this? As we advance in our reading of *The Castle*, we realize that, among many other things, the divine is *also* this. And yet is it possible that this is all? That the high Castle dreamt of by K. has nothing else to reveal to him? Perhaps the divine hides itself, conceals itself from the gaze, like the functionaries who do not like to be seen: it is not the true Castle; and we must not try to *see* the divine.

If we want to approach the divine, there is another path: the aural path—advised by many mystics, who preferred it to the visual one. The evening after his arrival, K. telephones the Castle. When he picks up the receiver, from it comes a buzz, a whisper, a rustle, that K. had never heard on a phone. The Castle does not articulate distinct and separate words, does not organize a discourse; this is "the undifferentiated murmur of language" which came before the word. "It was like the hum of innumerable childlike voices—but it wasn't a hum, it was a chant of distant, very distant voices: it was as though from this hum a single voice were inexplicably formed, acute but resonant, which struck the ear as if it were trying to penetrate beyond mere wretched hearing." The divine is infinitely distant, unattainable, beyond our every glance and the perceptions of our hearing; the divine is multiple, the very place where the innumerable lives, and yet it forms a single voice, because its seat is the One; and it has a childlike appearance, as we will come to know during the dawn spent by K. at the Lords' Hotel.

We have just discovered the inaccessible quiet of the Castle, which caused the human gaze to turn and slip away. Now we know that the divine *demands* something from us: it approaches and addresses us; it is not satisfied to reach the cavity of our ear, but insists on delving "more profoundly"— all the way to the heart, or to the ultimate root of our being. A more radical reversal could not take place; and we remember the other demand that the divine makes of Joseph K. in *The Trial*, through the priest and the Bürgel episode. Shortly before, K. had heard the Castle's bell: a winged and joyous sound, which descended from the darkness and "made the heart tremble at least for an instant—because the sound was also sorrowful—as though it were threatening to fulfill what the heart obscurely desired." The divine does not only ask, it does not only wish to penetrate our being: it fulfills what we desire without our knowing it, what we obscurely crave— even though the fulfillment, like everything that descends from the divine, has the sorrowful tone of a threat.

The acoustic path seems to have brought us much closer to the divine: to its distance, multiplicity, unity—and to its unexhausted and dolorous relationship with us. Some chapters later, Kafka offers us the rational explanation for the strange telephonic noises: at the Castle the functionaries use the phone continuously, and these uninterrupted communications are perceived by the village inhabitants, who hear them in the receiver, as that childlike chant which fascinated K. We also learn something more serious. When an inhabitant of the village calls somebody at the Castle, the phones of the lower sections ring up there: or, more precisely, they would ring if the bells in most of them were not turned off. Every so often, however, a clerk worn out by fatigue feels the need for a bit of distraction, especially in the evening and at night, and he reconnects the bells. And so the inhabitants of the village are answered. But the answer is just a joke—like the answer received by K. that evening. Should we therefore give up auditory contemplation of the divine—the only kind that seems to have brought us to its borders? Is everything nothing but an illusion of the senses? Or the deception of a functionary tired out by too much work? This is the most obvious explanation. As we know from *The Trial*, the divine deceives: it is one of its favorite games. But that hum, that rustle, that chant of innumerable, very distant, childlike voices which form a single voice—they are the voice of the divine. It has no other.

In *The Castle*, Kafka is much more polytheistic than in *The Trial*. He fashions a multitude of divine creatures, has us meet them, evokes others in the background, describes their ranks and hierarchies, with the imaginative and meticulous abundance of a Gnostic or a Chinese. At the top of the great divine ladder dwells absolute Being, invisible Being, inaccessible, incomprehensible, ineffable, unrepresentable, which here has taken the slightly frivolous name of Count West-West, the Lord of our and his sunset. When K. meets the teacher, he asks him: "You know the Count, of course?" "No," the teacher says, and turns to leave. But K. repeats the question: "How's that? You don't know the Count?" "How could I know him?" the teacher says in a low voice, and adds loudly in French: "Please have some consideration for the presence of innocent children." With these little games, Kafka reveals to us not only that the Almighty is unknowable, but that his name is taboo, and to repeat it in public, and all the more in front of children, is to offend the total otherness of the divine.

Shortly before, at the Bridge Inn, K. had seen a dark portrait hanging on the wall, which represented a fifty-year-old man, with a heavy brow, big hooked nose, his head bowed on his chest and one hand furrowing his thick hair. In his naiveté, which seven days of living around the Castle were not able to dissipate altogether, he asks: "Who's that? The Count?" "No," the innkeeper says, "it's the doorman." As in the Islamic world or among the Byzantine iconoclasts, a prohibition forbids the portrayal of God's effigy. After the first chapter, no one speaks about the Count again; we meet functionaries, secretaries, servants, inhabitants of the village; decisions are taken; but everything happens as though he did not exist. Count West-West, who because of a nervous ailment will spend his life confined to a room of the Castle or playing on a fashionable French beach, is a true and proper *deus otiosus*, as religious historians put it.

Below this secret and inaccessible God, there are the other gods: the high functionaries, such as Klamm, Sortini, Sordini, Friedrich; the secretaries, such as Erlanger and Bürgel, the former silent, the latter delightfully garrulous; the servants of superior rank, strong and large like angels, chosen for their stature and even more reserved than the functionaries; and finally the wild, frenzied mob of servants of inferior rank. The high functionaries resemble eagles, as K. observes apropos of Klamm. "The innkeeper's wife had once compared him to an eagle and this had seemed very ridiculous to K., but not anymore. He thought of his aloofness, his impregnable dwelling place, his silence, inter-rupted perhaps only by screams such as K. had never heard before, his penetrating gaze which fell from on high, which one could never point out or confute, and of the circles that from the depths of the abyss in which K. found himself could not be destroyed, the circles which he traced in accordance with incomprehensible laws, and which could be glimpsed only for a few instants—all this Klamm and the eagle had in common." Aloofness, inaccessibility, incomprehensibility, silence, penetrating gaze: all this the *deus otiosus* and the high functionaries have in common.

These inferior gods, or at least Klamm, have a particular quality: the transcendent, that which *is*, which subsists, which is equal to itself, is revealed in them through the games of appearance and illusion. Klamm is continually changing, like Proteus; and his perennial metamorphosis is the sign of the elusiveness of the divine. He is one thing in the village and another at the Castle: one thing before drinking his beer, another afterward: another when awake, when asleep, by himself, when conversing: he is different in stature, bearing, corpulence, beard; he changes in accordance with the mood,

intense emotion, the countless nuances of hope or despair of
the onlooker. Only one thing remains unchanged in him: his
attire—the black coat with its long tails. The single, stable
and fixed aspect of the transcendent, the single form that
defines it, Kafka says with marvelous irony, is its appearance,
what all of us change morning and evening, spring and
winter.

And yet this multiform Proteus always remains identical
to himself, just as the god is the same in his metamorphoses.
When Barnabas, who had compared all the testimonies
concerning Klamm's appearance, meets him in an office at
the Castle, he does not recognize him and for quite a while
cannot get used to the idea that this person is Klamm. But
when his sister asks him in what way that Klamm differs
from the current idea one has of him, he cannot answer; or he
answers giving a description of the functionary met at the
Castle which jibes perfectly with the idea everyone has of
Klamm. In his inexhaustible desire to see, K. manages to
catch a glimpse of Klamm: Frieda violates the taboo, opens a
small hole in the door and shows him Klamm, who is asleep.
And there, before his eyes: a fat, heavy man of average
height, with a face still smooth but already flabby under the
weight of years, very long black mustaches, pince-nez covering his eyes, and he sleeps sitting up in a comfortable round
armchair at a desk illuminated by the brilliant light of a lamp
hanging from the ceiling. We believe that K. satisfies his
curiosity by gaining access, though only once, to this *vision* of
the divine. But the dazzling lamp does not reveal anything:
that coarse, heavy, trivial face might belong to almost any
other person as well as Klamm. We have already experienced
this, in the winter morning before the Castle; and it is
confirmed for us by the innkeeper's wife, who has been to
bed with Klamm. The divine is invisible: our sight tells us
nothing about him and his secrets.

The civilization of *The Castle*, as of *The Trial*, is a
civilization of the Book and the written document. Up there,

on the hill, in the inner rooms, there are large open books that the functionaries consult standing up; we do not know what they contain, whether it is the Law or the interpretation of the Law. Every question or problem or difficulty is turned into writing: the offices exchange correspondences, compile reports, prepare documents, write letters to those on the outside, and the immense mass of written material fills the Castle's offices and even the superintendent's wardrobes and attic, which are unable to contain them. So we should not be surprised that the Castle is omniscient: "Who could ever hide anything from Klamm?" says the innkeeper's wife. And yet here again we encounter a new paradox of the divine, that *The Trial* did not know. Precisely Klamm, who seems to rest on an unstemmable deluge of written pages, never reads the documents and reports: "Don't bother me with your reports!" he always says. The gods stand above the written Law that they have laid down: they let the world be guided by papers copied by diligent secretaries: they let the papers save or condemn—and enclosed in their ineffable wisdom, they don't even glance at them. So then what is it that makes up Klamm's wisdom? His penetrating gaze, his lofty flight? Is it perhaps made of memory? Not even of this. Klamm forgets everything, and right away: the women he has loved as well as the documents. The gods live in darkness, without writings, without memory, without speech, similar to that high-pitched, distant and childlike hum that resounds over the telephones.

With a complete reversal, the gods now revolve upon themselves and, as in *The Trial*, they show us their other, contrary face. Precisely they, the incarnation of the transcendent and of inaccessible distance, are the gods of undifferentiated vitality: they oversee the most palpable, violent and sanguine human reality; they themselves are this reality—a mass of flesh that desires and covets. During their divine undertakings, they never grow tired, or if they do, theirs is the fatigue in the midst of a happy labor, something that seems fatigue and is instead indestructible peace; and yet they sleep a lot, beatific, like children, reacquiring in their sleep calm, strength, distance. Their privileged realm is eros; and perhaps one of them, Klamm, is the god of love. They do not know nostalgia, desire, fantasizing, long expectation, memory, dream, return, chains: but only immediate and brutal physical possession. They delight in obscenities, utter "shattering" vulgarities, because of their profound love of turpitude and because obscenity serves to bridge the distance that separates them from men. As in an eighteenth-century gothic novel, they exercise the *ius primae noctis* over the village girls: they take and abandon, possess and immediately forget; and the girls are grateful to the gods for being possessed and abandoned, because the erotic gift, not love, is the only gift that the gods give to the earth. Their sexual power is so exorbitant and explosive that they communicate it to the other creatures, as does Klamm, who irradiates the Assistants with his seed. So when they go down into the village, the Castle's servants abandon themselves to dances and unrestrained orgies, like a mob of wild animals. Nothing distinguishes them from their masters. In them sexual passion is joined to a profound desire for filth.

Low down, on the last rung of the divine hierarchy, are the Assistants Arthur and Jeremiah, whom the gods have sent K. to help and mock him. Who they are we shall know at the end of the book—they are only people like ourselves with an old, heavy human body subject to falling ill and limping, separate individuals who express themselves with such mediocre instruments as human words, fall in love and speak with good common sense. Nothing interests us in them when they appear as men. But with its extraordinary magic, its gift of metamorphosis and enchantment, at the beginning of the book the Castle transforms them into puppets, kobolds, who have a Shakespearean flavor together with strong suggestions of commedia dell'arte, Yiddish drama, romantic *féerie* and Jules Laforgue. We know none who are more delightful. From that moment on, if they were two they become a pair; if they expressed themselves with words, they express themselves with gestures; if their body was of flesh, it is now of wood. And here they are, in the village streets: lithe, their faces alike, their complexion dark brown, with pointed beards, thin legs, tight-fitting clothes, they walk along with surprising speed and seem to have flexible, disjointed limbs. They stuff themselves with food, sleep naked, covet the maidservants and Frieda, lubricious and erotomaniac, puerile, gluttonous, idiotic, angelic and frivolous like all their commedia dell'arte brethren. Now they embrace cheek to cheek and smile with humble irony; now they watch K., cupping their hands over their eyes like binoculars, pretending to smooth down their beards or sketching a military salute; now they huddle on the ground, amid laughter and whispers, cross their arms and legs, bunching up like a ball; they play with the scarves and winds of the night, fill the closet with papers, watch K. as he makes love, enter through the window, hop through the snow on one foot, rap on the windowpanes. Whatever they do, they transform the events that take place around them, even the most tragic experiences, into a farcical episode of wind and air.

They are not opposed to the Castle, just as the wild mobs of servants are not. They too are the Castle: the ultimate divine emanation, the ultimate revelation from on high. As they eat, covet and flex their elegant wooden limbs, the sacred frees itself of its weight. The great edifice that appeared in the winter morning was so heavy, gloomy and grim; often the gods are intractable, and now suddenly the divine mocks itself, shows that it possesses the flightiness of kobolds, the metaphysical grace of clowns, a kind of innocence that surrounds the enigma. All this is new in respect to *The Trial*, where the guards did not have this puppetlike grace. Kafka has recovered the delicate and anguished *clowneries* of his youthful books, the sad threadlike *clowneries* of "A Hunger Artist," and with delightful skill has injected them into his theological construction. But the Assistants do not always play with childlike grace. They are lemurs, spectral inventions; their old bodies have no joy, and often we get the impression that, in their games, the disquieting and sinister accompanies the comic.

The gods administer the world, or at least that lowest part of the world—the village—that they still have; and Kafka has us witness the wittiest and most tremendous discussion on the ordering of the world and on Theodicy since the times of Leibniz and Voltaire. When he arrives in the village, K. is confident: the speed with which during the night he is at first rejected and then accepted seems to him the sign of a systematic, concatenated, coherent service. Some days later he visits the gouty village superintendent, who gives him a solemn lecture on the Castle's bureaucracy. The first thing we learn is that it is an immense human machine, that it functions on its own, like a unique creature, so to speak without the functionaries' help, reaching "sudden and lightning solutions" that no one seems to have dictated. What interest can this great machine, which occupies all of the Castle's rooms, as in the past it occupied all of the nameless city's attics, have in the "cases" of real people, the fate of this or that creature, with his burden of desire and happiness and pain? The Castle's machine does not know what charity or love is: it is formalistic, like the Law in *Amerika*. This, coming from God, does not surprise us: God has always loved formalism, for administering his contradiction-riddled kingdom. We are, however, surprised—but with God we should never be surprised—that this triumph of form should be illegal: in the village the teacher draws up a report about a conversation he had never heard.

That very same day, the superintendent explains to us how the great machine works. "One of the principles regulating the administration's work is that one must never contemplate the possibility of making a mistake. This principle is justified by the perfect organization of the whole and is necessary if one wishes to maintain maximum speed in the handling of the cases." The superintendent makes two points: on the one hand, a theoretical principle that has the same absoluteness as a theological principle: that is to say, the Administration, in theory, does not make mistakes; on the other hand, an experimental fact: one has never seen the Administration make a mistake. Theodicy, therefore, is demonstrated twice over: on the theological plane as well as on the experimental plane. But let us examine a particular case: in the matter of the summons of the agricultural surveyor, the Castle made a mistake. What is the superintendent's answer? "The control system . . . is not meant to discover mistakes in the crude sense of the word, because mistakes are not made." And when K. insists: "Even if through an exception a mistake does occur, as in your case, who is to say that in the end it really is a mistake? Who is to maintain that the second office will judge it in the same way, and also the third, and the offices after that?" The Castle nullifies all experimental proof of the mistake; there are no mistakes, because there cannot be any.

Kafka's novel, which the Castle's authorities cannot refute, tells us what really happened: a catastrophe; the theoretical perfection of Theodicy covers the most absurd human muddle. A long time before, the commune of the village had received a decree from the Castle's section A (we say "A" to simplify matters, because the superintendent does not remember at all which section is involved), which sent down word in categorical fashion that an agricultural surveyor must be hired and the commune must prepare the necessary plans and drawings. The superintendent answered, with thanks, that he did not need any agricultural surveyor. The answer did not reach the section to which it was addressed—but by mistake it reached office B; what is more, only an empty envelope arrived, because its contents had been lost in the commune or along the way; there was only a note saying that the letter concerned the appointment of an agricultural surveyor. Section A completely forgot about the matter. But in office B, the empty folder fell into the hands of a most scrupulous employee, the Italian Sordini, who sent the folder back to the commune to be completed. By now months and years had passed since section A's first letter, and no one at the commune (where, for that matter, no files were kept) could remember what it was all about. The superintendent answered, in a vague sort of way, that he knew nothing about such an appointment and that he had no need for an agricultural surveyor. Sordini, who saw scoundrels everywhere, became suspicious and initiated an intensive correspondence, asking why he had so suddenly thought of hiring an agricultural surveyor. The superintendent answered; another answer from Sordini; and so on, ad infinitum. . . .

If we want a close-up view of the unimaginable confusion of human history, as administered by God, we have only to contemplate the superintendent's files, some of which are kept in a closet in his bedroom—bundles of papers rolled up and tied together like kindling—some in the attic, some in the teacher's house, some which have been lost, while in another closet there are the files of pending dossiers that will perhaps never be expedited. The superintendent's wife, holding a candle, searches for the lost document, while K.'s Assistants rip papers from each other's hands; the document cannot be found, and in the end the Assistants lay the closet flat on the floor, stuff in at random all the dossiers, and sit on the closet door, trying to close it. So then, this is history, as administered by God? We would be wrong to affirm this. The series of cases, of qui pro quos, of confusions, senseless correspondences and mislaid documents ends by forming a coherent destiny, such as is in fact K.'s.

Between the Castle's indecipherable world and those who are extraneous to it, like K. and even the small cosmos of the village, which lies at its feet and indissolubly belongs to it, there are no true and proper contacts. For the functionaries, appearing in public is torture; their only dream is to disappear: they think they are incapable, at least without lengthy preparation, of enduring the sight of a stranger; they even avoid the sight of the maids, producing indescribable complications in the functioning of the hotel. They interrogate defendants at night in order to better conceal themselves; they do not wish to receive any news that rises from below, from that obscure world in which the peasants live together with the stranger. We get the impression that they are afraid of the human world: that a kind of neurasthenia, fear or inner fragility prevents the gods—who are supposed to be so powerful—from looking men in the face. Sometimes, overcoming their embarrassment or hesitation, as though the passage from the divine to the human sphere were fraught with danger, they descend among men, like Greek gods, attracted by a female body. But they linger for so short a time in our beds! A few fleeting visits, a few embraces: they do not bring their beloved a gift, they only let them take a souvenir; and then they flee without ever again returning, without a motive, completely forgetting those they have possessed. As for men, those very few, in fact that single one—K.—who demands to see and speak with them, violating divine otherness, commits a most grievous sin: a sin of hubris. Far better to maintain with them the indirect, elusive and misleading relations that K. rejects, because to meet and perhaps love them can bring about only a tragedy, like the one that overwhelms Barnabas's family.

In the gloomy Castle, which sometimes must bore them and fill them with spleen, the gods write to men. Even though they despise writing, writing (or rather dictating) is their profession. In the Castle there is a huge office, divided into two parts by a lectern, which runs from one wall to the other. On the lectern there are large open books, one next to the other, more mysterious than the books of the Law in *The Trial*. Before them stand the functionaries who consult them, while, pushed close to the lectern, stand small, low desks at which sit the employees who write under dictation. The functionary stands in front of his book, reads it and suddenly, without warning, begins to whisper. The scribe hears him and starts to write, but often the functionary dictates in a voice so low that the scribe cannot hear him if he remains seated; he must stand up to grasp what is being dictated, sit down quickly to write, then jump to his feet again, and so on. Then the letter is not handed to swift messengers to take it to the men waiting impatiently. Time passes. The messenger is again in Klamm's office, one of the innumerable Klamms who have his face; and this Klamm suddenly wipes his glasses when the messenger approaches, and looks at him (granting that he sees him when he is without glasses: at such moments, with his eyes half closed, he certainly seems to be sleeping and to be wiping his glasses in a dream). Meanwhile, the scribe rummages through a pile of documents he keeps under his desk, and pulls out a letter: it is not a recent but a very old letter, which has been there for a long time. How can one believe, then, that a relationship can exist between the gods and our earth? These letters inspired by a book, whispered, badly understood, delivered after delay, written perhaps to one does not know whom, can contain only a series of deceptions and illusions, like the letters that Klamm sent to K.

Like a source of light, the Castle sends out "reflections" all around it: not divine reflections—human beings or things, which nevertheless contain the most delicate essence of the divine. The first reflection is the "girl from the Castle." K. meets her in a peasant hut during one of his wanderings. She half lies on a tall armchair in a corner of the room, a silk kerchief covers her head and half her brow, she has a nursing baby at her breast, she lies inert in the armchair; she does not look at the child, but her weary blue eyes, marked by an unfathomable illness, stare vaguely into space, and a snowy gleam which enters through the window and speaks of other worlds casts a silken reflection on her dress. K. observes this beautiful, sad and immutable scene for a long while: this Italian Madonna lost in the country where the cold reigns. We know only that the woman, wife of a shoemaker, is "one of the Castle's girls." The superintendent does not want to talk about her, as though it were forbidden. She has lived for some time above the snows, as a servant or mistress of a functionary; and now, for an unknown reason, she has fallen into the country of the snows. She is ill: she cannot tolerate the village air; the slightest incident, such as her casual encounter with K., is enough to force her to take to her bed for several days. Like a romantic heroine, she suffers from *Heimweh*, homesickness for the Castle: the melancholy of the separation and the expulsion consumes her soul; and with her melancholy, weary and blue eyes we begin to look on high.

The second "reflection," Barnabas, reminds K. of the Raphaelesque grace and snowy luminescence that envelops the "Castle's girl." He has a luminous and open face, huge eyes and a comforting smile, which shines mildly like the stars in the sky: he wears tight-fitting garments like the Assistants, he is slim and agile in his movements. He wears an almost white garment; the fabric is not silk, yet it has the iridescence, softness and solemnity of silk, like the girl's dress. As soon as we meet him in the village inn, we are enchanted. His gestures have such unearthly delicacy: when he passes his hand over his face, almost as though wanting to erase the imprint of a smile, or when he leans against the inn's wall and with one glance takes in the entire room, or when he looks down at the floor, or lightly caresses K.'s shoulder, or when he runs, "flies" through the snowy night. The essence of his nature never resides in what he does, but in the aura that surrounds him; and an invisible line keeps him at a distance from people and things, as though he could never mingle with any created person or object.

If every character in *The Castle* has one or more archetypes, Barnabas's archetype is the god of messengers: Hermes. Everything about him reminds us of the Greek god: his litheness, speed, grace, elusiveness, the talent of learning messages by heart. As we find out later, he is a rejected, excluded man; he is not a true messenger; and his tunic with its silken reflections when it is untied displays over his vigorous and square servant's chest a coarse, much mended shirt of a dirty gray color. And yet it is precisely to him that the Castle has entrusted that tunic which in appearance reminds us of the garments of angels, that starry smile, that quick step in the night—the elegance and light it cannot otherwise reveal.

The third "reflection" is a swig of cognac. K. slips into the courtyard of the Lords' Hotel—what beauty, what quiet down there, just after having left the snow-covered village!—and he sees Klamm's closed sleigh. He waits for him in vain, while the twilight's shadow turns into dense darkness. Violating a first taboo, he climbs into the sleigh of the gods, where it is pleasantly warm: all is "luxury, calm, voluptuousness"; the wooden bench is upholstered with blankets, pillows and furs, and wherever he turns he sinks into softness and warmth. At his side, in a closed cabinet, stand bottles of cognac: K. violates a second taboo, he takes one out, unscrews the cap and smiles: "the aroma was so sweet, so caressing, as when we listen to praise and kind words from a person very dear to us, yet we do not know exactly what is involved and have no wish to know and are simply happy that she talks to us in this way." So the coldness and impassivity of the gods are only a cliché? Do we love them and do they love us, and send us heavenly perfumes, ecstasies, praises and kind words? When K. drinks the divine nectar, that sweet and caressing aroma is transformed into a coachman's brew. As in fairy tales, the violation of the taboo and of divine distance is punished.

We have touched four times on the same motif, which constitutes one of *The Castle*'s principal themes. Seen from afar, the Castle is limpid, bright, weightless, ascendant;

whereas seen from close by, it proves to be a degraded
edifice, grim, without grace or upward thrust. The distant
hum of childlike voices, heard over the phone, that chant of
a single voice that tries to reach our heart, is nothing but a
mechanical effect. Barnabas's white tunic with its silken
reflections covers a coarse, dirty gray shirt: Hermes is a
messenger no one appointed. The heavenly scent of the
cognac which resembles the breath of a beloved person who
gives us praise and kind words is only a disgusting coachman's brew. From these repeated motifs we must not draw
the mediocre conclusion that the divine is simply a deceit,
unmasked by reality; or a fantasy of K.'s. The divine exists as
appearance, remote gaze, illusion, silken reflection, perfume;
and we must seize it when it reveals itself to us, know it, love
it, without subjecting it to the test of reality or demanding a
direct vision of it—just as Plutarch and Goethe seized myth
and the divine in their radiant "colored reflections."

Against the Castle's labyrinthine construction, its deceptions
and its gifts stands a single man, K. He has arrived in the
village on a late winter evening, poor, tattered, with a small
mountain pack and a staff, like the wanderer in the fairy tale,
like Ulysses returning home disguised as a beggar. We do not
know when he left his country: and he has traveled a long and
fatiguing road step by step, crossing the snowy desert that
surrounds Canaan, stopping who knows where, in the poor
desert hotels, or with peoples whose names we do not know,
or sleeping under the open sky. If he looks behind him, he
can see a past which is radiant only in his childhood: one
day—the empty and silent square was flooded with light—he
jumped onto the cemetery wall, saw the crosses stuck in the
ground, and felt greater than everyone, victorious over death
and men. His present bold undertaking springs from that
day. But for the rest his past is unknown to us. Does he have
a wife and a child, as he claims? Has he any knowledge of

medicine? Or is he lying? He is the absolute stranger, stranger in the world, stranger to himself: he gives off a cold shiver of indifference and loneliness; he possesses nothing— not even his own name, which even the poorest do possess. He lingers for a long time on the bridge, surrounded by the mists' "apparent void"; his choice is irrevocable, and he does not know that he is about to become doubly a stranger, estranged and rejected also in Canaan. He takes a step contrary to that of his author. During the months in which he began the book, Kafka had settled in the desert, whereas K., faithful to Kafka's old dreams, crosses the threshold that from the desert leads to the kingdom of Canaan.

Although he does not display a literary aura, we have already met K. many times: he has inspired writers, given his name to books, suggested interminable discussions, as though the essence of the West were concentrated in him. He is the combination of Faust and Ulysses in the heart of our century. No one is more aggressive, obstinate, tenacious, constant, single-minded, concentrated than he: from the very beginning, the relationship with the Castle, in which others might have seen a search or an expectation or a gift, is experienced by him as a battle in which he is the aggressor and from which he must issue victorious. "You know," he says in a variant text, "I can be ruthless to the point of madness. . . . I am here to fight." He does not accept gifts or favors from the Castle or anyone. He wants to force his way into the building on the hill—and goes down any road to attain his purpose: the love of women, the devotion of young boys, natural attraction. He does not know what experience is: experiences, for him, are only means; he does not stop to seize them, love them, enjoy them, and he burns them one after the other, without ever obtaining joy in the *here*. Slowing one's step, waiting, postponement and delay are unknown to him. Like Faust, he is devoured by *Streben*: anguish, anxiety, neurotic desire, the impatience to go ever further ahead; and in his impatience he abandons himself to dreams, incredible fantasies and hopes, and he cannot understand reality and other human beings.

K. is also the modern incarnation of Ulysses. His mind is sinuous, supple, mobile, crafty, disposed to adapt and yield like water: it knows the art of circumvention, of cunning and machinations, that the village people do not know. And since heaven deceives us, Kafka does not become at all indignant when his hero attempts to deceive heaven. But neither the aggressive desire for power nor the art of circumvention is of much help in a battle with the divine; and each time K. sees himself defeated by the lazy and sovereign nonchalance with which the Castle conducts its game of chess. And so he experiences the defeat that is always the lot of the too violent or too ingenious, and particularly of a Faust disguised as Ulysses. After having drunk Klamm's cognac, K. remains alone in the courtyard, undisturbed, in the freezing cold of the snowy night. He, the man who relies only on his energy and his ingeniousness, has achieved what he, at least apparently, wanted: independence, freedom, solitude, invulnerability. But nothing is more desperate and absurd than this freedom, this solitude, this waiting in the icy cold, that no person, gesture or gift from above will come to fill.

Together with the protagonist of "Investigations of a Dog," K. is the only other character to whom Kafka has entrusted an echo, albeit distorted, of his own search for God. K. does not accept what Castle and village teach in a thousand ways and with a thousand images: that God is *other*, distant, unattainable, invisible, incomprehensible. With the force of his desire, the impulse of his own *Streben*, with the ruses of his Ulyssean nature, he wants to meet the gods face to face, see them, speak to them, as Moses did on Sinai. If Kafka had said: "In theory there exists an earthly possibility of perfect happiness: that of believing in what is decisively divine and not aspiring to attain it," K. has no use for this kind of happiness. He tries to eliminate all mediations that keep divinity at a distance: those which are human (the innkeeper's wife, the Castle's bureaucracy) as well as those established by tradition and scripture. He wants to *speak* with Klamm (with him as a private person, as though God were not always one, in the multiplicity of his functions); and he waits for him in the night and freezing cold, but no one comes to meet him. He wants to go beyond Klamm, to meet the supreme God, Count West-West, the Lord of our sunset, whose portrait is invisible and whose name is taboo. What K. demands of the gods is not quite clear; perhaps it isn't even clear to his tortuous mind. On the one hand, he is the "agricultural surveyor"; therefore he wishes to "measure," to know the divine rationally, as theologians do. So far as we can sense, he desires a purified and rationalized divine: without anything awesome or morally ambiguous about it, without mystery and eroticism, just the contrary of the Castle's divine, and which does not impute sins to human beings. On the other hand, as the cognac scene reveals to us, he dreams of embracing the divine: perhaps of merging with and losing himself ecstatically in the divine without defenses, as al-Ḥallāj lost himself in God's indistinct unity. Though these allusions are extremely vague and Kafka does proceed with a hand more delicate than usual, it is probable that K. wants even more. That God for whom he yearns is a prey to be conquered: perhaps he would like to ascend to the Castle, take the place of the gods, wrest their secrets from them, become one of them.

When K. arrives at the Bridge Inn he knows very well where the Castle is and what sort of proprietor it has. Someone has informed him. He hasn't come to spend a night at the inn, like a vagabond beggar, but rather to be admitted to the village, to enter the Castle and live in the last country that is left to the gods. As soon as he arrives, he lies: "The innkeeper and these gentlemen here are witnesses, if witnesses should be needed. Meanwhile let me tell you that I am the agricultural surveyor whom the Count sent for. My assistants will arrive tomorrow by coach with the instruments." That he is lying is certain: the Assistants will never arrive, and an inner monologue of his shows that he knows he is lying. Something remains dubious. How could K. know that actually, years before, the Castle did need, or thought it needed, a surveyor? We could advance the hypothesis that, like Joseph K. in *The Trial*, who intuits the Court's secret intuitions, K. has mediumistically intuited the Castle's old wishes. But this seems excessive to me: in no other passage does K. possess Joseph K.'s magical gifts. However, it is not arbitrary to suppose that news about the search for a surveyor had spread beyond the Castle's circle: K. has picked up the rumor and presented himself, with a lie, as the agricultural surveyor requested some time before.

Every reader imagines that the celestial bureaucracy will challenge this lie; it would not be difficult for it, despite the disorder in which its files are kept. Instead the contrary takes place: first a phone call at night from the office manager in person, then a first letter from Klamm, head of the tenth section, then a second letter takes on K. in the Count's service. K. had falsely asserted that he had been summoned by the Castle, and the Castle receives him: he had said, no less falsely, that he was an agricultural surveyor, and the Castle accepts this; he had maintained, with a third lie, that he was waiting for his Assistants, and the next evening there arrive the two Assistants, whom he had never seen before and who claim they work for him. The Castle's technique is clear: it does not challenge lies, does not engage in any sort of struggle, does not impose the weight of coercive relationships; but it welcomes with ironic and indifferent benevolence all of K.'s claims, sanctions his requests, passively yields to his wishes. There is only one thing, but it is an essential one, that the Castle does not accept: to let K. enter the Castle and simply "see it." While it makes phone calls and sends exquisite and elusive letters, it spurns any real relationship and contact: its resistance is passive, undefined, amorphous, like Kutuzov's military technique in *War and*

Peace. We have completely left behind *The Trial*'s atmosphere, where God pursued man with an accusation, investigation, sentence and atrocious execution. This new God, who does not impose anything, who welcomes and accepts, this passive, ironic, indifferent God who does not summon us, has mislaid any relationship with us.

Amid false telephone calls and false letters, the Castle sends K. the two false Assistants, the light and threadlike wooden clowns whom, with a magical stroke, it had extracted from their old and flaccid human flesh. They know nothing about agricultural surveying: they have neither maps nor instruments; and with those pointy, disjointed limbs, which bump into all the doors, they concoct only mixups. Their presence makes a parody of K.'s arrogance: his high religious aims, his celestial dreams, his lofty sense of himself, his search for erotic power, his concealed childishness; and flings the vanity of his aims into nothingness. At the end of the book, when they have accomplished their mission, they explain it to the astonished K. The Castle has ordered them to divest K. of his tragic hero's seriousness, lightening the gravity of his gestures, bringing gaiety into his life, educating him to the limited life, without heroic goals, that he will have to lead in the village. I wonder whether with these words the Assistants aren't deceiving K. and us too. It seems unlikely to me that the indifferent Castle should care about a human creature, a "stranger," to the point of wanting to educate him. As for K., he hates his Assistants: he maltreats them, hits them, chases them out into the snow, not only because they cast a derisory light on his life, but because he cannot bear the humorous and buffoonish face that the gods assume in them. Unlike Ulysses, always willing to grasp the divine in the clownish, K. does not want to pursue the divine in the foolish laughter and disjointed limbs of these two puppets.

When K. begins his adventure in the village, he hears a sentence similar to the one that Joseph K. heard from Titorelli: "There's no difference between the peasants and the Castle." In the land of Canaan, ruled by the gods, the divine flows into the human smoothly and without a break; the Castle is reflected in the village; and the inns are the sordid places in which the revelation of the sacred takes place. This is not a comforting discovery. When K. goes through this soulless village, desolate even in the morning, with its deserted streets and all of its doors shut; when he sees those tormented faces, those swollen lips, those skulls which seem flattened by bludgeonings, those features shaped by the pain of blows, those dull expressions; when he comes to know that closed society, oppressed, avid and arid, in which the women are subject to the sexual power of the gods, he must think with horror of the longed-for land of Canaan, where he wants to settle at all costs. In the country of the gods, under the shadow of that squat, dispirited tower, there is not a trace of the divine. The peasants drive K. out of their homes, even though they are curious about him and, perhaps, would like to ask him something. The women understand that he belongs to another race: he is not a man from their country, who cultivates the virtues of obedience, faithfulness, constancy and reverence—but a hero who has come from below, who can hover at unknown heights, an adventurer who craves the unforeseeable, a fugitive, an astute maneuverer. They fall in love with him at first sight, and would like to be set free like the princess in the fairy tale, carried off to Spain or France, or who knows where. Some of them, among the Castle's lowest maidservants, dream that he will set fire to the Lords' Hotel or perhaps the Castle, and to everything—so strong are the destructive tensions that seethe in Canaan.

As he walks through the snow-covered streets, K. repeats the experience of *The Trial*'s protagonist in the attics of the Court, where the unbreathable air made him faint. That first moment, K. immediately feels tired, as never had happened to him during his journey in the snowy desert: he wears himself out walking through the streets, falls asleep from weariness in the first house he enters, clings to Barnabas's arm as to a rock, and at the end of the book, he will die of exhaustion. We would be wrong to attribute this condition to K.'s nervous tension. Just as the atmosphere in the attic was not made for Joseph's lungs, so the streets of the divine homeland are not made for a stranger, and condemn him to death.

Meditating on Klamm's first letter, K. imagines that the Castle is offering him two possibilities: either to be a worker in the village, connected with the Castle by apparent ties, or to preserve only the appearance of a worker and direct his life in accordance with instructions from on high. He chooses the first path, that of striking root, as though the desire to belong were stronger in him than his desire for the divine. But throughout the book he does nothing but follow the second path, and desperately tries to enter into a relationship with Klamm, his god. Perhaps he does not yet know himself: he does not know that the craving for transcendence, the anxiety to see it and possess it—this craving which can burn only in a stranger's heart—is immensely stronger in him than that of belonging to an earthly home, even though it be the homeland of Clamm

One of the first acquaintances he makes in the village is Gardena, the mistress of the Bridge Inn. a woman so gigantic that Frieda, standing up, barely reaches her shoulders as she sits knitting in a chair. Her enormous knees protrude beneath her thin dress, her voice howls, raves, offends; yet the broad face, furrowed by many tiny lines but still smooth, preserves some memory of the past beauty that made her sought after by the Castle's lords. In appearance, she is only a great maternal figure: a goddess of the hearth, a grotesque Demeter. No character is more imbued with an emanation of the sacred: no one worships more than she the capricious and inscrutable will of the divine world. Klamm has loved her three times; and then he left her without the slightest explanation. Now, deserted for over twenty years, she has become the figure that is the exact opposite to that of K.: the mystique of distance and separation from the celestial world. The gods are up there, invisible, unattainable, mute, unrepresentable, ineffable: we can only worship them, and venerate the few signs they leave to us—those reports, those writings that K., the mystic of divine presence, repudiates.

What a grotesque, puerile and heartrending figure this Gardena is! Precisely she who affirms the fatal separation from the gods has done nothing but ask herself why Klamm ever left her: all day long, sitting in the small garden of her house, and all the nights, together with her husband who tried in vain to fall asleep, she has thought about that desertion, which certainly should be quite clear to her. On the marriage certificate at the registrar's, there was Klamm's signature; the day of her wedding, unconcerned about her husband, she ran home, didn't even take off her wedding dress, sat down at her table, spread open the document, read and reread the dear name and with the girlish ardor of her seventeen years tried to imitate that signature, filling entire notebooks. Klamm had left her three mementos: a shawl, a nightcap, and the photograph of the messenger who had brought her his first invitation. During all the years of separation, Gardena has lived only on these worn-out numinous objects, trying to keep close to her heart that divinity whose irremediable remoteness she proclaims. One evening, at the Lords' Hotel, she hears Klamm's step as he leaves and returns to the Castle. On tiptoe she runs to the door that opens on the courtyard, looks through the keyhole, then turns to the others with staring eyes and her face in flames, beckons to them with a crooked finger, invites them to look at the divine figure as it moves away; then she remains alone, bent in two, almost kneeling, as though imploring the keyhole to let her through.

On the second evening of his sojourn in the village, K. arrives at the tap room of the Lords' Hotel. A young girl, Frieda, is drawing the beer, a slight blonde with melancholy

features and gaunt cheeks; a low-cut cream-colored blouse
rests like an extraneous object on her puny body, but her
fragile hand is extraordinarily soft. As soon as he sees her,
K. is struck by her air of superiority: her victorious and
triumphant glance, which seems to possess the secret of all
mysteries. He soon discovers the reason for this; Frieda is
Klamm's mistress and in a very short time has risen from her
lowly condition as stablemaid at the Bridge Inn to the tap
room in the Lords' Hotel. As soon as the disgusting horde of
Klamm's servants bursts in, Frieda grasps a whip and with a
high but somewhat uncertain leap, similar to the leap of a
small lamb, she swoops down on the dancers. "In Klamm's
name," she shouts, "all of you into the stable!" With incomprehensible terror the servants crush together at the end
of the room, run out into the open air and go into the stable.
Suddenly the frail and melancholy taproom girl has become
the goddess Circe, the witch-queen of animals, who dominates the bestial impulses of the divine servants. K. watches
the scene, immediately attracted by those triumphant
glances. He stares into her eyes and understands that in them
Frieda holds the secret of his destiny, which he senses in the
most confused manner.

The love scene that takes place immediately after, behind
the hotel's bar counter, and another scene at the Bridge Inn
are the only erotic experiences Kafka has ever described.
Klamm is asleep in his room; the servants are locked up in the
stable; the indifferent, idle conversation between K. and
Frieda comes to an end. The witch-queen of the animals
suddenly becomes a violently lustful Venus: she places her
small foot on the chest of K., who is hiding under the
counter, kisses him quickly, turns out the light, stretches
under the counter without touching him and whispers: "*Mein
Liebling! Mein süsser Liebling!*"; she lies on the floor with
outflung arms, as if exhausted by love; her frail body burns
under K.'s hands; they fall into a swoon which K. vainly tries
to shake off, spending hours of shared breathing and palpi-

tations; and in the morning, contrary to all her former caution, Frieda beats with her fist on Klamm's door, shouting: "I'm with the agricultural surveyor! I'm with the agricultural surveyor!"

As in *The Trial*, coitus is invasion by the foul and bestial: the coitus of K. and Frieda takes place amid small puddles of beer and the rubbish that covers the floor: as dogs desperately scratch in the dirt, they dig into each other's bodies and lick each other's faces. Love is a foreign country, where no one has ever penetrated: an unknown land where not even the air is at all like one's native air, where one loses one's way and seems to suffocate: a land like the divine land, since the divine is the supremely foreign place; and yet those two continue on ahead, go even further astray, proceed; both are searching for something, both furious, with contracted faces, they try to push their heads into the other's breast; neither their embraces nor their bodies, which plunge into each other, help them forget; on the contrary, they remind them of their duty to search further, disappointed, lost, probing one last happiness—in their insatiable, disappointed, exhausted craving for the infinite. In the end, beneath the grayish half-light that precedes dawn, K. feels lost. "What had happened? Where were his hopes? What could he expect from Frieda, now that everything was revealed? 'What have you done?' he said, speaking to himself. 'We are both lost.' 'No,' says Frieda, 'only I am lost, but then I have conquered you.' "

Is Frieda truly lost? While she was Klamm's mistress she lived immersed in the plenitude of divine love, as if in a quiet and potent water. The relationship with him filled her soul. Irritations, contentments, joys, the usual feelings of life, did not affect her: it seemed to her that all such things had happened many years before, or had not been her lot, or she had forgotten about them. This was mystical quiet: a happiness that, seen from below, seemed to resemble enervation and indifference. But Frieda did not adapt completely, like the mistress of the inn, to Klamm's ineffable remoteness. When she meets K. she clasps him in her arms, possesses him and is possessed by him, and advances with him into the foreign country where there is no longer stability nor quiet but eternal search and eternal going astray—she is happy at having escaped indifference. She wants passion, joy, tenderness: absolute love made of the present and lived in the present. She wants to devour K.'s body, remain at his side forever, in a desire of confinement and claustration, which concludes with a desire for death: "I imagine a ditch, deep and narrow, in which the two of us lie embraced as in a vise, I hide my face in you, you hide yours in me, and no one will ever be able to see us again." Thus she dreams of escaping Klamm's quiet plenitude: of leaving the village, the country of the gods, and of going far away to southern France and Spain, there to live in another space together with K. But at the same time she's terrified by that new love which has been revealed to her that night: "Why? Why was I the one to be chosen?" With her gaze drifting into the distance, her cheek against K.'s chest, it seems to her that this love too is under Klamm's protection. She cannot free herself from him and leave him with her mind. Smiling, she loves to discover the games of the gods in the Assistants, whom K. detests: it seems to her that their sparkling eyes look at her with Klamm's gaze and that their desire for her is simply an irradiation of Klamm's desire—quiet, ferocious, omnipotent, speechless.

Like Frieda, K. has gone astray in the foreign land of eros, experiencing for the first time the power of love. But he would have liked to be close to the gods: look into their eyes, speak with them; and he cannot grant Frieda the closeness she desires. He leaves her at home: he is always away, busy with his machinations with the teacher, the superintendent, Momo, Barnabas, Olga, little Hans. His love for her is only a means to establish a relationship that is almost physical, close to the point of a secret understanding, with the Castle's gods. So Frieda is doubly alone: she has lost the empty plenitude of divine love and has not obtained the presence of earthly love; she has neither Klamm nor K., but only the two lewd Assistants. In just a few days the freshness, the assurance, the victorious and triumphant look, which had enhanced that frail body, desert her: she loses her bloom, and cries without covering her face, turning her tear-drenched face toward K., as though he deserved the sad spectacle of her sorrow. Toward the end of the book, she leaves him. When K. sees her again, only a day has passed; but Frieda already looks at him with the tender and astonished eyes of memory and softly strokes his brow and cheek with her hand, almost as though she had forgotten his features and meant to call them back to memory. She rests her head on his shoulder; and slowly, tranquilly, almost with a feeling of well-being, knowing that she is granted only a brief moment of rest, she repeats her sentimental dream to him: "If we had left right away, already that same evening, we could have been safe somewhere, always together, your hand always close enough for me to seize it. How much I need to have you close to me! How deserted I feel since I know you, without your closeness! Your closeness, believe me, is the only dream I dream, and there is no other."

Interwoven with Frieda's story, like a more concentrated and dramatic novel in the quiet flow of the larger novel, toward the middle of the book the story of Barnabas's family winds its way in: the father, head instructor of the village firemen, the mother, the daughters Amalia and Olga, the son, the radiant young messenger who brings K. the truthful and illusory messages. The story begins three years before, on June 3, during one of the festivities in which Castle and village consecrate their proximity and their separation. That morning, Amalia is dressed with particular charm: she wears a white gathered blouse with rows of lace and a necklace of Bohemian garnet; but the grim, cold, piercing, impassive look which skims above the others, her haughty pose, her love of solitude mark her as a creature apart. One of the Castle's functionaries, Sortini, ignorant of the world, observes Amalia: he is startled when he first sees her, and leaves. During the night he writes her a letter in which love, haughtiness, solitude, the gods' maladroitness in speaking to men are turned completely around in the obscene language favored by the Castle. The girl's world collapses: perhaps she too is in love with Sortini; another woman from the village would have accepted the invitation, but confronted by the insult, Amalia raises her arm and tears up the letter right in front of the messenger who delivered it.

In the village, where the women welcome and seek out the offers of the gods, nothing like this had ever occurred. The Castle is silent, does not bring any charge whatsoever against Amalia and her family. In *The Trial* and "In the Penal Colony," the Law accused us, engraved our sins on our bodies with the most subtle and fantastic calligraphic embroidery, whereas here God brings no charge, enclosed in his absence and indifference, in his elusive grace. This is the most awesome fact of the new religion: the end of condemnation, where God and men used to meet and embrace. Barnabas's family is covered with shame: abandoned by everyone, afraid of the Castle, they spend the torrid July and August days in the house behind bolted windows. The village watches them. Had they left the house, forgetful of the past, and by their behavior shown that they had overcome the incident, no one would have talked about their story ever again, and the family would have recovered their old friendships. But Barnabas's family does not know how to forget. If heaven has given up the weapon of condemnation, in their hearts the guilt complex has not disappeared, this atrocious devourer, which tortures them for having violated an unwritten decree, for having evaded the divine embrace and offended the celestial messenger.

So the village expels them: it does not accuse them of rebellion against the gods; had they been able to overcome

misfortune, the village would have paid them very great
honors; but at seeing them bewildered by anguish, incapable
of freeing themselves of the thought of their sin, the village
excludes them, despises them, breaks every tie with them
and calls them the "Barnabases," after the name of their
youngest and most innocent member. Now the entire family
has become untouchable: the sin not vanquished in the heart
has saturated souls, thoughts, bodies, clothes, the very
house—and even K., a man rejected as they are, finds them
repulsive. The family cannot live like this, without light and
without hope: each in his way asks for grace and forgiveness,
hoping to be freed from suffocation. Faced by the father's
prayers, the Castle has an easy time of it: "What in the world
might he want? What had happened to him? What did he
want to be forgiven for? When and how had even a finger
been lifted against him at the Castle? . . . But what were
they supposed to forgive him for? they replied: there are
no charges against him, at least they aren't yet in any of
the reports. . . ." The father tries to bribe some clerks, and
he tries to talk privately with one of the functionaries, as if
the gods had a private life. Everything is equally futile. In his
most handsome suit and wearing a small fireman's badge, he
waits in the streets for the functionaries' coaches to go by, to
ask for forgiveness: he sits on the stone ledge of the gate to a
truck garden—together with his wife, he sits there all day
and in all seasons, under rain and snow. Nobody ever stops;
every so often a coachman recognizes him and playfully flicks
him with his whip. "How many times," his daughter tells us,
"we found them there, huddling against each other on their
narrow seat, cowering inside a thin blanket that barely
covered them, and all around nothing but the gray of the
snow and mist, and far and wide for whole days not a man or
a carriage to be seen."

Not even Amalia, the gloomy virginal creature, casts off
the feeling of guilt: no one suffers as she for having offended

the divine; her contracted and restrained gestures, rigid and
fixed, do not have the naturalness inspired by the harmony
and quiet with which heaven sometimes regales us. That
letter has taught her that God is evil: impurity, obscenity,
violence, oppression, virile darkness. This is the only reality
and truth, which has become forever fixed in her mind; she
cannot accept, like Olga (and perhaps like Kafka) the divine
in its infinite complexity: she loves a god of purity; and while
many lie when speaking of the gods and flattering the divine
with their poor theology, her clear intelligence does not agree
to call evil by other names. Amalia's figure takes on a tragic
aura: her gestures seem those of a great actress who is in
hiding, an Antigone who has fallen into Kafka's world. She
does not want to be reconciled with the Castle: she does not
accept any contacts with it—prayers, pardons, implorations
for grace, the service of messengers. She lives closed in her
despair, drawing nourishment from despair, knowing and
loving only despair: but her tragic experience, which perhaps
goes beyond the expressive possibility of any language, does
not utter a single word, while her gloomy eyes continue to
stare at Evil. After having rejected the gods' obscene vitality,
she observes the dictates of purity, asceticism, solitary
virginity. Thus she lives in her house, confined in her
negative dream, without seeing, without listening, and when
she does listen she does not seem to understand, and when
she does understand she seems not to care at all. Her cold,
clear and motionless gaze never looks directly at the object it
observes: it glides past it on one side, lightly, imperceptibly;
and this strange sidelong glance reveals a need for solitude
stronger than any other emotion. In the ice of her soul only
one affection survives: an Antigone-like affection for father
and mother, whom, though innocent, she has dragged into
sin; a Vestal's affection for the hearth. Almost insomniac, she
remains awake, fears nothing, is never impatient; cares for
her sick parents with pain-soothing herbs, while her brothers

and sister restlessly pace to and fro in their miserable house.*

The other virgin of the family, Olga, is blonde and mild, grave and quiet, as much as Amalia is gloomy and haughty; and she accepts the radical ambiguity of the sacred. Before the gods, who do not know love, and the village, which has forgotten the gift of *caritas*, she repeats the gesture of Christ. Like Christ, who went on the cross to take on the sins of men, Olga is a substitute victim. Whereas Amalia had refused her body to Sortini, she offers her body to the gang of servants who, twice weekly, come down to the Lords' Hotel in order to give free rein to their instincts in the stable; whereas Amalia had offended Sortini's messenger, Barnabas takes his place in order to carry messages between Castle and village. So this sacred prostitute, this Dostoevskian Sonya, sacrifices herself for her family, hoping to erase the guilt that weighs upon it and obtain reconciliation with heaven. But Olga is less fortunate than Gregor Samsa, who saved his family and the continuity of the natural cycle. Her sacrifice serves no purpose. None of the gods notices her, or if one does notice her, he remains indifferent to this episode of sin and repentance, guilt and expiation, in which God by now has no interest.

Barnabas is a substitute messenger, and he repeats the gestures of the distant and ever elusive messenger, whom Amalia had offended. He goes to the Castle, waits for two years to be called, becomes the man of expectation, of useless pause, of desperate procrastination, who always begins all over again without any possibility of change—which is exactly what the gods want from us, men vowed to an expectation that will never be fulfilled. As it does with K., the Castle, ironically benevolent, lets him do as he wishes,

* There is only one detail I do not know how to interpret. At one point it is said that Amalia has been to the Castle and has brought back a letter for Barnabas. This seems unlikely. Amalia does not go up to the Castle. One can think only that this is an oversight of Kafka's. If, however, it is not an oversight, one must think that Amalia is still cultivating a relationship with the Castle, even though she obstinately denies it.

allows him to enter its enclosure, and in the end, as though by chance, entrusts him with two messages for K. It seems to Barnabas that a new world is opening up before his eyes; he cannot endure the joy and fear of this new turn of events and hides the letter against his bare skin, continually bringing his hand to his heart to assure himself that he has not lost it. But he is a completely gratuitous messenger: he does not wear the regulation uniform, does not know whether the offices to which he has access are truly those of the Castle, does not know he is speaking with Klamm, does not know whether his messages are true messages or some of heaven's mystifications. Nothing is more problematic than his activity. And besides, even if he were a true messenger, what is a messenger? His begging to be taken on as a messenger is received like the wish of an idle child who pesters the grown-ups to be sent on an errand, just to have something to do.

And yet heaven is both repelled and attracted by those who are rejected, those who live without the Law, who inhabit the world's underground. Heaven loves guilt, even though it has given up accusing people of it. At the foot of the Castle it seems that only sorrow and misfortune can bring to bloom the grace of a message, the gift of a word that consoles. Barnabas is the last of the last—but his radiant garments with their silken reflections, his smile, his swift step, his Hermes-like elegance are in sum one of the very rare, precious "reflections" that heaven sends on the earth. And so perhaps the family's entire sorrow has been purified.

Toward the end of the novel, exhausted by insomnia and worn out by fatigue, K. by mistake enters the room of the Castle's secretaries at the Lords' Hotel. It is four o'clock in the morning. More than half the small room is occupied by a large bed; the electric lamp on the night table is lit, and beside it is a small suitcase. In the bed, hidden under the

blankets, someone is moving restlessly and, from a slit
between the blanket and sheet, whispers: "Who is it?" K.
looks at the occupied bed with displeasure and pronounces
his name. Then the man lying in bed lowers the blanket a bit
from his face, ready to cover up again should he see
something he does not like. But then he resolutely throws off
the blanket and sits up. He is a small man, quite handsome,
with childishly pudgy cheeks and childishly merry eyes; his
high brow and thin mouth betray mature thought; later, in a
dream, K. will see him in the guise of a young Greek god,
completely naked, who squeals like a girl being tickled.
Smiling, he introduces himself. He is Bürgel, Friedrich's
secretary, who maintains the liaison between Friedrich and
the village, between his secretaries at the Castle and his
secretaries in the village. And he must keep himself ready at
every instant to go up on the hill with his little suitcase. It is
late by now; Bürgel no longer feels sleepy, and invites him to
sit on the edge of the bed, with a confidence and familiarity
that K. had not yet encountered in the village. K. wants to
sleep; he accepts the invitation, sits down on the bed, leaning
against the headboard, and thus as he slowly passes from
wakefulness to sleep he listens to the delightful *bavardage*, the
effervescent and merry buffoonery of the small Greek god–
secretary. This is what often happens: the ultimate truth of
things, what we've always wanted to know and no one has
ever revealed to us, is offered us by a comical chatterbox,
without our even realizing it.

   In order to pass the time, or because he is charged with
delivering the revelation to K., toward the end of the night
Bürgel begins a long discourse. "Now pay careful attention,"
he says, "sometimes opportunities arise that almost are not in
accord with the general situation, opportunities when a
word, a look, a confidential gesture can obtain more than
certain exhausting efforts prolonged for a lifetime." These
opportunities arise at night: when the functionaries must
hear the parties right after an inquiry is completed; and

when, under artificial light and before sleep, it is easier for the gods to tolerate and forget all ugliness. But although the Castle and village are sunk in darkness, in winter and eternal twilight, the divine world is a diurnal space. At night it is subject to terrible perils: in the dark nestles the small gap, the invisible crack, that can bring down the Castle's squat wall. At that time the barrier between gods and human beings, although externally it appears intact, beings to crack: the Law is weakened; the gods begin considering things from a private point of view, lose themselves in the sorrows and vexations of men, mislay all distance and all impassivity, forget indifference, give in to pity—exactly as we do, mediocre, sentimental, lachrymose human beings.

Thus the unthinkable, the impossible, the never seen before, can happen—when strange human beings, strange flecks, agile and thin as fish, try to slip through the holes of the Castle's exceedingly close-woven net. While god and man stand face to face, the complete reversal takes place. We knew that man considered the Castle unreachable, and now it is the god who considers the bold human being, the extremely astute Ulysses, unreachable. We knew that the Castle is "the never seen, the always awaited, awaited with true craving," and now it is man who is awaited with infinite craving. We knew that the god loved the Law exclusively, ignoring souls and hearts, and now he seems to draw nourishment only from tortuous and obscure human psychology. We knew that the god did not hear prayers, and now he hears only prayers. We knew that he did not care, did not help, did not come to the rescue, and now he comes to man's rescue like the most compassionate of mothers. At this moment, there fall away distances, separations, oppositions, which, through the centuries, had been formed between gods and men; and a true *unio mystica* is created between divided bodies and souls. The old god dies, and he is happy and desperate and intoxicated over his death. Overwhelmed by the lacerating triumph of universal love, by the passion for sorrows and sufferings till now unknown, he announces his own end: an end that will occur at night, in secret, but then will be proclaimed on every day of the universe. His evangelist is Bürgel, the small, merry secretary who announces it with ecstasy, with a desire for dissolution, with despair and, above all, with sparkling, winking buffoonery.

Should we therefore believe that the times are about to change, beginning with this night? That the God of *caritas* will take the place of Count West-West, the empty, indifferent and obscene god? And that in place of the squat, degraded Castle with its sinister, disquieting tower, there will rise a light, slim bell tower, pure as the sky, nourished by childish voices and the peal of bells? And that Barnabas, with his grace and in his tunic rippling with silken reflections, will become the true messenger of the gods? And that the cognac will always disclose its caressing fragrance? We must not delude ourselves: Kafka is not a utopian. With a sudden reversal, Bürgel is anxious to let us know that, in his experience, the nocturnal surprise "is an unusual thing, known only by hearsay and never confirmed by the facts": God, until now, has never been pitiful, has never granted grace to anyone, as we know from *The Trial*. The same applies to the future, and above all to the present, this decisive moment for the history of mankind, which we are going through while K. has gone to sleep. "And even," Bürgel insists enigmatically, "if that extreme impossibility were suddenly to take shape, would everything perhaps be lost? On the contrary. That everything should be lost is even more improbable than that extreme improbability." The possibility remains mere possibility. There is no salvation. And so now Bürgel shows us a new face: he of all people, who had theorized about exceptional grace, the ecstasy of *caritas*, the end of the old world, becomes the theoretician of providential harmony in *this* world. "It is an excellent arrangement: we could not imagine another more excellent." Perhaps—he adds with the best of good graces and the most

delicious irony—"from a different point of view it is dismal."
But there is nothing but this world: as Kafka knew.

What we have described here is not a theoretical discourse
that the buffoon metaphysician weaves around the different
faces of God, around *caritas* and Theodicy. The small, plump
secretary is speaking to K.: the "nocturnal discovery" of
which he speaks is the nocturnal discovery that we have just
witnessed. He says: "With the loquaciousness of someone
who is happy, one must explain everything to him. One must
describe to him minutely and without neglecting anything,
all that has happened and for what reasons it has happened,
how the offered opportunity is extraordinarily rare and great,
how the petitioner [K.] stumbled upon it with the lightheartedness that is typical of him, but how at this point, if he so
wishes, Mister Agricultural Surveyor, he can control events
and therefore has only to manifest his desires, whose fulfillment is already prepared, indeed flies around you." So there
is hope for K.: the door is open, he will be able to ascend to
the Castle and see the gods. We are here in the same situation
as in *The Trial*, when the Court sends the priest to reveal to
Joseph K. that the splendor of the Law awaits him.

The solution is identical. Just as Joseph K. does not
understand the meaning of the fable, K.—this strange small
fleck, agile and thin, which has by chance penetrated the
Castle's net—does not know how to take advantage of the
opportunity offered him. To take the gods by surprise, one
must remain awake at night, like Kafka, who wrote "The
Metamorphosis" and *Amerika* and *The Trial* and *The Castle*
instead of sleeping. But K. is exhausted by the efforts of
penetrating the divine space. Precisely he, who seemed to
defy with reason the exigencies of the body, is the body's
victim. Precisely he, presumed to be a nocturnal man (but in
reality, too diurnal, rational, Western), he who planned to
enter the Castle at night, is defeated by the night, which this
time, with its usual irony, protects the gods. While salvation
is announced to him, he sleeps—blinded by heaven, which

makes him fail when he could win. While Bürgel reveals to him the "coming fulfillment" of his wishes, K. does not hear, shut off from all that happens. His head, at first reclining on his left arm which is stretched out on the bed's headboard, slips down in sleep and lolls freely, dropping lower and lower; he props his right hand and by chance grasps Bürgel's foot, which sticks out from under the blanket. He dreams: and in his dream he triumphs over Bürgel, who is disguised as a Greek god; and never was a triumph more derisive, while his definitive defeat was consummated. Chattering volubly, confiding and despairing, growing enthusiastic and effacing himself, the secretary—turbulent and insolent as a little boy—makes fun of him. So the old story is repeated once again. God has left the door open to man; and if man did not cross its threshold, it is his own fault, because he does not understand enigmas or is sleeping. As we know already, heaven is always innocent.

At five o'clock, still sleepy, K. leaves Bürgel's room, and after a brief visit to Erlanger, he finds himself in the hotel's deserted corridor. It is almost dawn. Suddenly both sides of the corridor are animated by an extremely gay bustle: now it sounds like the exultance of children preparing for an outing, now like the awakening in a chicken coop, the joy of the cocks and hens at being in full harmony with the rising day, and one of the functionaries even imitates the cock's crow. The corridor is still deserted, but here and there a door opens a crack and closes again hastily: the entire passage buzzes with that opening and shutting of doors; above the partitions, which do not reach the ceiling, appear and disappear just-awakened, tousled heads.

In the distance appears a servant pushing a small cart full of documents. A second servant accompanies him: he holds a list in his hand and checks the numbers on the doors against those on the documents. The cart stops in front of almost every door: the door opens and the papers, at times simply a small slip, are introduced into the room. If the door remains closed, the documents are carefully piled up on the threshold. But now the difficulties begin. Either the list is wrong, or the documents are hard to find, or the gentlemen protest for some other reason: a delivery here and there must be canceled; then the cart goes back and through the crack in the door there is a restitution of papers. Whoever believes he is entitled to the documents becomes very impatient, makes a tremendous racket inside his room, claps hands and stomps feet and shouts the number of the documents, which is always the same. One servant calms the impatient man; the other, in front of the closed door, tries to get the restitution. Often the blandishments have the effect of irritating even more the impatient man, who refuses to listen to the servant's words and demands his documents; through the crack in the door one of them spills a whole basin full of water on the servant. The negotiations are protracted. Sometimes an agreement is reached: the gentleman gives up part of the documents and requests other papers in exchange; but it also happens that someone must give up all his papers—and with sudden resolve, angrily, he flings them down the corridor, so that the string comes undone and the sheets fly away. Sometimes, instead, the servant gets no answer and remains before the closed door; he begs, implores, cites his list, brings up the regulations: all in vain, not a sound comes from the room, and the servant does not have the right to enter without permission.

All around the interest is enormous: everywhere there is chattering, all doors are in movement; looking out from above the partitions, the functionaries' faces, curiously wrapped in cloth, follow the events. One of the two servants never gives up: he grows tired, but he immediately bounces back, jumps down from the cart and gritting his teeth makes straight for the door that must be conquered. Even when he is repulsed by that diabolical silence, he does not admit defeat and has recourse to cunning. He pretends he is no longer interested in the door, lets it exhaust its silence and turns to other doors; but soon after, he returns, obstinately and in a loud voice calls the other servant and begins to pile up documents on the closed threshold as though he had changed his mind and were supposed to deliver, not remove, documents. Then he goes farther, but he keeps an eye on the door. When the gentleman cautiously opens the door, with two jumps there he is, and he sticks his foot in the gap, forcing the functionary to deal with him face to face. Only one gentleman refuses to calm down: he falls silent and goes wild again, just as violently as before. It isn't quite clear why he screams and protests like this so much: perhaps it isn't because of the distribution of the documents; his voice continues to echo stridently through the corridor, and the other gentlemen seem to agree with him, encourage him to continue, with shouts and approvals and nods of the head.

Only at the end of the scene does K. understand that the reason for this turmoil, which upsets a normal "Functionaries' Dawn," is in fact he with his heavy human body. The functionaries do not like to be seen by strangers: barely awakened, they are too bashful to expose themselves to a stranger's eyes, and even though perfectly dressed they feel naked. They would have driven K. away, but they are so polite that they didn't raise their voices. Meanwhile the turbulent gentleman has discovered the button of an electric bell in his room: happy with this relief, he begins to ring the bell uninterruptedly. A murmur of approval rises from the other rooms. From the distance the owner of the Lords' Hotel already comes rushing, dressed in black and buttoned up to his chin, and at every shriller sound of the bell he takes a small leap and rushes along more quickly. The hotel owner drags K. away; the bell resumes its ringing and other bells begin to resound, no longer out of necessity now but playfully and with an excess of joy. After K. goes by, the doors are flung wide open, the gentlemen come out, the corridor becomes animated, traffic develops in it as in a narrow, busy lane, while all along the bells continue to ring without pause, as though to celebrate a victory. This delightful Functionaries' Dawn, perhaps the Castle's only passage of pure entertainment, is orchestrated like a comic opera, with a hundred singers who do not show themselves, and a hundred mute voices, and the first servant as orchestra conductor. The musical execution could not have been more exquisite. How childish the divine is! And at times, on bright mornings, how scintillating, gay, light and irresistibly comical it can be!

Perhaps this bogus roosters' crowing already announces K.'s last hour. He is worn out by tension, insomnia and fatigue; Frieda has deserted him; Olga has robbed him of every hope as regards access to the Castle; the road that takes him to Brunswick's wife can only prove to be the road to failure; and he has understood that he will never meet Klamm and contemplate the gods. Kafka says almost nothing about his desolation: in the book there is a great void, like those which mark Karl Rossmann's disappointments; the optimistic pride and euphoric hubris of the first day have given way to an atrocious feeling of failure. K. is defeated in both body and soul. In his long dialogues with Pepi, he disavows his own nature. He understands that, in his life, there's always been too much tension, too much effort, too much *Streben:* he has never known calm, spiritual quiet, the gift of living in the quotidian; and now, exhausted, he dreams of an "always more absolute lack of occupation." But he has not changed, as some interpreters believe. Driven by his mad Faustian heroism, he does not give up his search.

We do not know how K. spends his last days. Perhaps at Gerstäcker's, as a watchman in the stable? Or perhaps even lower down, in the ultimate underground of the divine? The maids spend their lives confined in warmth and darkness, in certain sepulcher-closet-burrows where they huddle next to each other without ever seeing the light. They invite him down there, to share their beds and their bodies, for the entire duration of the interminable winter. K. had never reached so low; he had never come to know so profoundly the horror of darkness, of debasement and claustration. Had he gone down there he would have become like Karl Rossmann, the servant in the brothel, renouncing all his celestial dreams. But destiny, or the Castle, or life, or whatever we might call that something which ends novels, spares him this degradation. According to Max Brod's account, K. dies of exhaustion: men are not born to breathe the atmosphere of the divine. The people of the village gather around his deathbed. At that precise moment the message comes from the Castle, according to which K. is permitted to work and live in the village, though without the right of citizenship. It isn't easy to understand a text from a friend's account, even a scrupulous and faithful friend. But it seems impossible to interpret this conclusion in a "positive" manner, as many do. Grace arrives, ironically, at the point of death, when K.'s body is about to be carried to the grave. And besides, what did K. care about living and working in the village, in the *here*, the limited, among men—together with Gerstäcker, Pepi, Brunswick, even Hans? K. wanted to live only among the gods.

CHAPTER TWELVE

"The Burrow," "Investigations of a Dog"

Although Kafka never loved stories told in the first person, during the last years of his life he wrote two of them, perhaps his most extraordinary, in which one character says "I." This "I" can be a literary convention, a fictitious screen elegantly flung between the world and the person who writes. And yet we have the impression that, this time, Kafka is approaching himself as he had never approached himself before: that he is there, before our eyes, strangely desirous of making himself known; he had never led us so deeply inside the mysteries of his art of darkness, nor had he ever communicated to us his most secret thoughts. As though to find a foundation, Kafka takes a leap backward, all the way to *Notes from the Underground*. All external events are abolished; the traditional ruses of storytelling are done away with; concentration, flights, return, search and revelation take place only in the Narrator's mind; nothing allows us to affirm that, outside, there exists a real world with which we must establish relations; at each step we realize that we are moving within the enclosed, abstract and echoing space of a mind, which envelops us from all sides like a prison. We too are prisoners, victims of a monologuing and solitary voice, which narrates, comments, reveals itself, disguises itself, advances hypotheses, demolishes hypotheses, performs laborious calculations in a fantastic and intellectual delirium which substitutes itself for the created universe.

"The Burrow" is the most grandiose attempt at claustration that was ever accomplished in literature. The protagonist—seen by the commentators as a badger or a mole or a hamster, all hypotheses which are correct and useless since the exact term is deliberately omitted—is a kind of perfidious self-caricature of Kafka: a selfish celibate, astute, voracious, cruel, misanthropic, narcissistic, who many years before, perhaps in his early youth, had built himself a burrow. What a marvelous work had sprung from his labors! At the center a fortress, filled with supplies of piled-up meat, which send their odors everywhere: from these depart, each according to the general plan, ascending or descending, straight or curved, widening or narrowing, the silent deserted tunnels. Every hundred meters the tunnels widen out into small round clearings, where the animal can comfortably curl up, warm himself from his own heat and rest. No animal had ever suffered so much; the soil of the fortress would collapse: the animal then hammered it with his bleeding forehead until it was compact, just as Kafka had drawn his books from the painful labor of his forehead and his body. The great monologue does not speak of any other burrow, of any other beast at work. In Kafka's universe, there exists only *this* burrow: the edifice created by the animal's brain and paws is exclusive; any other project would have threatened the uniqueness and existence of his project.

Although the story speaks of the fortress and tunnels, parading a vague militaristic terminology, the burrow is not a defensive work; and it is not even useful for storing supplies, despite its being pervaded by a very sharp odor of game. The burrow is the archetype of the nameless animal. It is the realm of silence: with what joy the animal glides through the tunnels for hours on end, only rarely hearing the rustle of some little beast that he immediately silences, crushing it between his teeth; with what well-being he stretches out in the fortress, warms himself in his own heat and sleeps; with what ecstasy he awakens from sleep and listens, listens in the silence, which reigns unchanged day and night and is actually not an empty, passive silence but active and resounding, possessing its own noise. Kafka had never expressed the ecstasy of concentration and segregation so profoundly and with such abandon. But the burrow is above all the maternal home, the home of regression to childhood, where the animal can curl up like a small boy, fall beatifically asleep, lie dreaming: the home of being; the home of life and death. When he is in the tall stronghold, he feels it is his to such a degree that he could even accept a mortal wound from his enemy, since his blood would imbue the ground and would not be lost—such is the tragic greatness of his project. Outside the burrow stands finite time: inside, infinite time. Outside the burrow stands weakness: inside the burrow, strength. Outside the burrow is light: inside the burrow, darkness, which is the only thing the unknown animal (and Kafka) wants to explore.

The burrow represents Kafka's work such as he contemplated it in 1923, when it was almost completed, with the three great novels, the myriad of short stories and aphorisms, and the letters as a cortege—very few printed pages, and thousands of pages covered with his dense handwriting. At that moment he had a revelation: his work was not only the most jealous of secrets, but something external and visible—a place, a burrow, with a stronghold, dozens of tunnels and small fortresses. He lived inside *Amerika* and "The Metamorphosis" and *The Trial* and *The Castle* and "The Burrow" which he was now writing; around, all was quiet and silence; he listened to the silence and realized that it was a subterranean work, a true Pit of Babel, like the shelter of the unknown animal. Despite his dreams, he had never had anything to do with the light. His work—the maternal home, the

stronghold, the childlike regression, life, death, substance
—gave him a very strong feeling of stability and firmness,
such as he had never experienced. It was a nucleus that no
weakness could damage, no aggression could destroy, no defeat could shake. Even if he were to die—as he knew he must
soon die—his blood would consecrate it.

The animal's burrow is not safe. The entrance is located
very far from the stronghold, covered only by a light curtain
of moss, and from there the enemy could enter. "In that place
in the dark moss I am mortal and in dreams there is always an
avid snout there that snuffles incessantly." But why, then,
didn't the animal close it with a thin layer of pounded earth?
He wanted to be able to flee into the open, if some impassioned predator, blindly probing the burrow, should slip into
one of its passages or if the subterranean beasts of legend
gave chase to him inside it. The unknown animal is more
terrified by the burrow (which should defend him) than by
the open space (from which all dangers ought to come). It
is the act of building burrows, defending oneself, shutting
oneself up, concentrating oneself, isolating oneself, protecting
oneself that gives rise to danger, as Kafka's life demonstrated.
If there were no burrows, there would be no dangers either;
and the animal lives at the mercy of his anguish, moves about
and drags supplies with his teeth from one clearing to another.
Thus Kafka realized that in his work, grown around him like
a cocoon, were hidden all the enemies who could do him harm.

At times the animal comes out of the burrow and goes
into the open, hunting. At the start he does not feel free:
imprisonment has caused him to lose all pleasure in freedom.
But then he begins to look at the burrow: he splits in two and
observes himself as he sleeps in his prison, with a happiness
he had never had when shut away in his abyss. "It seems to
me I am not standing in front of my house but in front of
myself as I sleep, and that I have the good fortune to be able
to sleep deeply and at the time watch myself attentively. . . .

I would reach the point where sometimes I was overcome by the puerile desire not to go back into the burrow, but settle in the vicinity of its entrance, spending my life watching it and always having it before my eyes, considering to my great joy how much safety the burrow could give me, if I were inside it." As always his anguish is produced by the burrow: joy, happiness, quiet are offered him by life in the open, while the mind fantasizes that it is inside. So then will the animal renounce the burrow? Will Kafka abandon his art of the underground, of the unconscious and darkness? Will he narrate what happens in the world of light? Will he reject claustration? It is impossible. While he is outside the burrow, the animal is not really observing himself *inside*, precisely because he is not inside: the situation is not identical, as he thought, but pure fantastication. In this situation, a stranger to the burrow, Kafka is unable to bring together the two spiritual conditions that he must concentrate in one and the same attitude. He controls (from the outside) the darkness of his unconscious, but he cannot identify (from the inside) with darkness, as he desperately needs to.

So the animal must return to the burrow; and Kafka to the Pit of Babel, which is the only place where he can write. Nothing could be more difficult, because the others might be watching him. He makes several attempts: during a stormy night, he swiftly tosses a prey into the burrow; the operation seems successful; or at a sufficient distance from the true entrance, he digs a short trial tunnel, slips into it, closes it behind him, patiently waits, calculates short or long stretches of time, comes out to record his observations. At times he is tempted to resume his old life as a vagabond, bereft of all security. Then he tells himself that such a decision would be true madness, "brought about only by living too long in absurd freedom." He wants to go back inside; but he is afraid—a true anguish of persecution, an obsession that is continually regenerated—and everywhere he sees animals spying on him, watching him from the back, just like Kafka when he went back into his prison. The danger is real. Possibly some small repugnant animal is following him out of curiosity and, unwittingly, acts as guide to the hostile world; or perhaps it is someone of his own species, a connoisseur and admirer of burrows.

If at least it came right away—if at least it began to probe the entrance, lift the moss, if it succeeded, if it would take his place or had already entered—he would pounce on it furiously, free of all scruples, and would bite it, tear it limb from limb, savage it, bleed it to death, adding its corpse to his other booty. No one comes. So he no longer avoids the entrance, circles around it, and it seems almost that he himself is the enemy lying in wait for the right moment. If at least there were somebody with whom to make an alliance! The *other* would cover his back, as he enters the burrow. But this too is impossible: in the first place, he wouldn't want the other to go down into the burrow, and then, besides, how can you trust someone at your back whom you cannot see? "And what shall we say about trust? If I trust someone when I look into his eyes, would I be able to trust him just as much when I don't see him and we're separated by the moss covering? It is relatively easy to trust someone, if at the same time you watch him or at least can watch him, perhaps it is even possible to trust at a distance, but to trust from inside the burrow, that is, from another world, someone who is completely outside, seems impossible to me." Finally he makes up his mind: he thinks about his burrow, his stronghold; incapable of reflecting because he is so tired, his head lolling, tottering on his legs, almost asleep, feeling his way rather than walking, he approaches, gingerly lifts the moss, slowly descends, leaves the entrance more uncovered than necessary and finally lowers the moss.

Back in the burrow, the animal carries out an inspection; his weariness is transformed into fervor; he lugs his prey through the narrow, fragile tunnels of the labyrinth or pushes them down one of the main tunnels, which descends along a steep incline to the fortress. Everything is in order: only a little damage here and there, which he will be able to repair easily: he inspects the second and third tunnels, and through the latter he goes back to the fortress, after which he again returns to the second tunnel. Suddenly he is overtaken by apathy: he curls up in one of his favorite spots and yields to the desire of settling down as though he were going to sleep, in order to find out whether he can sleep as well as in the past. He sleeps deeply, for a long time. When he awakens—his sleep by now is very light—he hears an imperceptible hiss, which wounds and offends him: the beauty of the burrow coincides with its silence. The hiss is now a kind of whistle, now the breath of a sound; now there are long interruptions, now brief pauses; and he realizes with terror that wherever he strains his ears, above or below, along the walls or on the ground, at the entrance or in the interior, there is the same noise, which grows slightly in intensity.

In a delirium of hypotheses, a frenzy of conjectures— Kafka's art had by now chosen this path—the animal interrogates himself as to the causes of the noise. Perhaps the little beasts in the burrow, not watched during his absence, have cut out a new passage, which has crossed an old passage; the air is swirling around there, producing the hissing sound. But the animal immediately cancels his hypothesis, because the noise resounds everywhere with the same intensity. So he advances a new hypothesis. Perhaps it is a large unknown wild beast. It digs through the earth feverishly, at the speed with which one strolls in the open; it works with its muzzle, by a succession of thrusts, powerful tears; the hiss is the drawing in of air between one thrust and the next; the earth trembles because of that digging, even when it is over, and this successive vibration mingles with the noise of work very far away. Convinced by his own thoughts, the animal begins to make plans. In an attempt to recapture the strength of his youth, he will dig a large tunnel in the direction of the noise. Then he abandons the project. He imagines the wild beast has already traced several circles around the burrow; and he understands that danger is definitively installed in his old oasis of peace.

Who then is the *Enemy*? Where does the noise spring from? Is the hiss that of another animal? Or does the same burrow animal split into two hostile figures? Is the hiss then a mere obsession, born from a mind contaminated by solitude and silence? Kafka's text is ambiguous. We can say only that the hiss, with its short and long intervals, the imaginary or real Enemy occupies the animal's mind as soon as he abandons himself to the pleasure of sleep and the abyss, forgetting to control them. If he had not entered the burrow, or had continued to guard it and inspect it, he would never have met the Adversary. Kafka knew that the menacing figures, the images of nightmare, horror and danger pierced his spirit, tearing it apart whenever he abandoned himself passively to the darkness, from which he must draw his treasures as a writer. The identification with the unconscious, which he had attained in sleep, was not all. He could not forgo knowing it and representing it.

The story breaks off toward the end. By now the animal's fate is sealed: for him there is no possibility of salvation; the huge unknown beast will spring from his obsessions and will bite him, tear him limb from limb, bleed him to death, just as he in his imagination had killed many enemies. At the supreme moment, he returns in his mind to a project of his youth, which he had abandoned out of negligence. At that time, he had thought of isolating the fortress from the surrounding earth; he would have left the walls intact to his own height, and above that, all around the clearing, he would have created an empty space as high as the wall. Thus he would have dug a burrow inside the burrow, a void inside the void, hiding himself ever more profoundly in the darkness. From there, from that void, he would have protected the stronghold, like the most invisible and steady custodian, holding it firmly between his claws. Like Gregor Samsa, who walked along the ceiling in his room and let himself drop playfully to the floor, he would have played the clown: pulling himself up into the free space, sliding down, tracing somersaults, abandoning himself to games of his imagination. "Then there would not be any noises in the walls, no impudent excavations would be made all the way to the clearing, peace would be guaranteed, and I would be its guardian; I would not have to eavesdrop with disgust on the diggings of tiny animals, but would listen with ecstasy to something that I now completely lack: the rustle of silence in the fortress."

With these pages, written during the last months of his life, Kafka sealed his farewell to literature. The youthful project of the lord of the burrow was the literary project to which he had always been faithful, from the time of "The Metamorphosis" down to that of *The Castle* and "The Burrow." When he wrote novels or short stories, he did not control the darkness of the unconscious from the outside, seated outside his abyss, like a split observer who pretends he is inside. He did not surrender himself passively to darkness and fantasies of the unconscious, in sleep or in ecstasy, like an intoxicated visionary. He lived immersed in the ultimate profundity of darkness, excavating yet another abyss inside the abyss, a burrow inside the burrow: he was *inside* like no one else; and yet he maintained a detachment, a control drawn from the very heart of darkness, indistinguishable from the darkness. He played with the unconscious, leaped, walked the rope, like the lithe, frail, desperate acrobat of the night that he had always been since the days of his youth.

In "Investigations of a Dog," written approximately a year earlier, we do not find this smell of burrow and the hunt, these lethargies, these cruelties, these densely, heavily bestial odors. The dog who says "I" does not smell of the canine world: he is a double metaphor for a Jew and a man. He is old by now, and he no longer lives among dogs. But he makes a point of saying that ever since his youth he has always felt a stranger. Even then he realized that "something did not fit," that a small, imperceptible fracture divided him from the others. He felt a slight discomfort; it could be provoked not only by the great collective manifestations of the crowd but also by the mere sight of another dog, of a friend; and this filled him with embarrassment, fear, perplexity, even despair. This awareness of his nature as a stranger forced him to forgo the warmth of cohabitation and devote himself—all alone—to his small, fruitless investigations. At times he asked himself whether in the history of dogs there had ever been a combination like his—so strange, so eccentric. At times the knowledge of his diversity was less acute, and others produced in him a less keen unhappiness. He too, perhaps, was like all dogs: a bit more melancholy, cold, reluctant, shy, calculating. Like all the others, the double reason for his existence was his frenzy to ask questions and to remain silent.

With the passing of the years, his feeling of estrangement is alleviated. He no longer protests: a subtle veil of disappointment, bitterness and irony (what men call wisdom) envelops his words. He lives in perfect accord with his own nature. At the bottom of his disappointment he finds tranquility. When we remember the effusive sweetness of the old dog (nameless, like the lord of the burrow) we ask ourselves who he might be. Certain details—the despair into which he could be plunged at the sight of a single human being—evoke Kafka's youth, in the streets of Prague. But what about the tranquility of old age, renunciation, the ironic and disappointed gaze cast on human affairs? Kafka probably wrote "Investigations of a Dog" around the middle of 1922, while working on *The Castle* or immediately after. During those months he did not at all resemble his dog. The dog was a projection he had made of himself: the dream of an old age that he would have been able to know, when the time of the great questions was over.

Like Kafka at Zürau, the dog has a profound theological passion and puts questions to himself about the prime problem: the creation of man, Eden, Adam and Eve, sin. Then the human-canine race was young, memory was free: our total silence was not yet born; there were words, or at least a possibility of speech, which today is completely lost. The iron destiny by which dogs cannot be but dogs, men cannot be but men was not established. Death did not yet exist. "The true word could still have intervened . . . and that word existed, was at least close, on the tip of the tongue, everyone could learn it." It hung like a fruit from the tree of life: it could have changed the destiny of the human-canine race; and men could have become gods or angels or gone beyond the distinctions among men, angels and gods, without death and silence. Our progenitors never spoke that word: they were lazy, indolent, lingered at the crossroads which led to the gods and to men, and hesitated to turn back, toward the origins, because they wanted to enjoy a little longer the human-canine life which seemed so beautiful and inebriating to them. They did not see Eden and the tree of life, and they went astray forever, without thinking that they were definitively lost. Thus men and dogs were born, and the grim destiny of humanity, of silence and death, was established. As for us, today, we are "more innocent" than Adam and Eve: we have not committed the sin, although, perhaps, taking into account the unconsciousness and futility of the human race, we might have committed it. "I would almost say: Lucky us who weren't those who had to shoulder the guilt, and can instead go to meet death, in a world already darkened by others, within an almost innocent silence." Now we have forgotten the dream of becoming gods: ours "is the oblivion of a dream dreamt a thousand nights ago and a thousand times forgotten."

Many thousands of years after the incomplete investigations into the "true word," the old dog continues his small
religious-philosophical inquiries. He has always had a passion for analysis: he splits every fact into its parts, compares
it to other facts, attempts analogies, experiments, inductions;
he investigates the origins and causes of the alimentation of
dogs; and he thinks that only these inquiries can give him the
gift of happiness. Like the final Kafka, he nourishes a hope.
He does not want an individual investigation, like the sort
carried out by the dogs before him: dog-Plato, dog-Aristotle,
dog-Kierkegaard, dog-Nietzsche; but an investigation carried
out by all the dog-men who together possess knowledge and
together also have the keys to it. "Iron bones, which contain
the noblest marrow, can be won only by the common bite of
all dogs," a crossed-out page says. But is this dream realized?
During the investigation the dream of the Great Wall is
realized: "Chest against chest, a dance of the people, blood no
longer imprisoned in the puny circle of limbs, but flowing
softly with perpetual ebbs through infinite China"? The
dream remains utopian. The marrow, the aim of the inquiry,
contains "the poison": the dreadful poison of knowledge and
art, which had infected Kafka's limbs throughout his life.
Although the dog apparently wants the bone to open under
the pressure of the common forces, he then wants to suck the
poisonous-beatific marrow absolutely alone, we do not know
whether out of egoism or a desire for sacrifice. Not even in
these last pages, where Kafka seems to release and free
himself from himself, is there born a collective art and a
science of the people. The writer remains the "scapegoat,"
who is sacrificed for all men: the dog-Kafka alone sucks the
poison, which must transform itself for the others into an
almost innocent story.

The dog-men do not want our dog to investigate, because
they do not want to know the truth—the marrow of the iron
bone. Some of them, perhaps, know more than they let on
and do not want to admit it; all of them keep silent, protected

by a silence that nobody has broken since the time of Eden; and this silence, of which they naturally hide both cause and mystery, poisons the life of the dog-investigator. He cannot bear the silence: he questions, and again questions, and then questions again; he interrogates the dogs and heaven and earth—although he hates anyone who asks questions and despises anyone who interrogates every which way, at random, as if they wanted to wipe out the traces of the real question. He wants answers or, if there are no answers, not a word. Thus also the dog-investigator ends by belonging to the race of those who remain silent, either because he does not know the answers or because he does not want to communicate them. In reality, there are no answers. There is only silence, eternal silence: all the dogs remain silent and will remain silent forever; and also the dog-narrator will die remaining silent, almost in peace, certainly with resignation, resisting all questions, also his own, from behind that bulwark of silence that he is. This is Kafka speaking, while writing *The Castle*. There was indeed no answer to any of K.'s questions, despite all that Kafka did depicting the gods, all that he had played and parodied and danced in an effort to evoke heaven and the night—the final answer was simply that there was no answer.

In the years of his old age, the dog-investigator protects himself by remaining silent: he comes to resemble the animal of the burrow, who delighted in silence, listened to its rustle, its buzz and rumble, and died when it was violated by the imperceptible hiss, generated by the profundity of his sleep. But at the time of his youth and his audacious maturity, the dog had violated the silence. He had gnawed the iron bone all alone, searching for the "noble marrow," breaking the silence with the most audacious metaphysical inquiries. He had asked what was art and what was God. The gods, mild for a change, had descended to meet him and had answered him.

The first experience took place in his youth: during that beatific, inexplicable period, when everything had pleased him and he imagined that all around him were happening great things, to which he must lend his voice. It was dawn; the day was already bright, just a bit misty, with a wave of confused and intoxicating odors. The dog lifted his eyes and greeted the morning with timorous whimpers. Suddenly, seven musical dogs stepped out of the darkness. Unaccustomed to music, the dog heard only "a horrendous din such as he had never heard before." But the dogs were not playing trumpets, violins, double basses, flutes or clarinets. They lifted and tapped their feet, moved their heads, ran about or stood still, clustered together; one of them placed his front paws on the next one's back, and then they lined up so that the first one standing upright supported the weight of all of them; or they would crawl about with their bellies almost on the ground and form a nearly intertwined figure. The dogs were acrobats, dancers, gymnasts, like so many Kafkian acrobats of the darkness; and magically their gestures became sounds.

The music came from everywhere, from on high, from below, from all sides, surrounding the young dog, flooding over him like a sea, crushing him like a stone, annihilating him and shrilling victoriously over his annihilation, so close as to be already remote, like a barely perceptible fanfare. The dog let himself be overwhelmed: it was Kierkegaard's demonic music, Nietzsche's Dionysiac music, the voice of seduction. But in the seven-dog orchestra, one became aware, toward the end, of something that surpassed all sounds and perhaps even literature and the forms of human expression: "a limpid, severe sound which remained always the same, which issued unchanged from a great distance, perhaps true melody in the midst of crashing noise," vibrated and made his knees bend. It was the extreme experience, driven beyond the limits, to which everyone is in danger of succumbing. Meanwhile, in the din of the inaudible, the young dog watched the musicians. That apparent calm with which they played in the void was in reality a supreme tension, a tremor, terror in the presence of the revelation; that apparent need for help, that making an appeal to the warmth of cohabitation was the meaning of solitude; that impeccable play of gestures was the experience of guilt and shame. The seven dog musicians shared the experience of literature that Kafka had known: tremor, solitude, guilt.

Much later, the dog had the second revelation. With his eyes closed, he had begun a fast in the forest, to provoke the intervention of the gods. He lay down, sleeping or awake, dreaming or singing. He imagined, fantasized, cried, deeply moved about himself. Then came hunger, his gut was on fire: hunger, which was not something different from him, a sensation, a pain—but nothing else but himself, which spoke inside him and mocked him. "The way passes through hunger," he comments when old: "supreme things can be reached, if they are reachable, only through extreme efforts, and this extreme effort is among us voluntary hunger": the descent of the gods must be provoked by our tension and our will to die. Almost beside himself, he licked his hind paws, chewed them, sucked them in despair. He began to dream of Adam and Eve; he detested them, because they had imposed a man's life on man, a dog's life on the dog; and he thought that the fast he had undertaken was at odds with canine and rabbinical law. Despite prohibition and pain, he continued his fast and held to it avidly. "I would roll about my bed of dry leaves, I could no longer sleep, I heard noises everywhere, the world which had slept during my previous life seemed awakened by my hunger, I had the impression I would never again be able to eat, because I would have had to reduce the freely noise-filled world to silence again and would not have been able to do so; but the greatest noise I heard was in my belly, I often laid my ear on it and my eyes must have been filled with terror because I almost couldn't believe what I heard." Overcome by intoxication, he began to smell imaginary food odors, the odors of his childhood— the perfume of his mother's teats. Then his last hopes

vanished. What good were his investigations, childish attempts at a childishly happy time? Heaven was silent. He
had the impression of being distant from everyone and of
being about to die—not from hunger but from abandonment.
No one cared for him, no one below the earth, no one above
it, no one in heaven; he perished because of their indifference.
Yes, certainly, he accepted death—not to end in this world of
mendacity, but to arrive there, in the world of the true word.

He was alone in the forest, exhausted, delirious, immersed in a puddle of blood, when a large, strange dog
appeared before him: a hunting dog, gaunt, brown, with
white patches here and there, long legs and a beautiful,
energetic, inquiring look in his eyes. "What are you doing
here?" he asked. "You must leave." "What renunciation
would be easier for you," our dog answered, "to renounce
hunting or renounce sending me away?" "Renounce hunting," the strange dog answered without hesitation. Despite
the omission of the name, painful though it may be to fill the
blank left by Kafka with the fullness of a name, the large
hunting dog with white patches is a form or shadow of God.
As always with Kafka, he is the God of power; he cannot live
together with man; he must push him away, far away into
the regions where he is not, at the cost of renouncing the
beloved practice of hunting; and man experiences "horror"
before the revelation of the sacred.

This extraordinary page, this page of blood and shudders,
terror and ecstasy, has no parallel passages in Kafka's work.
In his texts, God has never revealed himself to men: he had
sent off, for an instant, before our death, "inextinguishable
splendor"; or a messenger who will never arrive, before His
death. Now he is here and he speaks to us, breaking the
silence which for thousands of years closed the mouths of
men. While he was writing *The Castle*, where God was
absent, invisible and unattainable, Kafka had flung himself to
the other side and tried the opposite road, meeting God in
the guise of a dog.

From imperceptible details that perhaps no one else would have been able to notice, our dog became aware that the big hunting dog was preparing to sing, and he felt invaded by the new life aroused by his terror. The dog began to sing from the depths; he was already singing without knowing it, the melody hung in the air by its own law, and passed over his head, as though it did not belong to him; the sublime voice became ever louder, the crescendo was without limits and shattered the eardrums. The melody was aimed only at the dog-investigator, existed only for him, in the grandiosity of the forest; as the priest in *The Trial* and the chant of *The Castle*'s telephone have hinted, God's song belongs not to God, but to each of the men to whom it is addressed. Our dog was completely enchanted; he could not resist; he was beside himself, lost in the ecstasy that alone produces the supreme experiences, and he plunged his face into his own blood, his own pain, because of the anguish and shame that we feel before the sacred.

This communion between the divine and the human, which in other writers would have been transformed into a long everyday affinity, lasts barely an instant: Kafka can experience only a vertiginous moment of revelation and terror. The large dog does not forget that he is the God of power. He does not keep the dog-investigator with him, because the voice of God drives us away; it reveals to us the song composed for us only to make it clear to us that we will never be able to live together, that the relation between divine and human is one of distance and separation. But what did this distance matter? Despite everything, the strange dog had manifested himself: God had been revealed: his sublime voice continued to sing; and our dog, "driven by the melody, with stupendous leaps," strengthened and lightened, flew from the encounter that could destroy it.

Our dog does not openly reveal to us the conclusions he has reached by his little inquiries. The limpid, severe, always equal sound, coming from a great distance, hidden in the soundless music of the seven dogs, and the sublime song of the strange dog, which grows boundlessly and hangs in the air by its own law, are the same music. Music and religion, art and metaphysics are the same thing. At the end of his life, hidden in the guise of a dog, Kafka had understood that, through so many meanderings and bleedings, buffooneries and sorrows, he had done nothing but investigate the One.

CHAPTER THIRTEEN

1924

Then came the last months. In July there was the stay at
Müritz, on the Baltic, where he met Dora Dymant, an
Eastern Jew: in September there was the move to Berlin,
together with Dora—peaceful streets on the city's periphery,
Miquelstrasse, Grunewaldstrasse, Heidestrasse. When he
left the house in the warm evening, from the old luxuriant
vegetable gardens, botanical gardens and woods he was met
by an overpowering fragrance such as he had never before
experienced. There was inflation, poverty, no money for
newspapers and electric light; food packages sent from home;
the mild light of the kerosene lamp that lit his nocturnal
vigils; study of the Talmud at the Superior School of
Hebrew Sciences, a place of peace in tumultuous Berlin;
there was the dream—the ironic dream, which was known to
be impossible—of going to Palestine and opening a restaurant there, with her the cook and him the waiter, while all
he was granted was "to pass a finger over the map of
Palestine."

There was the story of the doll, we do not know when.
He had met a little girl who was crying and sobbing
desperately because she had lost her doll. Kafka comforted

her: "Your doll is traveling, I know, she has just written me a letter." The child was very doubtful: "Do you have it with you?" "No, I left it at home, but I'll bring it to you tomorrow." Kafka went home to write the letter. He sat down at his desk and began to compose it as though he were writing a short story, giving free rein to the great Dickensian game of warmth and fantasy that had always inhabited him. The next day he went to the park, where the child was waiting for him. He read the letter aloud to her. In those pages—perhaps interminable, like the ones written to Felice—the doll politely explained that she was tired of always living with the same family: she wanted a change of air, town and country, leaving the little girl for a while, even though she loved her very much. She promised to write every day, giving a detailed account of her travels. So for some time, by the light of the kerosene lamp, Kafka described countries he had never seen, described adventures that were dramatic and had happy endings, and took the doll to school, where she made new friends. Over and over the doll assured the girl of her love, alluding, however, to the complications of her life, to other duties and interests. After a few days, the child had forgotten her loss and thought only about the fiction. The game continued for at least three weeks. Kafka did not know how to end it. He thought, thought again, searched at length, discussed it with Dora, and finally decided to have the doll marry. He described the young fiancé, the engagement party, the wedding preparations, the young couple's house. "You will understand," the doll concluded, "that in the future we must give up seeing each other."

When he arrived in Berlin, he said that the spirits—the old spirits that had inspired all of his books—had lost sight of him: "This move to Berlin has been a wonderful thing, now they look for me, but they don't find me, at least for now." But spirits have excellent informers. At the end of October he already wrote to Brod that the "nocturnal phantoms" had tracked him down: "But even this is not a reason to go back;

if I must be their victim, better here than there." He feared
the spirits, who avidly sucked into their insatiable throats
what he wrote to Milena or anyone else. He sensed the chasm
at his feet, into which he could sink. So one day he had Dora
burn all his manuscripts, diaries, short stories, a work for the
theater. He often repeated: "Who knows if I've escaped the
phantoms?" What he wanted to write must come *afterward*,
after he had acquired his freedom. Did he ever acquire it?
Did he really become another man? It seems right to doubt
this. The ritual pyre served no purpose. In January 1924 he
dedicated this sinister self-portrait to Max Brod: "Now even
if the ground beneath his feet were solid, the chasm before
him filled, the vultures around his head driven away, the
tempests above him calmed, if all this were to happen, well,
then, things would be quite all right." "The Burrow,"
written in Berlin (perhaps in a single night) is a grandiose
interpretation of everything he had composed during the
long years in which the phantoms dominated him. If he
really had new hopes and dreams and revelations and desires
for something absolutely different, he kept his lips closed,
with an art of silence more delicate than that of his wise
old dog.

In March 1924, his temperature reached thirty-eight
degrees, permanently. He rose at seven o'clock, only to go
back to bed two hours later, and his cough tortured him from
morning to night. He stopped his walks to the Botanical
Garden, stopped the Talmud lessons. On March 17 he
returned to Prague; he saw an old schoolmate and smiled at
him with a smile identical to that of his adolescence—but his
voice was reduced to a whisper. In April he was taken to a
sanatorium: first in the Wienerwald; then near Klosterneu-
burg, close to Vienna, in a beautiful room adorned with
flowers, which looked out on the greenery. Tuberculosis had
affected his epiglottis and prevented him from speaking,
swallowing and eating.

He had never remembered willingly. Now he remem-

bered the youthful friendship with Brod; the baths at the
swimming school together with his father, that enormous
man who held a frightened bundle of tiny bones by the hand;
a few hours of joy in the country with his family; and
Karlsbad and Merano and beer gardens. Sometimes he
raved. He did not read: he played with the books, opened
and leafed through them, looked and closed them again, with
the old happiness. After he finished reading the galleys of his
last book, tears came to his eyes, as had never happened to
him before. What did he mourn? Death? The writer he had
been? The writer he could have been and whom perhaps he
had seen in the last pyre? He praised wine and beer, and
asked the others to drink in deep gulps those liquids—beer,
wine, water, tea, fruit juices—he was unable to swallow.
Whenever he could do so, he ate strawberries and cherries,
after having long inhaled their perfume. He had never
described a flower in his books, or almost never a tree or a
green thicket; and now he worried with maternal care about
the flowers with which Dora and his friend filled his room.
"One should also see to it that the lower flowers in places
where they are crushed in the vases aren't harmed. What
should one do? Best of all would be to use very large bowls."
"I would like to take particular care of the peonies because
they are so fragile," he wrote on small sheets of paper. "And
put the lilac in the sun." "Do you have a minute? Then do me
a favor and spray the peonies." "Please make sure that the
peonies don't touch the bottom of the vase. That's why they
must always be kept in bowls." "Look at the lilacs, they're
fresher in the morning." "Indoor flowers," he recommended,
"must be treated in a completely different way." "Let me see
the aglaia, it is too bright to stay together with the others."
"The red hawthorn is too hidden, too much in the dark."
"Would it be possible to have some laburnum?" Then, with
a leap into the utopia that he finally granted himself: "Where
is the eternal spring?"

Many years before, he had said that "he would be content

to die" if there wasn't too much pain. But the pain was tremendous, and yet he still wanted to live. On the morning of June 3 he asked for morphine and said to Robert Klopstock: "You have always promised it to me, for four years now. You torture me, you have always tortured me, I don't want to speak to you any more. This is how I will die." They gave him two injections. After the second injection he said: "Don't make a fool of me, you're giving me an antidote. Kill me, or else you're a murderer." When they gave him the morphine, he was happy: "This is good, but again, again, it isn't taking effect." He fell asleep slowly, woke up in confusion. Klopstock was holding his head and he thought it was his sister Elli: "Go away, Elli, not so close, not so close. . . ." Then with a brusque and unusual gesture he ordered the nurse to leave the room; he forcefully pulled out the tube and threw it into the center of the room. "Enough of this torture. Why go on?" When Klopstock moved away from the bed to clean the syringe, Kafka said to him: "Don't go away." "No, I'm not going away," Klopstock said. With a deep voice, Kafka answered back: "But I'm going away."

Acknowledgments

As in my other books, this book does not have bibliographical references. Here, however, I would like to thank those writers to whom I owe ideas and information: Beda Allemann, Günther Anders, Giuliano Baioni, Evelyn T. Beck, Peter U. Beicken, Friedrich Beissner, Walter Benjamin, Charles Bernheimer, Hartmut Binder, Hartmut Böhme, Jürgen Born, Bianca Maria Bornmann, Max Brod, Massimo Cacciari, Elias Canetti, Claude David, Kasimir Edschmid, Wilhelm Emrich, Karl-Heinz Fingerhut, Ulrich Gaier, Eduard Goldstücker, Ronald Gray, Erich Heller, Ingeborg C. Henel, Clemens Heselhaus, Heinz Hillmann, Werner Hoffmann, Wolfgang Jahn, Gerhard Kaiser, Hellmuth Kaiser, Jörgen Kobs, Winfried Küdszus, Paul L. Landsberg, Eugen Loewenstein, Claudio Magris, Ferruccio Masini, Ladislao Mittner, Robert Musil, Gerhard Neumann, Malcolm Pasley, Ernst Pawel, Heinz Politzer, Franco Rella, Marthe Robert, Laurence Ryan, Jost Schillemeit, Carlo Sgorlon, Richard Sheppard, Jean Starobinski, Johannes Urzidil, Klaus Wagenbach, Martin Walser, Luciano Zagari, Giorgio Zampa, Anna Zanoli. But, among all of them, I take special pleasure in recording the names of Maurice Blanchot and Walter H. Sokel.

Among the many reasons for gratitude that I have toward Roberto Calasso and Federico Fellini, there is also that of having read the typescript of this book and having given me advice. I am also grateful to Hartmut Binder, Bianca Maria Bornmann, Ida Porena and Luciano Zagari for their opinions concerning details of Kafka's life.

JULY 1986

Notes and Bibliography

Numbers in Roman type indicate pages; the numbers in italics indicate lines.

10, *5–6: Br.F.* 79

12, *15–18: Br.F.* 352

13, *16–18: Tgb.* 100

14, *18: E.* 34

14, *34–37 / 15, 1–7: Br.* 9–10

15, *10–12: Br.* 19

15, *17–19: Br.* 20

16, *17–33: Br.* 14

17, *10–11: Hoch.* 10

17, *28–31: Be. I–II* 106

18, *33–36: E.* 134

19, *3–8: Tgb.* 497

19, *20–22: Tgb.* 9

21, *4–9: Tgb.* 129

21, *24–26: Tgb.* 400

21, *33–37 / 22, 1–2: Br.F.* 140

22, *10–11: Tgb.* 121

23, *12–22: Br.F.* 71

23, *33–37: Tgb.* 223

24, *31–33: Tgb.* 334

24, *36–37: Tgb.* 344

25, *3–12: Br.F.* 693

25, *34–37: Tgb.* 393

26, *5–6: Hoch.* 305

26, *37 / 27, 1: Tgb.* 15

27, *14–23: Br.* 164

28, *7–9: Tgb.* 20

28, *11–14: Tgb.* 319

28, *28–35: Hoch.* 418

28, *35–37 / 29, 1–5: Be.* 216

29, *11–13: Be.* 216

29, *27–28: Be.* 222

30, *3–4: Be.* 222

30, *27–29: Tgb.* 9

30, *34–37* / 31, *1–14: Tgb.*
　97, 218, 222, 343
34, *1–4: Br.F.* 61–2
34, *30–31: Tgb.* 204
38, *2–4: Br.F.* 45
38, *17–26: Br.F.* 43
40, *9–13: Br.F.* 181
43, *7–9: Br.F.* 172
43, *17–21: Br.F.* 186
45, *29–37: Br.F.* 214–15
46, *13–18: Br.F.* 211
46, *29–31: Br.F.* 208
47, *10–16: Br.F.* 384, 389
48, *37* / 49, *1–3: Br.F.* 175
49, *13–14: Br.F.* 93
49, *24–27: Br.F.* 206
50, *1–6: Br.F.* 101–2
50, *12–17: Br.F.* 107, 235
51, *2–6: Br.F.* 352
52, *4–8: Br.F.* 320
52, *13–24: Br.F.* 328–9
52, *26: Br.F.* 343
53, *15–17: Br.* 85
53, *25–27* / 54, *1–2: Tgb.* 20
54, *10: Br.* 100
54, *27: Tgb.* 212
55, *12–14: Tgb.* 210
55, *25–26: Br.F.* 67
56, *14–16: Br.F.* 197
57, *31–37* / 58, *1–4: Br.F.*
　250
60, *10–11: Tgb.* 203, 312
61, *33–37* / 62, *1–3: Br.* 254
69, *10–11: E.* 85
69, *34–37* / 70, *1–3: E.* 86
70, *7–8: E.* 86–7

71, *1: E.* 89
71, *30–33: E.* 91
73, *9–10: E.* 98
74, *9–13: E.* 99
74, *21–23: E.* 100–1
77, *12–14: Br.* 107
79, *20–24: Br.F.* 204
82, *18–19: Hoch.* 30
87, *12: Ver.* 40
103, *18–27: Ver.* 387
106, *9–20: Ver.* 388
106, *37: Ver.* 401
108, *10–11: Ver.* 412–13
109, *3–4: Tgb.* 344
110, *19–20: Pr.* 7
114, *2–4: Tgb.* 225
114, *13–18: Br.F.* 433
114, *23–32: Br.F.* 402–3
114, *34–37* / 115, *1: Br.* 122
115, *12–17: Br.* 420
115, *26–29: Tgb.* 226
116, *1–8: Br.F.* 408
116, *11–13: Br.F.* 450
116, *24–26: Br.F.* 472–3
116, *28–31: Br.F.* 464
116, *35–36: Br.F.* 479
117, *11–18: Br.F.* 512
118, *6–14: Br.F.* 272
118, *37* / 119, *1–13: Br.F.*
　533–4
120, *5–6: Br.F.* 548
120, *12–14: Br.F.* 560
120, *19–20: Br.F.* 567
120, *23–25: Br.F.* 577
120, *30–32: Br.F.* 650
121, *1–7: Br.F.* 572

121, *11–13: Br.F.* 532
121, *16–19: Tgb.* 275
122, *18: Tgb.* 293
122, *25–31: Tgb.* 293
122, *33–34: Br.* 131
123, *6: Tgb.* 299
123, *12–13: Tgb.* 315
123, *24–27: Tgb.* 300
123, *35–37: Tgb.* 294
124, *22: Tgb.* 301
125, *18–19: Tgb.* 317
126, *13–15: Tgb.* 290
126, *24–25: Tgb.* 291
130, *11–12: Pr.* 103
137, *29–32: Pr.* 11
140, *5–6: Pr.* 132
153, *24–26: Pr.* 181
153, *30–31: Pr.* 189
154, *3–4: Pr.* 182
155, *10–11: Pr.* 189
159, *34–36: Pr.* 193
160, *20–25: Pr.* 194
161, *12–15: Tgb.* 393
163, *8–9: Be.* 55
164, *11–15: Be.* 56–7
166, *34–35: Be.* 59
167, *37* / 168, *1: Be.* 59
168, *11–25: Be.* 59–60
172, *11–19: Br.* 279–80
172, *36–37: Hoch.* 71
173, *17–20: E.* 115
174, *7–11: Br.F.* 757
174, *34–36: Br.* 161
175, *11–16: Br.* 177
175, *26–29: Br.* 167
176, *3–4: Br.* 179

176, *21–23: Tgb.* 381
176, *24–27: Br.F.* 758
176, *36–37* / 177, *1–2: Hoch.* 72–4
177, *9–10: Br.* 186
177, *18–19: Br.* 161
178, *12–13: Hoch.* 73
178, *22–27: Br.* 198
180, *5–6: Tgb.* 382
180, *18–19: Hoch.* 52
180, *37* / 181, *1: Hoch.* 53
181, *13–14: Hoch.* 55
181, *17–18: Hoch.* 61
181, *30–31: Hoch.* 52
182, *6–7: Hoch.* 52
182, *9–11: Hoch.* 61
182, *21–22: Hoch.* 60
182, *37: Hoch.* 36
183, *17: Hoch.* 65
183, *20–21: Hoch.* 79
184, *10–22: Hoch.* 80
184, *26–28: Hoch.* 75
184, *32–35: Hoch.* 69
185, *2–7: Hoch.* 69, 83
185, *10–12: Hoch.* 69
185, *14–22: Hoch.* 67, 71
185, *22–26: Hoch.* 67, 75
185, *30–32: Hoch.* 66, 77
185, *33–34: Hoch.* 67
186, *8–10: Hoch.* 69
186, *10–12: Hoch.* 72
186, *15–17: Hoch.* 62
186, *20–21: Hoch.* 71
186, *29–32: Hoch.* 249, 259
186, *33* / 187, *1–6: Hoch.* 53, 59, 63

223, *31–33:* Tgb. 403, 404, 405

224, *18–22:* Tgb. 406

224, *23–33:* Br. 370–1

224, *37* / 225, *1:* Br. 374

225, *2–3:* Tgb. 412

225, *12–15:* Tgb. 414–15

225, *17–22:* Tgb. 416

226, *18–20:* Br. 386

226, *35–36* / 227, *1–2:* Br. 386

227, *13–25:* Br. 384–6

229, *1–2:* Br. 415

230, *1–6:* Schl. 7

232, *1–2:* Schl. 19

232, *6–7:* Schl. 298

233, *14–15:* Schl. 17

234, *7–8:* Schl. 18

234, *16–21:* Schl. 156

235, *7–13:* Schl. 36

235, *31–33:* Schl. 29

236, *37* / 237, *1–6:* Schl. 20

237, *34–37* / 238, *1–7:* Schl. 183–4

239, *27–28:* Schl. 182

239, *32:* Schl. 182

243, *7–12:* Schl. 103–4

243, *21–27:* Schl. 104–5

248, *20–24:* Schl. 174

250, *19–21:* Schl. II 116

251, *26–28:* Br. 279–80

252, *24–27:* Schl. 9

252, *27–29:* Schl. 12–13

254, *23:* Schl. 20

258, *33–36* / 259, *1–2:* Schl. 69–70

259, *21–24:* Schl. 218

259, *29–30:* Schl. 77

260, *27–33:* Schl. 398–9

262, *18–23:* Schl. 335

262, *33–36* / 263, *1–2:* Schl. 344

266, *26–30:* Schl. 410

267, *17–18:* Schl. 422

268, *11–13:* Schl. 421

268, *18–21:* Schl. 421–2

268, *26–29:* Schl. 425

268, *36–37* / 269, *1–7:* Schl. 423–4

273, *4–5:* Schl. 480–1

276, *36–37* / 277, *1:* Be. 132

277, *22–30:* Be. 140–1

278, *18–19:* Be. 143

279, *3–11:* Be. 144

281, *22–25:* Be. 153

282, *18:* Be. 180

283, *22–25:* Be. 200

284, *4–10:* Be. 200

284, *23–25:* Be. 192

284, *27–30:* Be. 54

286, *13–14:* Be. 182

286, *32–36:* Be. 185–6

287, *18–21:* Be. 208

287, *30–37* / 288, *1:* Be. 210

288, *17–21:* Be. 211–12

289, *32–35:* Be. 213

292, *24–26:* Brod 172

292, *27–30:* Br. 451

293, *3–7:* Br. 472–3

294, *8–11:* Brod 180–1 294, *11–23:* Br. 485, 488, 490

The abbreviations and page numbers in the list of quotations refer to the following volumes:

Be. Beschreibung eines Kampfes. Novellen-Skizzen-Aphorismen aus dem Nachlass, ed. Max Brod (Fischer, 1980).

Be. I—II Beschreibung eines Kampfes. Die zwei Fassungen, Text edition by Ludwig Dietz (Fischer, 1969).

Br. Briefe 1902–1924, ed. Max Brod (Fischer, 1975).

Br.F. Briefe an Felice, ed. Erich Heller and Jürgen Born (Fischer, 1976).

Br.M. Briefe an Milena, expanded new edition, ed. Jürgen Born and Michael Müller (Fischer, 1983).

Br.O. Briefe an Ottla und die Familie, ed. Hartmut Binder and Klaus Wagenbach (Fischer, 1974).

E. Erzählungen, ed. Max Brod (Fischer, 1980).

Hoeb. Hochzeitsvorbereitungen auf dem Lande, und andere Prosa aus dem Nachlass, ed. Max Brod (Fischer, 1980).

Pr. Das Prozess, ed. Max Brod (Fischer, 1980).

Schl. Das Schloss, critical edition, ed. Malcolm Pasley (Fischer, 1983).

Tgb. Tagebücher 1910–1923, ed. Max Brod (Fischer, 1983).

Ver. Der Verschollene, critical edition, ed. Jost Schillemeit (Fischer, 1983).

Brod Max Brod, *Über Franz Kafka* (Fischer, Taschenbuch Verlag, 1974).

Index

l

A NOTE ON THE TYPE

This book was set in a digitized
version of Janson. The hot-metal version
of Janson was a recutting made direct from type
cast from matrices long thought to have been made by the
Dutchman Anton Janson, who was a practicing type founder in
Leipzig during the years 1668–1687. However, it has been
conclusively demonstrated that these types are
actually the work of Nicholas Kis (1650–1702),
a Hungarian, who most probably learned his trade from
the master Dutch type founder Dirk Voskens. The type is an
excellent example of the influential and sturdy Dutch
types that prevailed in England up to the time
William Caslon (1692–1766) developed his own
incomparable designs from them.

Composed by American-Stratford Graphic Services, Inc.,
Brattleboro, Vermont
Printed and bound by the Haddon Craftsmen, Inc.,
Scranton, Pennsylvania
Designed by Mia Vander Els